What News?

Communication and Society
General Editor: James Curran

What News?

The Market, Politics and the Local Press

Bob Franklin and David Murphy

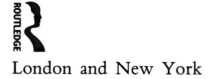

London and New York

First published 1991
by Routledge
2 Park Square, Milton Park, Abingdon, Oxon, OX14 4RN

Simultaneously published in the USA and Canada
by Routledge
a division of Routledge, Taylor & Francis
270 Madison Ave, New York NY 10016

Transferred to Digital Printing 2007

© 1991 Bob Franklin and David Murphy

Typeset in 10/12pt Bembo by
Intype, London

British Library Cataloguing in Publication Data
Franklin, Bob
    What news?: the market, politics and the local press. –
(Communication and society)
    1. Great Britain. Newspaper publishing industries
I. Title   II. Murphy, David   III. Series
338.47072

Library of Congress Cataloging in Publication Data
Franklin, Bob,
    What news?: the market, politics and the local press / Bob
Franklin and David Murphy.
      p.   cm. – (Communication and society)
    Includes bibliographical references and index.
    1. Community newspapers – Great Britain.   2. Free circulation
newspapers and periodicals – Great Britain.   3. Local government
and the press – Great Britain.   I. Murphy, David.   II. Title.
    III. Series: Communication and society (New York, N.Y.)
PN5124.C63F7   1991
072'.91 – dc20   90–27270

ISBN 0–415–06172–5
ISBN 0–415–04049–3 pbk

Publisher's Note
The publisher has gone to great lengths to ensure the quality of this
reprint but points out that some imperfections in the original
may be apparent

Contents

Tables

Chapter 1

The local press: defining the new boundaries

From the end of the First World War until the beginning of the 1970s, there was a remarkable uniformity and continuity in the British local press. Young people embarking on a career in journalism in the 1960s were schooled by the older professionals who began their working lives on newspapers in the 1920s and 1930s. Fundamental journalistic practices and news-gathering routines which they learned at that time, however, were not in essence different to those which they passed on half a century later: how to take accurate shorthand notes in a ring-backed reporter's notebook; how to develop a garrulous but trustworthy source on the local council; the correct form of address for a bishop. In the 1960s typewriters would probably be small, portable, grey Olivettis instead of black-and-gold Remingtons, and there were probably new neon strip lights to illuminate the same dusty, paper-filled, smoky, linoleum-floored offices. Otherwise little had changed. There were some differences of practice. Most reporters no longer had to collect the names of mourners as they left the funerals of local worthies. Newspapers printed bigger pictures, and there were more of them.

The presses on which the papers were printed were mostly rotary, although some flat beds were still in use, and compositors still set pages by hand from lines of lead type produced by men operating Linotype machines. Reading through the Rexine-bound files in the libraries of such papers, continuity and similarity of concerns were discernible across the decades: the same parochial obsession with courts and councils; the same attention to the *rites de passage* of local individuals, their births, marriages, golden weddings, diamond weddings, ninetieth birthdays, hundredth birthdays and deaths; the records of communal rites: pageants, carnivals, fêtes, annual prize-givings, mayoral inaugurations and local elections.

The political complexion of the papers remained the same. They almost all described themselves as independent or conservative, which were two ideological states of mind the difference between which was not detectable with any known instrument of measure. They all cleaved to a local patriotism which put forward the notion that Birmingham, Stafford, Bishop Auckland, Castleton, Accrington or Folkestone was the best town in the world surrounded (notwithstanding the carping of the ignorant stranger) by some of the finest countryside in existence and inhabited by good-hearted, hard-working, literate, tolerant, clean, law-abiding, reasonable, sober inhabitants who none the less always managed to provide each issue of the local paper with a helping of court-room drama comprising violence, theft, drunkenness, rape, domestic disturbance, child molesting and, at regular but decent intervals, the occasional murder.

It was easy to caricature local newspapers in this way and to assume a uniformity of organizational structure and ideological disposition. The typical stereotype presented local newspapers as insignificant, harmless distractions, reporting little more than uncritical celebrations of local culture in tandem with eulogies of local personalities – a curious if not perverse forum for collective introspection.

This perception of the local press, however, is undermined by two observations. First, the local press, judged in terms of the number of titles published, the variety and range of publications it embraces, the levels of advertising revenue it generates and its importance as a source of news – especially political news – is a highly significant component in local media networks as well as in the more general setting of the British press. Second, the stability and continuity which seemed to typify the local press have, since the early 1970s, been more apparent than real, concealing undercurrents of profound change. These changes have not been confined merely to local newspapers but have extended to other local media as well as the more important news sources of the local press.

THE IMPORTANCE OF THE LOCAL PRESS

The presumed insignificance of the local press is underscored by the scant attention which academics have paid to the local media in general, and to the local press in particular, since the mid-1970s. Around that date, a flurry of academic activity produced a useful crop of detailed studies, typically focused on the way the local press reported, or more accurately failed to report, local politics.[1] Subsequently, however, media research has become increasingly national in its focus and relatively unconcerned with the press, whether in the national or local setting.

This relative neglect is perhaps unsurprising given the national character and concentration of both the media and political structures in Britain. It remains none the less somewhat curious at a time when the local press is flourishing and when the long-term decline in regional press circulations apparent since 1947 seems to be reversing to some degree. It should not be forgotten, however, that the vitality of the local press, like that of all other sectors of the media, is not uniform. Indeed, the short life and early closure of the *North West Times* in November 1988 attest to the uncertainties involved in establishing a new provincial newspaper. Six factors underline the significance of the local press within the British media.

First, the overall number of published titles remains extremely high, with *Benn's Directory* claiming 797 weekly paid newspapers, 931 free newspapers and 70 daily papers published in England in 1988.[2] There are a further three Sunday papers published in New-castle upon Tyne, Plymouth and Birmingham, with the latter enjoying a circulation in excess of 150,000.[3] These figures suggest a phenomenal diversity of newspapers, reflecting differences in the size of circulation area, frequency of publication, price, focus of contents on national, regional or local affairs, size and number of published pages. The eleven daily morning provincial papers, for example, range from the relatively modest *Leamington Morning News* to the prestigious Leeds-based *Yorkshire Post* and include the *Daily News*, a free morning newspaper which distributes over 320,000 copies to 86 per cent of Birmingham homes and claims 587,000 readers daily.[4] A similar diversity prevails among the evening and weekly papers.

Publishers in Wales, Scotland, Northern Ireland and the Channel Islands produce a distinct range of morning, evening and weekly newspapers, reflecting their unique national and cultural concerns and making their own contributions to the diversity of the local press. In Northern Ireland the forty-eight regional papers constitute two mutually exclusive elements within the local press, distinguished by their expressed attitudes towards the nationalist or unionist cause. The daily *Irish News*, for example, established in 1855, is read exclusively by the nationalist community; the *Newsletter* (founded in 1737 and formerly the *Belfast Newsletter*) enjoys a readership composed exclusively of unionists. Newspapers' ideological postures in reporting certain stories must be carefully chosen to complement readers' political attitudes in a community where 'few would buy or even have an opportunity to read "the other side's" daily', where 'the very act of purchasing a newspaper is an act of self-identification'.[5]

A second factor signalling the importance of the local press is the substantial circulation figures achieved by this diverse range of local papers. Readership figures are also extremely high. The Maud Report on local government claimed that 80 per cent of its survey respondents were regular readers of local newspapers.[6] A more recent study of local newspaper reading habits in Richmond-upon-Thames, undertaken by MORI, showed that only 14 per cent of respondents did not read a local newspaper, while 72 per cent were regular readers of the local press.[7] In 1987 the annual report of the Press Council claimed sales in excess of 7.5 million copies daily for local morning and evening papers, 7.7 million for local weekly and bi-weekly papers and an additional 2.7 million copies of regional Sundays.[8] Table 1.1 contains a breakdown of these figures by nation, region and type of newspaper.

The same Press Council report suggested that circulation figures for free weekly papers distributed within the UK had reached in excess of 37 million, a figure which has continued to grow subsequently – see Table 1.2.

There are, of course, enormous variations in circulation size within the various newspaper categories set out in the tables. Morning circulations range from the *Paisley Daily Express* (11,886) to the *Glasgow Herald* (126,000), while evening papers embrace both the *Manchester Evening News* (276,665) and the *Nuneaton Evening Tribune* (12,976).[9] Weekly paid-for and free papers reveal an equivalent range of circulations. Despite the existence of papers

Table 1.1   The paid-for newspaper press, 1987

Region	Class of newspaper	Number	Circulation (000)
National	Morning	12	14,920
	Sunday	9	18,100
London	Evening	1	488
	Weekly and bi-weekly	73	739
English	Morning	10	619
regions	Evening	60	4,247
	Sunday	3	331
	Weekly and bi-weekly	527	5,015
Wales	Morning	1	74
	Evening	4	230
	Weekly and bi-weekly	47	410
Scotland	Morning	5	1,202
	Evening	6	449
	Sunday	2	2,274
	Weekly and bi-weekly	106	1,040
Northern	Morning	2	85
Ireland	Evening	1	148
	Sunday	1	59
	Weekly and bi-weekly	42	418
Channel Isles	Evening	2	42
and Isle of Man	Weekly and bi-weekly	7	60
UK total	Morning	30	16,900
	Evening	74	5,604
	Sunday	15	20,764
	Weekly and bi-weekly	802	7,682

Source: The Press Council, *The Press and the People*, 34th annual report, 1987, p. 288.

with very small circulations, aggregate figures are surprisingly high. If total weekly sales for the national and local press are compared, they are almost equivalent, with the former circulating 107.5 million and the latter almost 91 million. The comparison is not wholly legitimate, of course, not least because the local press figure includes free newspapers, which, unlike nationals, are distributed free without the need to 'win' a circulation. None the less the comparison is both suggestive and useful in demonstrating the sheer scale of local press operations. One aspect of local press circulation which is particularly important is that the large majority of morning and evening provincial papers enjoy a local monopoly within their circulation areas.[10] This leads directly to a third factor underpinning the significance of the local press.

Table 1.2 The free newspaper press, 1987

Region	Class of newspaper	Number	Circulation (000)
London	Weekly and bi-weekly	108	5,688
English regions	Morning	1	278
	Sunday	1	81
	Weekly and bi-weekly	633	28,550
Wales	Weekly and bi-weekly	34	1,119
Scotland	Weekly and bi-weekly	37	1,504
Northern Ireland	Weekly and bi-weekly	7	175
Channel Isles and Isle of Man	Weekly and bi-weekly	1	28
UK total	Morning	1	278
	Sunday	1	81
	Weekly and bi-weekly	820	37,064

Source: The Press Council, *The Press and the People*, 34th annual report, 1987, p. 329.

Local newspapers, because of their monopoly, are highly influential in defining news for their readers and are likely to be the single most important source of news, especially political news, within their area. In any particular circulation area where a successful local paper achieves a high penetration, somewhere in excess of 80 per cent of households may be reading the same newspaper each day. It seems unlikely that even a top-selling tabloid such as the *Sun* could equal such readership levels in any given locale. Golding cites research conducted on an inner-city council estate in Leicester which revealed that while 56 per cent of residents read the *Sun* and 25 per cent read the *Daily Mirror*, 83 per cent read the *Leicester Mercury* and 94 per cent the local community paper produced by the local council.[11] The potential of such local newspapers for agenda-setting discussions of local matters cannot be overstated. Table 1.3 illustrates the importance of local newspapers as a source of local news.

There is, moreover, growing evidence to suggest that free newspapers may, in some areas, be supplanting the traditional weekly paid papers as the primary source of information about local matters. A MORI poll conducted in Harlow, Essex, for example, discovered that the most common sources of information about the council were the *Harlow Star* (72 per cent), the weekly free newspaper, the *Classified* (48 per cent), a second weekly free paper, the *Harlow Gazette* (41 per cent), a weekly paid-for paper, and the *Harlow News* (40 per cent), a civic monthly free paper.[12]

Table 1.3 Sources of most local news (percentages)

	1981	1982	1983	1984	1985	1986	1987
Television	12	12	14	18	16	17	19
Radio	13	12	10	13	14	12	12
Newspapers	56	58	59	54	55	56	56
Magazines	1	1	1	1	1	—	—
Talking to people	13	13	12	11	11	10	9
Don't knows	5	4	4	3	3	5	4

Source: *IBA Yearbook*, London, IBA, 1988, table 16.

The significance of the local press can also be measured by the considerable advertising revenues it generates. In 1987 the regional press attracted £1,280 million of advertising, which represents 36 per cent of total press advertising and 22 per cent of the national advertising revenues total for all media. In 1970 the equivalent figure was 35.8 per cent, suggesting considerable stability of market share which is consistently almost 30 per cent greater than national newspaper revenues at 26.9 per cent of total market share in 1987.[13] The overall figure for regional press advertising revenues, however, conceals a variety of financial fortunes for daily, weekly paid-for and free newspapers – see Table 1.4.

Table 1.4 Regional newspaper advertising by type of publication (£m.)

	Daily (morning/ evening)	Weekly paid-for	Free	Total
1977	244 (61.6%)	123 (31.1%)	29 (7.3%)	396
1978	298	150	35	483
1979	359	181	53	593
1980	378	178	84	640
1981	393	187	104	684
1982	405 (54.9%)	196 (26.6%)	136 (18.5%)	737
1983	430	207	180	817
1984	474	223	224	921
1985	506	234	263	1,003
1986	544	243	314	1,101
1987 (first half)	294 (47.0%)	131 (21.0%)	200 (32.0%)	625

Source: *AFN News*, April/May 1988, p. 10.

Table 1.4 shows that in the decade following 1977 the dailies' share of regional advertising dropped by 15 per cent, and the paid-for weeklies' by 10 per cent, with the beneficiaries being the free newspapers, which picked up 25 per cent of market share in the same period. The year 1987 ended with free newspapers showing a 29 per cent year-on-year increase and with advertising revenues reaching £405 million. Free newspapers are consequently growing in advertising terms at roughly twice the rate of television and national newspapers.[14] The divergent fortunes of the different components of the regional press are also evident if increases in advertising revenues are examined. Total regional newspaper advertising revenues rose by 49 per cent between 1982 and 1987, but revenues expanded only by 34 per cent for dailies and by 24 per cent for paid-for weeklies during that period. Free newspapers, however, increased revenues by 132 per cent, thereby bolstering the total regional paper increase. It was the same very striking growth in free newspaper revenues which for the first time in 1986 allowed regional weeklies to overtake regional dailies in terms of total advertising revenues.[15]

Two other factors illustrate the importance of the local press. First, it continues to serve as a training ground for young people entering journalism who aspire to progress from the humble position of junior reporter on a weekly to a job on the local daily and eventually to journalism on a national paper. The limited number of national job opportunities means inevitably that not all aspirants will be successful. It remains none the less a goal. As a municipal journalist on a local paper confided, 'Most of us who work here are frustrated *Guardian* or *Independent* writers.' Local journalists' enthusiasms for a job on a national paper have a predictable spin-off. They supply news in the form either of a 'tip-off' or of a fully written-up story to the national newspaper network, ever hopeful that an editor might spot their talent. Local stories can, by this route, structure national news agendas. This happened when a Birmingham hospital was unable to perform very urgent and necessary heart surgery on young children because of a shortage of resources. After a number of airings in the local media, the story contributed substantially to making the hospital crisis a national news story which ran throughout the winter of 1987 to 1988. But, as Hetherington observes, such 'snowballing' effects require considerable determination on the part of the local journalist, and there may be a good deal of initial reluctance to run a local story in the national media.[16]

Finally, the local press is significant because it may provide a relatively open and pluralistic forum for public discussion and debate at a time when large sections of the British national press are increasingly speaking with a monotonously homogeneous voice, too often suffused with what Stuart Hall has described as 'the porno-racist ethics of the *Sun*'.[17] To characterize the British press as politically right wing is an uncontentious designation. Evidence to support the claim is abundant. In the 1987 general election, for example, the press overwhelmingly supported the Conservative Party. Among the tabloids the only exceptions were the *Mirror* (Labour) and *Today* (Alliance); but the latter has subsequently been purchased by Murdoch's News International and its advocacy and partisanship in the next general election are unlikely to prompt any great uncertainty or speculation.

Prior to the 1987 general election, moreover, the tabloid press orchestrated a concerted campaign against Labour politicians in certain local authorities, labelling and stigmatizing them as the 'loony left' and presenting their activities and policies as ridiculous and anti-democratic. James Curran's study of this tabloid coverage suggests that, to achieve these ends, editors were guilty of promoting bias, omission of fact, fabrication of stories and simple lies.[18]

Local newspapers undoubtedly express a great diversity of opinion. This plurality may simply reflect the fact that there are a greater number of papers (almost 1,800), but it also expresses, at least in part, their commitment to reflect diverse local opinions and to promote a local patriotism. A study of reporting of the 1986 board-and-lodging regulations in the national and local press confirmed that local newspapers reported and responded to the issue more heterogeneously than the national press. National papers broadly supported the Conservative government and alleged that young people were exploiting what had previously been over-generous levels of benefit for homelessness and unemployment. Since the press allegation was that young people were effectively on a well-paid holiday, stories were often headlined 'Costa del Dole'. But local papers responded to the issue less uniformly, and many were sympathetic to the difficulties of young people who were demonstrating their homelessness by living in tent communities in city centres. Local papers were also much more likely to quote the views of sympathetic pressure groups such as Shelter.[19] Increasingly monopolistic ownership of the national press is likely to exacerbate existing tendencies towards ideological uniformity, and consequently the importance of the local press as a potential counterbalance, and source of a more extensive range of opinions, should not be underestimated.

DEVELOPMENTS IN THE LOCAL PRESS

There have been major developments in the local press during the last decade. The growth of free newspapers, changing structures of ownership and the application of new technology have radically altered many aspects of the organization, production and content of the local press.

The rapid and substantial growth of the free press, in terms of both numbers of titles published and advertising revenues generated, has been referred to above. The rate and significance of free newspaper growth cannot, however, be overstated. In 1975, 185 free newspapers were published, but by 1987 the figure had reached 822, with aggregate circulations exceeding 37 million. In 1970 advertising revenue was £2 million, and by 1981 it was £100 million; but in 1987 it reached in excess of £400 million.[20] The phenomenon has proved to be European-wide, with an estimated 4,000 free newspaper titles distributing 200 million copies throughout Western Europe.[21] The free newspaper business can be risky and unstable, however. The net increase of 49 new titles recorded in 1987 masks much larger shifts of fortunes, with 85 new papers launched but 36 closing during the year.[22] The first daily free newspaper, the *Daily News*, was launched in Birmingham in October 1984. The paper claims to reach 86 per cent of households in the area, attracts 25 per cent of total advertising revenue in Birmingham and claims a dramatic effect on the sales of its local and national competitors.[23] This last point is significant because the increased competition from free newspapers has resulted in a substantial and permanent reduction in the circulation of the traditional paid-for weeklies. In 1977 the figure had been constant at 11.8 million for almost thirty years, but by 1987 it had fallen by 35 per cent to 7,682,000 – a reduction which accounted for virtually the whole drop in newspaper circulation over the decade.[24] Regional evening papers declined by 17 per cent across the same period. Competition from free newspapers, moreover, has exacerbated those tendencies which Simpson in the mid-1970s characterized as the 'commercialisation of the regional press'.[25] The distribution of free newspapers has constrained weeklies from raising their cover prices, and consequently they now attract a mere 14 per cent of their revenues from sales, whereas regional dailies attract 38 per cent of their revenues from readers. Simpson suggested that, as advertisements come to constitute a more significant component in revenue than sales, financial and commercial interests will prevail over journalistic interests, imposing substantial constraints on both the range and the quality of stories published. If Simpson's logic is correct, the advent of free newspapers might be expected to precipitate a considerable change in the quality of editorial in the local press.

A second set of changes, relating to the structure of ownership and economic organization of the local press, is equally significant. There has been an accelerating tendency to shift from independent or family ownership to ownership by the chain newspaper groups – a process accompanied by an involvement of national chains in the local press. Associated Newspaper Holdings and the Observer Group, for example, are now major owners of local newspaper companies, while United Newspapers own the prestigious *Yorkshire Post* and *Yorkshire Evening Post* as well as the *Sheffield Star*, the *Sheffield Telegraph* and forty-five other local newspapers.[26] The consequence of both these tendencies has been to consolidate the monopoly character of the local press. More than half of the daily morning and evening newspapers published outside London are controlled by eight groups, while nine (mostly the same) groups control 35 per cent of the paid-for weekly press.[27]

There has been an equivalent increase in concentration of ownership of the free press. Initially free newspapers were established by independent buccaneer entrepreneurs, classically cast in the Eddie Shah mould. Their occupational background was not typically in newspapers, and their attitudes towards the larger traditional newspaper groups were competitive and confrontational. They were attracted to the free newspaper industry by the high profits which the market promised. Many of these pioneer publishers have recently sold their newspapers to the older, well-established companies. In 1985, for example, Paul Morgan sold Morgan Communications to Reed International for £9.7 million,[28] while in May 1988 Thomson Regional Newspapers bought Keith

Barwell's Herald Newspaper Group, which published twenty-six free newspapers, for an estimated £20 million.[29]

Monopoly and concentration have developed apace as the free newspaper industry has matured. More than half of all free newspapers are now published by just ten companies, while the leading twenty-two publishers (each producing over half a million copies a week) account for over 70 per cent of total weekly production – see Table 1.5.

Table 1.5 Major publishers of free newspapers

		Copies per week	Percentage of production
1	Reed Regional Publishing	5,765,254	86.3
2	Thomson Regional Newspapers	2,229,290	24.9
3	Yellow Advertiser Group	2,215,792	100.0
4	United Newspapers	1,772,553	31.5
5	EMAP	1,763,505	56.0
6	Westminster Press	1,586,885	32.8
7	Argus Newspapers	1,447,501	79.6
8	Northcliffe Newspapers	1,336,467	19.6
9	Manchester Guardian Group	1,271,234	38.7
10	Southern Newspapers	1,024,000	47.5
11	Trader Group	836,991	100.0
12	Eastern Counties Newspapers	806,647	35.8
13	Goodhead Publishing	705,249	100.0
14	Johnston Group	659,028	64.8
15	Portsmouth and Sunderland	634,081	34.0
16	Recorder Newspapers	617,683	100.0
17	Middlesex County Press	592,799	86.9
18	Ingersoll Publications	560,524	19.8
19	Midland News Association	545,916	21.1
20	Messenger Newspapers Group	542,789	95.8
21	Adscene Publishing Group	533,142	88.1
22	Trinity International	529,888	23.6

Source: *UK Press Gazette*, 15 August 1988, p. 17.

Only one of the ten top publishers, the Yellow Advertiser Group, is a relatively new publishing concern among a group dominated by traditional publishers. The competitive threat of the innovative free newspapers has been systematically absorbed by the traditional newspaper houses and the profits they generate harnessed to bolster existing publishing projects. As one writer commented: 'A listing of the top free publishers is . . . not very different from a listing of the well-known paid operators.'[30]

Concentration of ownership of the local press in large newspaper groups has been accompanied by a process of horizontal
integration within the local media. Local press groups now possess substantial holdings in regional television companies. Pearson
Longman Plc, for example, owns a 21 per cent share in Yorkshire
Television Ltd; D. C. Thomson & Co. and Pergamon Foundation
(Liechtenstein) each own a 20 per cent share in Central Indepen-
dent Television Plc; while The Guardian and Manchester Evening
News Plc holds a 50 per cent share in Anglia Television Ltd.
Local press groups have acquired similar financial interests in
local radio. They enjoy a 32 per cent holding in Birmingham
Broadcasting Ltd (BRMB), 24 per cent in Capital Radio, 22 per
cent in Hereward Radio, 19.5 per cent in the London Broadcasting Company, 31.9 per cent in Midland Community Radio Plc
(Mercia Sound), 20.5 per cent in North-East Broadcasting (Metro
Radio) and 17 per cent in Piccadilly Radio. In a number of other
independent local radio stations, press holdings exceed 10 per cent
of total voting shares.[31] For their part, some local radio stations,
like Red Rose, have launched free newspapers, blurring further
the dividing lines between local media.[32] This process of horizontal integration has complemented and reinforced tendencies consequent on concentration within local newspaper markets.

The final area of major developments in the local press in the
last ten years has been the introduction of a new printing technology. For many owners of newspapers, the new technology
seemed to offer unprecedented opportunities to lower production
costs, improve the technical quality of their product, undermine
restrictive trades union practices, lower staffing levels and introduce a more flexible division of labour between journalists and
printers. Trades unionists, although to different degrees in the
National Union of Journalists, the National Graphical Association
and SOGAT, viewed new technology apprehensively, but universally perceived it as potentially threatening to job security and
to their respective positions in a finely gradated hierarchy of
newspaper workers.[33] The introduction of new technology into
the provincial press has consequently proved contentious. The
Press Council's view, that 'the changes in newspaper production
techniques which provided the opportunity for a revolution in
Fleet Street, proved far less traumatic outside the capital', is as
curious as it is misleading.[34] It is difficult to imagine how the
daily scenes of violent confrontation between police and union

pickets outside Wapping might be matched in any provincial setting, but this does little to support the thesis of the introduction of new technology without resistance.

The winter of 1983–4 witnessed some near-equivalent battles between as many as 1,200 trades unionists and police officers outside the Messenger Group premises on Tuesday and Wednesday nights when Eddie Shah printed his newspaper using new technology imposed on an NGA workforce.[35] In the upshot the battles at Warrington proved more portentious for the national than the local press. Following the Messenger dispute in autumn 1985, the NUJ and NGA signed an accord which established joint committees for negotiating new technology agreements, to ensure a unified trades union response to management on issues concerning new technology.

None the less, the introduction of new technology has been rapid. In the subsequent two years seventy initial agreements were signed within the framework of the accord, and between December 1985 and autumn 1987 direct input facilities were introduced into all Thomson Regional News centres,[36] as the company discovered that an evening paper could now go into profit with a circulation as low as 10,000.[37] A survey published in 1987 showed that increased payments for journalists following the introduction of new technology varied between nil and £40.[38] In some newspaper houses, management have imposed direct inputting technology without agreement. There have been a number of long-term strikes on local newspapers – for example, at the *Sheffield Star* and in a number of London free newspapers owned by the Morgan Communications Group.[39] The impact of new technology on the local press is already substantial. Judgements concerning whether new technology will generate low-cost opportunities prompting a proliferation of new titles and innovative formats, however, or reinforce the concentration of monopoly control of the larger established press interests, would be premature; certainly both claims have been made.[40]

DEVELOPMENTS IN THE LOCAL PRESS ENVIRONMENT

The local press operates within a well-established network of local media which are its rivals both for audiences and, perhaps more critically, for advertising revenues. Recent and proposed developments in local radio and regional television are consequently extremely significant for their potential impact on local newspapers. The local press, moreover, in common with other local media, generates news stories in co-operation with a range of local sources: from the allotments society offering copy about its recent vegetable show, to more important and routine sources such as a friendly sergeant at the local police station who will alert the local hack when a potentially interesting story arises. Recently, however, two major new sources of stories have entered the arena of local communications, reflecting developments in public relations activities in both local and central government. The implications of each of these changes are considered in turn.

The local press faces competition from both local radio and regional television as alternative news sources, although a study by Local Radio Workshop was extremely sceptical about the quality of local news broadcast by the three major local radio stations broadcasting in London.[41] The BBC boasts forty-nine local radio stations in the UK, broadcasting local news programmes in the morning, at midday and in the evening as well as updating bulletins on the hour. Forty-seven independent local radio (ILR) stations similarly broadcast local news throughout the day but can also draw on a UK-wide network news service from the London Broadcasting Company (LBC).[42] Changes in local radio make it uncertain whether or not it will grow or diminish as a competitor to the local press. Both BBC and ILR stations face financial problems. In 1988, as part of a more general regime of savings, the BBC announced 10 per cent cuts in local radio budgets, with inevitable consequences for quality of output. Since news gathering is expensive, it may be expected that in the short run the quality of news broadcasting will decline.[43] The economic viability of ILR stations is extremely variable, reflecting the circumstances of individual stations and their relative commitment to expensive high-quality programming, but also the strength of competition from other local media.

Radio Wyvern, for example, had reduced its news-room staff from six journalists to one within four years of its launch, to avoid bankruptcy.[44] Some ILR stations, like Viking in Hull, Sheffield's Hallam and Bradford's Pennine, have amalgamated to create greater markets for advertising revenues to ensure their survival. In the North-East, Radio Metro has absorbed Radio

Tees, while Red Rose in Preston has taken over Leeds's Radio Aire. But in this process, prompted by the need for economic survival, a regional rather than a local independent radio network is emerging. There are almost inevitable shifts in the focus of news output away from the local to regional and national stories.[45]

The existing local radio network, moreover, faces radical restructuring as a result of government policy. The Home Secretary's statement in the House of Commons on 19 January 1989 confirmed many of the proposals for changes in local radio outlined in the green paper of February 1987 and the white paper on broadcasting published in October 1988.[46] The main proposals of the 1990 Broadcasting Act relating to local radio suggest that the BBC should continue to provide public service broadcasting, but in the independent sector there will be several hundred local and community stations, a new radio authority and a 'lighter' system of regulation which would not require such stations to carry local news or current affairs. Douglas Hurd envisaged that 'there will certainly be greater competition for audiences and revenue', among the local media, but that 'radio could substantially increase its share of total advertising revenue'.[47] If such speculations become fact, local radio could squeeze local press profits and viability.

Initially only twenty community radio stations have been established, with the pioneers coming on air in autumn 1989. They vary in their possession of financial and human resources, audience reach, range of programming and advertising revenues. Some stations like West London Radio are targeted at ethnic minorities and are unlikely to threaten newspapers' wider audiences. Sunset Radio in Manchester, however, possesses a staff of twenty-four, including a news editor and three other journalists, plans to provide a diet of local news and anticipates raising £1.1 million in advertising revenues in its first year on air.[48] A number of such community stations could substantially deplete the pool of local advertising revenue and might establish themselves with audiences as alternative sources of local news. Both possibilities would present the local press with considerable difficulties.

Regional television likewise offers competition to the local press as a source of regional news. There are regional early-evening news and current affairs programmes as well as brief news bulletins throughout the day broadcast by the thirteen BBC and eighteen ITV regional and sub-regional centres. As with local radio, the structure of regional television and the character of its news output are changing. Some BBC regional news rooms tend to survive with spartan budgets and staffing levels which are relatively low compared to their ITV counterparts. BBC Midlands, for example, has a news room with 21 journalists, while the equivalent figure at Central Television is 84. Shortage of journalists is not the BBC's only difficulty. Since the early 1970s the Corporation has engaged in a number of very public skirmishes with the Conservative government concerning allegations of bias in the reporting of certain issues such as the Falklands war and the US bombing of Libya. A conviction has developed among news reporters at the BBC that the Board of Governors would not support any producer making critical programmes. What Hetherington describes as the 'play-safe disease', initially incubated in the stuffy corridors of the BBC at national level, 'has filtered through to regional news rooms'.[49] As a result, BBC regional television news may have lost much of its previous vitality.

Independent television companies are confronting major reform as a consequence of the proposals to deregulate the system contained in the Broadcasting Act. The IBA was replaced in January 1991 by the Independent Television Commission (ITC), which subsumes all existing commercial channels under its remit, but operates with a lighter touch. The ITC will allocate franchises to regional television companies, but applicants will first be required to pass a 'quality threshold' and then put in a financial offer.[50] The ITC is then required, other than in exceptional circumstances, to accept the highest bid. This auction system means that the new Channel Three regional companies will be under great pressure to maximize profits and minimize costs once the franchise has been granted. Ironically, the white paper also specifies that companies must 'show high quality news and current affairs . . . in main viewing periods'.[51] But the need to adopt a 'mini-max' philosophy towards news broadcasting, which is implicit in many of the white paper reforms, could sound the death knell for expensive programming such as regional news.[52] If such a pessimistic prognosis proves correct, the local press may become more significant as a source of local news, but subject to greater competition for local advertising revenues.

Two other developments in the local press environment are

noteworthy and both concern changes in local newspaper sources of news. First, the period since the early 1970s has witnessed a dramatic growth in the public relations activities of local government. The growth was prompted by a desire to raise public awareness of certain areas of local government activity and service provision and to improve the rather dull and bureaucratic public image of local government. The size of public relations departmental staff and their budgets varies considerably across different types of local authority, with the larger departments residing in the county, London borough and metropolitan district areas. But across all types of local authority, public relations activities have expanded.[53] The implications of this development for the local press are threefold.

First, local government public relations officers overwhelmingly identify as their highest priority the need to promote good working relationships with the local media.[54] They are employed to manipulate/construct local news agendas to promote the most favourable view of the local authority and its activities. To this end, PROs employ advertising and marketing techniques, stage press conferences and issue substantial numbers of press releases each month. Nor should it be assumed that these press releases are simply rejected. PROs seem to be extremely successful in using press releases to stimulate stories about local government in the local press. A recent research survey revealed that 82 per cent of public relations officers claimed that more than 75 per cent of their press releases generated stories in the local press.[55] Local government PROs have become a 'fifth estate', to borrow Baistow's phrase, which seems to enjoy an increasingly significant agenda-building role in the context of the local media.[56]

Another important and direct way in which local government public relations officers can influence local news agendas is by publishing, and distributing for free, their own 'civic' or 'municipal' newspapers. The number of such municipal newspapers has expanded considerably during the 1980s, and they enjoy a wide readership within their constituencies. They are discussed in more detail below.

The third implication for the local press arising from developments in local government public relations reflects the tendency of local journalists to migrate into public relations as part of an increasingly common career development. Local government pay and conditions are typically superior to those prevailing in the local press. Overall, 40 per cent of local government public relations officers have worked previously in journalism, while in the counties and London boroughs, where the larger departments are sited, the figures are 65 per cent and 68 per cent respectively.[57] One line of argument in *The Silent Watchdog* suggested that local journalists may become dependent on their local authority sources for news and thereby constrained from being strongly critical. Journalists, so the argument ran, should not bite the hand that feeds them. This maxim has become increasingly literal truth, as investigative local journalists writing hostile copy about a local authority may risk offending a future employer and damaging future career opportunities.[58]

Developments in information sources in central as well as local government are important in their implications for the local press. The Conservative government under Mrs Thatcher, but especially some of its members such as Lord Young, was an enthusiastic advocate of the possibilities provided by using a range of marketing strategies and public relations techniques to promote key areas of government policy. The Central Office of Information (COI), as it always has, issues a daily flood of press releases into national and local communications networks from its centre in London and its various regional offices, designed to raise public awareness of certain policies.[59] However, allegations have been made concerning the partisan content of much government advertising. The press officer at the Institute of Public and Civil Servants, which represents many of the civil servants who write these press releases, complained that civil servants are being asked to 'advocate, rather than explain, government policy' and to fulfil 'a role more suited to Conservative Central Office rather than the government information service'.[60]

A further but interesting innovation during the 1980s has been the decentralization of the Conservative government's 'agitprop' activities into the major departments of state, with ministers controlling very substantial advertising and public relations budgets. Advertising and PR expenditure for 1987–8 for the Manpower Services Commission, for example, was £32.2 million. Some departmental budgets have increased stupendously. Lord Young's budget at the Department of Trade and Industry grew from £1,997,288 in 1986 to £12,216,000 in 1987. Similarly at the Department of Environment the 1986 figure of £1,163,093 rocketed to £24.6 million in 1987. The aggregate figure for government expenditure on public relations and marketing, including COI expenditure, was a staggering £368,057,396 in 1987. It is hardly surprising, given these figures, that in 1987 the government over-took Unilever to become the largest single advertiser in the UK. Much of the resulting publicity and propaganda materials were targeted at the local media.[61]

Unpopular or contentious policies such as the poll tax have received particular attention and prompted the government to engage in 'a substantial PR exercise to explain and promote the community charge', in which 'local papers have been identified as a major avenue for communication with the public'.[62] To date, the campaign has also involved distribution of glossy pamphlets, a tour of the provinces by local government ministers Michael Howard and Christopher Chope, a video and fact sheets, with 'enormous efforts being targeted at local newspaper editors'.[63] Central government public relations involves using the local press as a conduit to its readers, to structure local agendas and, by aggregation, to create a national climate of opinion receptive to the particular policy in question. Research suggests that local newspapers' willingness to use these press releases tends to reflect their financial and journalistic resources, with free newspapers proving the most receptive.[64]

The Central Office of Information also tries to structure local news agendas via local radio. In 1985 it distributed 400 tapes to local radio stations in the hope of securing free air time. The tapes may, for example, contain interviews with the minister for housing at the Department of the Environment discussing 'the right to buy council houses', with questions being posed by a civil servant. The tapes provide a free 'filler' for local radio, although take-up rates may again reflect stations' journalistic and financial resources. The COI concedes a distinct difference in the take-up between BBC and ILR stations. 'The commercial sta-tions', it claims, 'are more adventurous and less likely to dismiss our output as establishment material.'[65]

These developments in local and central government public relations activities, in tandem with the deregulation of local radio and regional television, signal a shifting and changing environ-ment for local press operations.

DEFINING THE NEW BOUNDARIES OF THE LOCAL PRESS

There are two quite distinct, but not necessarily compatible, tendencies in the various developments in the local press discussed above. First, there has been an apparent movement towards monopoly in the market, combined with extensive capital investment in large-scale industrial production methods. Local papers, subsumed into national chains, are now printed in regional centres on the same sort of massive rotary presses staffed by the same massive oily-handed Morelocks that one could see in the national daily offices of Fleet Street, Manchester or Glasgow. Smaller weeklies have become mere editions of larger newspapers differentiated only by one page slipped in (the 'slipped' edition) or perhaps by different front and back pages. Larger weeklies have sometimes become little more than digests of the week's news from the evening paper serving the same town. A move towards giantism, based on economies of scale, appears to characterize the ownership, marketing and production methods of the local press.

The second tendency has been the development of a new technology, moving away from the old hot-metal mechanical engineering production towards one using computer-based control systems and photo-setting. As the new technology has developed, production skills have been gradually eliminated, to be replaced by a 'black-box' production process, whereby small numbers of individuals with relatively short periods of training can undertake typesetting by use of microchip-controlled typesetting systems. Early in the development of these processes, photographic setting along with cut-and-paste page make-up meant that capital entry costs for small local publications could be measured in a fraction of previous costs. Jobbing printers were available using the new print methods, and this meant that small firms could start up easily and offer competition for the established monopolies.

This is not to argue a simplistic 'new low-cost technology led to ideological variety' view. There are factors in the market and facets of the large corporations which have militated against such a simple equation of the free market with a burgeoning variety of viewpoints competing equally for public acceptance. None the less, it is the case that the new cheaper technology has created the opportunity for a number of new developments in the local press. These developments, moreover, create problems for any understanding of the mass media as institutions producing and articulating a unitary capitalist ideology which merely reflects their structural roots in monopoly capitalism.

Our purpose here is to examine these developments in detail and to consider precisely how they pose such problems. We begin with a brief discussion of these empirical developments in the local press and the theoretical problems implied. This will constitute the outline of the argument pursued in the rest of the book. The developments that have taken place have included those emanating primarily from changes in the market but which have ideological implications, while others have ideological origins which have been made possible due to market changes consequent upon technological change. We will examine them in that order.

THE FREE NEWSPAPER REVOLUTION

In the early 1960s virtually all newspapers had a cover price. A newspaper's income was in part revenue from sales and in part from advertising. Advertisers normally required some evidence of a newspaper's circulation, and there was consequently a connection between economic viability and a successful editorial section. A newspaper containing news, features and sports pages, which attracted high numbers of readers and sold well, attracted advertisers and meant that the newspaper could charge high rates for its advertising space.

The apparently immutable syllogism linking cover price to editorial content, and both of these in turn to advertising, proved less reliable than expected. 'Freesheets', as they were called in the early days of their development, were distributed free, but were normally entirely devoted to advertisements. They were not considered 'real' newspapers because they had little or no journalistic content, and they were distributed rather than sold so there was no guarantee that the people who received them would even look at them. They were judged to pose no real threat to the traditional local papers.

By the mid-1970s entrepreneurs using the new typesetting and printing technology were producing a radically different type of free newspaper. The most celebrated of these was Eddie Shah, the former Granada TV employee who established and owned the Messenger series of free weekly newspapers based in Stockport and distributed throughout the south of the Greater Manchester conurbation. These papers were based on a similar mix of advertising and editorial to that which underpinned the traditional commercial local press, but differed considerably by opting for maximum distribution numbers – rather than winning a high circulation – low production costs and a cheap distribution network, with district organizers commanding an army of low-paid schoolchildren, instead of sales through newsagents. The major difference between this new breed of free newspaper and its free-sheet predecessor related to editorial content, which in quality and quantity increasingly tended to expand until it became comparable to its traditional weekly paid rivals.

The low costs were partly the outcome of new-technology-based printing. But they also reflected the minimum provision of office space and small journalistic staffs – one or two reporters instead of four or five. The logic of this cost-cutting process resulted in one free newspaper opening which employed no journalists.[66] For some free newspapers one way of squaring the circle within these parameters was to encourage the local community to write their own papers. The local worthies who previously acted as sources, providing journalists with information with which to manufacture news, now themselves became reporters. Journalists would then correct or rewrite what was sent in and in this way became sub-editors for the community newspaper. Another simple but cost-effective way of filling space was to use readers' letters, which reflected the opinions of the locality and further underlined the identification of such free newspapers as papers of the community. The most important sources of free copy, of course, were the rapidly expanding local government public relations departments. PROs circulated local papers with selected extracts from council and committee meetings which could quickly be used to generate stories. Temptations to use such press releases were great, since they obviated the need for a reporter to attend the meeting.[67] Press officers also issued press releases to local papers which could serve as ready-made stories. The practice became something akin to a public subsidy for the local press.

The existing traditional local newspapers responded in one of four ways. The least successful were unable to compete and either folded or drew in their horns and withdrew from circulation areas where the new free papers were most dominant. The more successful either bought up the companies issuing free newspapers or launched their own in direct competition. The rumoured arrival in Manchester of a new free newspaper backed by Robert Maxwell was sufficient incentive for the *Manchester Evening News* to launch its own *Metro News*.[68] A fourth alternative has been simply to fight the free paper as a traditional cover-price commercial newspaper would be fought.

The free newspaper industry remains in a state of flux. Despite the tendency towards monopoly dominance and professionalization of news output implicit in this dominance, new titles continue to appear, while others vanish with an equivalent rapidity. But while the highly polished free products of the big evening paper companies tend to revert to the traditional professional modes of news production, the new model free weekly newspapers continue to offer editorial space to other news sources, with implications for the ideological nature of the press. In brief, this creates a pluralism in the nature of content and the authorship of news which the professional manufacture of news in the traditional commercial press makes impossible. How transient or trivial this pluralism will prove to be remains to be seen.

Two other sources of ideological pluralism have manifested themselves in the local press during the past decade and a half: the 'alternative' or 'community' press and the 'civic' or 'municipal' free newspapers. Both have been the product of tendencies encouraged by the new print technology and have been users and originators of associated new modes of news production requiring a redefinition of what constitutes news and newspapers. Much of the momentum behind the establishment of both has, moreover, been a self-conscious desire to offer a different ideological posture towards not only the news stories of the day but the broader prevailing political climate within the community. Both types of new papers have embraced explicit agitprop objectives. The local alternative or community press has been based on co-operative forms of ownership and work organization and dedicated to a definition of news which accentuates a community based on communality rather than hierarchy.[69] The municipal free newspapers, produced and published by local government public relations departments, as sources of information for local residents, have been judged by Conservative politicians, certainly in central government, as little more than outlets for 'propaganda on the rates'.

THE ALTERNATIVE PRESS

The alternative local press began to manifest itself in the late 1960s and early 1970s. It derived in style and content from the low-cost radical magazines of the anti-Vietnam and hippie groups in the United States and similar politically left-oriented publications such as *Oz* in Britain. All of the content was an alternative to the traditional commercial press. It provided what was not available elsewhere. There were alternative news, alternative politics, alternative art, alternative good food guides and alternative advertisements. The bread-and-butter basis of these magazines (in the sense of what enabled them to sell and survive) was and remains the 'what's on' guide. This was reflected in the title of the London-based forerunner of the rest: *Time Out*. Consequently there was an inherent tension between the aims and appeal of such publications. On the one hand, they espoused the radical left-wing politics which was manifest in the news and political features which they carried. On the other, the advertisements and consumerist feature articles subscribed and appealed to a sort of modish radical chic.[70] This was expressed in an ephemeral, egocentric hedonism which judged the latest form of indulgence to be the best. So long as the political right was identified and presented as the force which opposed and repressed innocent, youthful self-expression in the form of sexual freedom, experimental drug taking or apparently degenerate forms of art and music, there was a natural synergy between the left politics and the hedonistic modishness of such publications. But, with hindsight, it seems that such a synergy was contingent on the social and cultural ambience of the time rather than any inherent characteristics of the two aspects of the local alternative press.

In recent years the potential for dissonance between commercial necessity and radical politics and news production has been apparent in such publications. It is thus their nature that many do not survive for long and are often replaced by others with similar short life expectancies.[71] But many of the present crop are simply 'what's on' guides, without any left-wing or other overt political content and little news content. However, while some papers struggle with the conflicting desires to pursue radical politics through journalism and the need to survive in the market, other alternative magazines cater for specific groups. In these instances, access to specialist markets of both advertisers and readers

depends upon political attitudes in the magazine which underlie
its validity for its audience. The clearest examples of such publications are those written by and for homosexual audiences and
ethnic minorities. In gaining access to sales to homosexuals and
establishing themselves in the market for specifically homosexual-
oriented advertisements, it is necessary to carry news and views
which reflect a homosexual view of the social and political world.
And given the political right wing's opposition to pro-homo-
sexual policies, such gay news and views tend to identify with
left radical politics (even though this tends to be one-issue-domi-
nated). We will examine in Chapter 5 how the contradictions in
the aims and the practices of the alternative local press manifest
themselves and how the publishing co-operatives attempt to cope
with them.

THE MUNICIPAL FREE PRESS

The third development in the local press which has radically
disturbed the old homogeneity has been the development of local
government free newspapers. The growth of such papers has been
a response by predominantly Labour councils to two tendencies:
first, the prominence in the local commercial press of newspapers
owned by large national chains and increasingly professing support for right-wing political views which characterize their sister
national newspapers; second, the remarkable number of legislative
reforms of local government enacted by the Conservative government since 1979, including restrictions on the powers of local
government public relations departments, which many local politicians have interpreted as a sustained attack on local government
demanding a response. It is also possible to argue that the development of the new municipal press is part of a more general process
of the overt politicization of the bureaucracy, especially the information services, in both local and central government. It is, of
course, possible to overstate this argument, since the official version of the civil service as 'non-political' was always a highly
suspect account of events. Numerous academic studies have dem-
onstrated that bureaucrats exercise power in a covert way which
is unacknowledged and often uncontrolled. But, more recently,
civil servants working in the Central Office of Information, their
colleagues who handle the substantial press, public relations and
advertising budgets in the departments of state and the press staff

at No. 10 Downing Street have become overtly concerned with promoting party political issues. In local authorities, the expansion of professional public relations personnel has prompted similar allegations that they are local civil servants paid to undertake political advice and propaganda activities.

The identification of this Labour municipal journalism as 'propaganda on the rates' by the Conservative Party in the national press implies, however, that there is something specific and pathological about such municipal newspapers. In fact, as we show in Chapter 6, civic free newspapers have been produced by Conservative local authorities without arousing national comment for some years. Whether these are less propagandist or not depends on the identifications of bias made by those judging the issue. There is, however, a systematic difference between newspapers published by Conservative and Labour local authorities. Labour civic newspapers are more likely to report the provision of services for disadvantaged groups and to give advice on rights for the unemployed, whereas the Conservative municipal press is more interested in the local resident as consumer. This, in turn, is reflected in the amount and type of advertising carried by each category of newspaper. The Conservative papers devote 50 per cent of their space to advertisements, which is about twice the figure for their Labour counterparts. While the Conservative advertisements are from private enterprise business, moreover, the Labour advertisements are likely to emanate from departments within the publishing authority that wish to publicize their own policies and service such as housing benefit centres and AIDS helplines.

Local authority free newspapers are now under considerable pressure as a consequence of two government policies. The first is the direct attack on 'propaganda on the rates', which takes the form of specific clauses in the 1986 and 1988 Local Government Acts debarring councils from publishing and distributing materials which may be specified as party political propaganda, and, as in the case of Clause 28 in the 1988 Act, promoting controversial causes such as homosexuality. Both Acts also delegated powers to the relevant minister to draw up a statutory code of conduct to regulate local government public relations activities. Second, the Department of the Environment's constant downward pressure on local government spending means that Labour councils in the big cities, which have lost heavily in central government financial support since the 1979 elections, have also experienced rate and community charge capping. As a consequence there is a persistent pressure to reduce all but vital expenditure.

Most Labour authorities have exhausted the possibilities of creative accounting which many regarded as a gamble on a Labour victory in the 1987 general election; and, as a consequence, departments which do not contribute directly to the provision of visible council services have been cut back. Public relations departments fall into this category. In Manchester, where even the refuse collectors have faced staffing level reductions, two free magazine publications have disappeared. *Manchester Magazine* and *Police Watch* have both ceased to publish. Over the country as a whole a number of municipal newspapers have decided it is easier to cease publication than risk offending the vaguely worded prescriptions embodied in the various clauses of the 1988 Act and a ministerial code of conduct. None the less, in the larger urban areas, local authorities continue to publish a growing number of increasingly professional publications with distribution figures approximating in some cases to almost a million copies per issue. In terms of both journalistic quality of editorial and technical quality of presentation, these papers very closely resemble the standards achieved by their commercial counterparts.

All these developments, which we shall examine in detail, mean that a simple view of the local press as an undifferentiated ideological monolith sustaining the power of capital is not adequate. Academic analysis of the mass media has typically drawn upon the Marxist notion of ideology, constructing the latter as a supportive apologia for the inequalities of economic and social structures of the capitalist system. On this account, ideology is located, like the state, as an element of the superstructure owing its existence to its legitimation function. This analysis ignores many features of the nature of the mass media, not least that they themselves are rooted in both the infrastructure and the superstructure of society. They produce goods and services which are sold in the market, but they also have direct ideological inputs and consequences. Second, where, like the BBC and the municipal free papers, they are part of the state, the pluralistic nature of capitalism invalidates the simple syllogism that 'the state is capitalist; some aspects of the mass media are parts of the state; therefore these parts of the mass media are pro-capitalist'. We need an analysis of the production of ideology which allows for the variations in the products of the mass media – for the Labour-controlled free newspapers and for Channel Four and BBC–2 television drama, documentary and current affairs departments. It may well be that a tendency exists for such elements within the mass media to be eliminated over time. But it may also be the case that, over time, 'deviant' channels emerge, or conformist parts of the system may be colonized by subversive practitioners. We consider these possibilities in the context of the local press.

Chapter 2

The corporation and the parish pump

The traditional, but limited, academic treatment of the local press in Britain has tended to focus on it in its institutional, political form. The question which has been asked has tended to be how it fits into the local polity. Whether this interpretation has been functionalist and uncritical,[1] or has taken a radical perspective,[2] writers have at most called on the market only as a device to explain some characteristic of the political and institutional nature of the local press. Murphy, for instance, emphasized the role of the market in explaining why, and how, cost limitation and avoidance, combined with profit maximization, led to a limitation on the investigative function of the local press.[3] Whitaker pursued the same sort of argument.[4] Both the functionalist and the critical / radical approaches, in other words, have tended to accept that it is a parish-pump phenomenon, to be defined, explained and understood within the limits of this parochialism.

In the USA, studies of the press are studies of the local press by definition. These again have tended to take one of two forms. On the one hand, there are functionalist explanations of the role of the press in the integration of local communities through the provision of a communal identity and the articulation of local community values.[5] On the other, writers have taken up the tradition established by the critical community-power studies of the 1930s, where the aim has been to show how the local press supports the power structure, or how owners tend to impose social control on their journalistic staffs and thus produce an ideological conformity.[6]

In some ways such analyses may be less problematic in looking at the press in the USA. There may well be a better case for identifying considerable overlap between the local economy, the local political system and local social relationships, with this degree of overlap being represented in part by a locally owned newspaper. In the UK, however, this situation, by and large, does not exist. A centralized political system has become yet more centralized over the past decade. An economy dominated by a small number of very large firms often multinational in form and ownership has become more dominated by such corporate structures. This is heavily reflected in the ownership and control of the local press. A small number of firms, generally conglomerate in nature and generally multinational in scope, own the voice of the parish pump in Britain. The localism of the British local press is ersatz; it is the product of an international corporate capitalism whose form would delight any unreconstructed Trotskyist.

Seaton and Curran describe the reduction in the available choice in local newspapers, showing how competition has been eliminated and choice restricted through corporate dominance in all sectors of the local press.[7] Cities in the UK with a choice of directly competing local morning or evening papers were reduced by 1974 to London, Edinburgh and Belfast.[8] Subsequently, this competition among London regional papers has ceased once again after the *Daily News*, Robert Maxwell's attempt to provide a competitor for the *Evening Standard*, failed to attract enough advertising to survive, despite readership levels which would have guaranteed survival for a regional evening or morning paper elsewhere as the provincial local monopoly. Referring to the Royal Commission on the Press of 1977,[9] Seaton and Curran show that in 1975 only 18 per cent of towns with local papers had a choice of local weeklies under separate ownership, a proportion that was little over half of what it had been in 1961. 'In short,' the Royal Commission argues, 'the *deus ex machina* of liberal theory which makes the consumer "sovereign" and proprietors accountable had been seriously eroded in much of the regional press.'[10]

'The last commission', says the report,

found some solace in the emergence of freesheets, a development which has become even more pronounced since it [the commission] reported. However, the rise of freesheets has caused a further reduction in the number of paid-for weeklies. Due to their dependent relationship to advertisers, freesheets do not constitute an independent voice. Ironically many of them are now published by the major chains. In 1985 the five largest publishers of freesheets were responsible between them for 220 free publications: the same publishers also controlled a further 266 paid-for papers.[11]

The report goes on to consider the argument that the tendency towards greater concentration of ownership will be reversed by the development of new technology arising from labour cost reductions which will allegedly result in fewer closures of existing newspapers and facilitate the launch of new ones. Such arguments, it says, should be treated with caution, and it identifies three reasons for this. The first is that the cost reductions are only of the order of 20 per cent and therefore do not negate the fact that massive inputs of capital are required to found newspapers; the second is that increased competition results in additional promotional costs which will increase set-up costs and weaken already weak papers. And the third reason is that the new technology will not nullify the fact that the wealthy and successful have more resources to take advantage of the new technology than the poor and the powerless.[12] It is not hard to see that this last point tends to undermine all the optimism about the beneficial effects of the new technology producing a newly invigorated pluralism through a combination of the market and benign technological determinism. Given that all can take advantage of the beneficial effects of the new technology, there is clearly no reason to think that those with less wealth will be differentially advantaged by it. Far from it: one would expect big companies to be able to take advantage of economies of scale from vertical and horizontal integration with the new technology as they did with the old.

All the evidence we have of developments since Seaton and Curran wrote in 1985 suggests that the concentration of ownership in the local press has continued to intensify and that big corporations, as they suggested, have been advantaged. As we showed in Chapter 1, p. 12, 70 per cent of freesheet production is in the hands of twenty-two leading publishers, of whom the six largest are: Reed Regional Publishing, part of the Reed International empire; Thomson Regional Newspapers, part of the International Thomson empire; the Yellow Advertiser Group; EMAP; United Newspapers (who also own 31 per cent of the

Yellow Advertiser Group, as well as Express Newspapers); and Westminster Press. These companies, apart from the Yellow Advertiser Group, also dominate the paid-for local press. We also indicated that this concentration is part of a general concentration in the whole area of freesheets, paid-for weeklies and the local morning and evening press. As we also indicated, this is associated with ownership of national newspapers as well as other media operations, such as broadcasting, book and magazine publishing, marketing and exhibition organizations. Six companies – Reed International, United Newspapers, International Thomson, Pearson Longman, EMAP and Ingersoll – own over half the market by value of the UK local press. With the addition of three other companies – The Guardian and Manchester Evening News Plc, Lonrho and BET – we can account for two-thirds.

It would be wrong to regard this state of affairs, however, purely as the chance operation of the market under capitalism, although it might be argued that there are characteristics of market operations in the local press which particularly predispose it to monopoly. Local newspapers depend on advertising revenue, and in particular on the income from small classified advertisements. Where two papers are competing in the same town, there is a downward pressure on prices due to the aim of each to take as much advertising as possible and an upward pressure on costs through the need to give news coverage and to run promotional circulation drives in every locality in the area where new readers can be found. Once one paper gets the edge, either it can charge higher rates because it has a larger readership, or more probably it can offer special rates because it is attracting more advertisements and sales and thus drive down the income of the competitor. In order to find extra readers, the losing competitor makes costly attempts to beef up its product, and is thus faced with increased costs and decreased revenue. After a time, as debts mount, rescue packages are attempted through bailing out by banks, sales of assets and voluntary redundancies. Because the local press by definition operates within territorial limits, every gain the winning competitor makes is at the expense of the loser; it is a classic zero-sum game, in which there is one inevitable result: the elimination of competition as a result of competition.

This is how the monopolization of the local newspaper market occurs in the first place. But this state of affairs could be consonant with a large number of local firms throughout the country, each monopolizing its own area. This is not the case, however. A few large firms, generally multinational conglomerates, dominate the business, and they do so because they pursue corporate ownership as part of a management strategy: as a means of gaining control over the market. In doing so they develop among themselves a mode of competing and compromising with one another. Generally the process is one of ruthless competition in which one firm triumphs by the elimination or acquisition of another. But gains for one firm are not always at the expense of losses by another. When countervailing power is involved, the structure of competition can be negotiated and competition restrained; then a form of cartelization takes place. Let us examine how these processes of competition and compromise occur.

The number of papers which exist at any given time and the identity of those owning them are not static. Freesheets are constantly being started up, being taken over or failing. The paid-for sector in both weekly and evening papers is shrinking. Ownership changes both because of the take-over of groups by one of the conglomerate corporations and as a consequence of movements in shareholdings among individuals. In early 1989, for instance, Associated Newspapers acquired a 5.05 per cent holding in Portsmouth and Sunderland Newspapers from David Sullivan, the publisher of the *Sunday Sport*. In 1986 Westminster Press, a subsidiary of Pearson Longman Plc, which is 20 per cent owned by Rupert Murdoch, closed the *Darlington Evening Post*. In one week in 1990 *Journalist's Week* reported the suspension of publication of the 'quality broadsheet' paid-for *Hull and Beverley Independent*, the launch of a new freesheet, the *West Bromwich and Barr Observer*, and the relaunch of the West Midlands 'Focus' series as twenty titles instead of thirty-nine.[13]

The biggest undertakings are not necessarily those with the biggest operation in the local press. And it is hard to compare a company which owns ten evening papers in towns such as Nuneaton with a company which owns one evening paper only, in Manchester, with the biggest evening circulation outside London. It is, however, possible to identify the major corporations which dominate the local newspaper industry and often the men who control these undertakings. Reed International, International Thomson, United Newspapers, Associated Newspapers, Westminster Press, EMAP (East Midlands Allied Press) and Lonrho all combine extensive involvement in the local press with large-scale business activity elsewhere. Lonrho is more dominated than the others by non-publishing activities, and EMAP is the most clearly based in the local press as a major focus of activity.

The concentration of ownership of the local press developed in the 1980s along with the growth of free newspapers at the expense of the paid-for local weekly. The total income from advertising of paid-for local weeklies is 87 per cent. This means that by a marginal loss of income at an existing readership level a paper can achieve a circulation of up to 100 per cent of households in an area, with a consequent increase in advertising revenue. The introduction of a freesheet into an area is also an effective way of eliminating an existing paid-for newspaper. An efficient way for an existing newspaper owner to prevent this is to convert to free distribution, to start a second free newspaper to block competition or to buy out any free competitor that appears. All such stratagems favour the big company with access to large funds. The local weekly newspaper market changed from 11 per cent freesheets in 1982 to 30 per cent in 1987 to more than 50 per cent by 1989. This is reflected in the activities of the big corporate owners whose weekly empires are made up of paid-for and free newspapers in about equal proportions. We will now examine the activities of the biggest six owners of the UK local and regional press.

ASSOCIATED NEWSPAPERS

Associated Newspaper Holdings Plc dates back to the 'press barons' era of the inter-war period, in that the company remains in the hands of the same family. The present Lord Rothermere is chairman of the group and over recent years has been buying shares on the market to increase the family share of ownership. In other respects, however, Associated Newspapers is in the mould of the modern newspaper empire. It is both conglomerate and multinational.

In addition to Mail Newspapers Plc, Evening Standard Co. Ltd and Northcliffe Newspapers Group Ltd, Associated Newspapers also owns Blackfriars Oil and Gas Ltd, Euromoney Publications Plc, Bouverie Investments Ltd of Canada and Continental Daily Mail SA, which is incorporated and operates in France. The subsidiary Associated Investments Harmonsworth Ltd controls twenty further companies. These include the sort of media-related businesses which might be associated with newspapers: National Opinion Polls Ltd, NOP Market Research Ltd, IJK Survey Research Associates Ltd, Angex Ltd (exhibition organizers) and GAT Publishing Ltd, who publish *Girl about Town* and other magazines. But there are also, among others, a security firm, a builders' merchants, a building contractor and a manufacturer of light fittings. A further holding company, Associated Newspapers North America, controls Whittle Communications Limited Partnership, who produce 'targeted media', and the American Lawyer Newspapers Group Inc., who publish the *American Lawyer* and other legal newspapers.

The *London Evening Standard* operates alone as a direct subsidiary of Associated Newspaper Holdings Plc. Rothermere's other local newspapers are controlled by the Northcliffe Newspapers Group Ltd, which controls twelve provincial dailies and seventeen local weekly newspaper groups. Like its competitors, the firm has a policy of sales and acquisitions of shareholdings in other groups as a means of obtaining control over markets and gaining economies of scale. In 1988 it acquired the *Hull Property Guide*, in an area where it already owns the *Hull Daily Mail*, which is being re-equipped with new plant and premises. The extra series means that fuller use of plant becomes possible within the same company structure.

Northcliffe Newspapers' local press holdings are concentrated in three main areas. In their main area of activity, the South-West and South Wales, they own the Cheltenham Newspaper Co., the *Cornish Guardian*, a 94 per cent holding in the Cornishman Newspaper Co., Gloucestershire Newspapers, the *North Devon Journal Herald*, the Swansea Press, the West Briton Newspaper Co., the Western Morning News Co. and the Western Times Co. On the east coast they own the Lincolnshire Publishing Co., Hull and Grimsby Newspapers (which publishes the *Hull Daily Mail*, among other papers) and the Essex Chronicle series. In the North Midlands they own the *Derby Daily Telegraph* and the Staffordshire Sentinel series, publishers of the *Stoke Evening Sentinel*.

EMAP

EMAP Plc is involved in five areas of activity: publishing consumer magazines, publishing business magazines, organizing exhibitions, publishing newspapers and printing newspapers. It publishes 88 titles: 40 paid-for and 48 freesheets. Of this total, four are dailies: the *Leamington and District Morning News*, the *Northamptonshire Evening Telegraph*, the *Peterborough Evening Telegraph* and the *Scarborough Evening News*. The remainder are weeklies. The ethos of this company is reflected in this mix of activity. All of these activities are marketing-related. The consumer and business magazines serve the demand and supply side of consumerism; the exhibitions are the organization of marketing; and the newspapers are vehicles for advertising. The annual report of EMAP for 1989 reveals a total commitment to the ethics of the marketplace: 'It is a vital aspect of our launch programme that we set rigorous targets for every title. If these targets are not met, continuous publication is seriously questioned.'[14] The report reveals that some titles were closed in that year because they did not reach their targets. These were *Analyst International* and *Mortgage Business and Risk* (a nice, if unintended, irony here). Even in the world of hard-headed business, euphemism still prevails over directness. 'Seriously questioned' means 'closed down'.

Weekly newspapers fit into the business plans of the corporation along with consumer magazines. The 1989 report refers to the launching of three magazines: *More*, a fortnightly magazine for young women, *Today's Golfer* and *Old Glory*, a magazine devoted to old boats, tractors and cars. These are bracketed along with the acquisition of the *Northampton Citizen*, 'the most ambitious free newspaper in one of Britain's fastest growing towns'. The expected success of the *Ashford People* is related to the fact that it operates in a Channel Tunnel boom town.[15]

The method of growth of activity pursued by EMAP in the local press industry is referred to by the company as 'strategic acquisitions': the purchase of Associated Kent News, which was merged with SENews, which was added to the company a year previously; the purchase of 75 per cent of the Citizen Group of Newspapers; and the acquisition of Courier Press Holdings. The monopolistic aim behind the corporate strategy is frankly acknowledged: 'Shareholders and colleagues will know that our business is built on targeting, leading and dominating markets. We operate from this position of strength in more than 75% of our businesses.'[16] During 1988 EMAP spent £57.5 million on nine acquisitions.

This aggressive business policy has characterized EMAP's operations in the local press in particular. Robin Miller, the group chief executive, reported that the addition of four publishing companies 'marked an active year even by our standards', and claimed that the company now dominated the market in four of the country's fastest growing areas: East Anglia, the South-East, the West Midlands and the South Midlands. Mr Miller's description of the acquisition of the Citizen Group is couched in the language of a military campaign: the surrounding and the capture of territory, the elimination of the enemy and territorial domination. Competition with other companies is not referred to. It is certainly not regarded as a permanent and healthy feature of business life.

Miller writes:

> Indeed the acquisition not only strengthens our already dominant position in Milton Keynes, Bedford and Hitchin, it also provided a thrust at the heart of the opposition in Luton and a strategic launch in Northampton – a town we have bordered on for many years and, with the acquisition of *The Courier*, now surround. Free newspapers are the fastest growing area of the media and it is important that we capitalize on this growth with all the expertise at our disposal.[17]

This language and substance almost suggest that the English civil war is still in progress in its battlegrounds in the rolling hills of south Northamptonshire. What it certainly shows is that the main market which concerns the managers and owners of EMAP is not that of newspapers or even advertisements but of shareholdings and companies.

EMAP structure

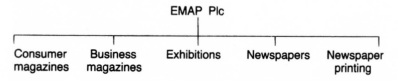

EMAP Plc

| Consumer magazines | Business magazines | Exhibitions | Newspapers | Newspaper printing |

The structure of the company as shown in the diagram reflects this process. EMAP Plc is a holding company under which it controls its main subsidiaries. EMAP Newspapers Ltd, under its chief executive, Martin Lousby, is then the holding company for a number of other companies which are the management companies for groups of regional papers which the company has bought up over the years. Many of the owners or managing directors of these groups become members of the board of EMAP Newspapers Ltd, or are retained to manage their own groups after take-over. In the case of the Citizen Group of papers, Bill Alder and Jerry West, the men behind the group as a successful independent business, retained a 25 per cent stake in its ownership. Thus there develops a management structure which is designed to take over existing independent businesses and which is in turn the result of this process of take-over. Ownership is thus not something which can be distinguished from management and control; it is part of the process of management and control. The take-over of other firms is equally not simply the means whereby the newspaper business is more successfully carried out, although this is part of the reason for it. The take-over is an integral *part* of the business of this modern local newspaper conglomerate.

PEARSON LONGMAN

Pearson Longman Plc, which is 20 per cent owned by Rupert Murdoch, is the publisher of the *Financial Times* and owns 50 per cent of *The Economist* and all of the Viking Penguin book publishing group. It recently acquired the leading French financial daily, *Les Echos*. The company has a 25 per cent share in the *Canadian Financial Post*, which was launched in 1988, and it also has a 35 per cent share in the Spanish financial daily *Expansión*. Pearson also produce a number of business newsletters and run similar information services. Such a company may seem to occupy rather a rarefied atmosphere to be involved in the humble business of publishing the *Watford Observer*, but it does so through its component company Westminster Press which contributed £19.4 million to the total newspaper business profit in 1988 of £54.4 million (not entirely due to the efforts of the staff of the *Watford Observer*).

Unlike the other major corporate owners of the local press, with the exception of Associated Newspapers, Westminster also date back in an unbroken line to the era of the press barons in the shape of Lord Cowdray, who in 1908 bought a small interest in the *Westminster Gazette*, a failing Liberal evening paper. In 1920 another Liberal newspaper business, the North of England Newspaper Co. of Darlington, combined with the *Westminster Gazette*. The new company was named Westminster Press, and the Pearson family were the principal shareholders. The present distribution of the company's papers reflects these origins, despite the fact that they sold the *Westminster Gazette* in 1928 and closed the *Darlington Evening Post* in 1986. Their activities are concentrated in the South around London, Essex and Kent and in the North-East. In 1973 they bought a number of Kent and Sussex papers from Morgan Grampian, who are now a subsidiary of United Newspapers. They also own some papers in Yorkshire and in the area from Oxford to Bath. In all, they own 11 evening newspapers, 56 weeklies and 18 controlled-circulation papers with a total circulation of 6 million. The evenings include the prestigious *Northern Echo* as well as the *Bath and West Evening Chronicle*, the *Bradford Telegraph and Argus*, the *Brighton Evening Argus*, the *Darlington Evening Dispatch*, the *Oxford Mail*, the *Basildon Evening Echo*, the *Southend Evening Echo*, the *Swindon Evening Advertiser* and the *Yorkshire Evening Press*, which is published at York.

REED INTERNATIONAL

Reed Regional Newspapers are part of the holding company Reed Publishing UK, an arm of Reed International, the multinational conglomerate based on paper manufacturing. Reed Publishing alone – who own in addition to their newspapers Reed Business Publishing, Reed Telepublishing and Butterworths – in 1988 had a turnover of £432 million and made profits of £64.4 million. They claim to be the 'number one free newspaper publisher', and, like the other conglomerates so far referred to, have in the region of 100 paid-for and free local papers. In this case there were 109 titles in 1988 with total sales of 6.75 million copies a week. Of these, one, the *Daily News*, is a free daily, and there are four evenings: the *Bolton Evening News*, the *Colchester Evening Gazette*, the *Hereford Evening News* and the *Worcester Evening News*.

Reed's newspaper activities, like those of EMAP, are entirely concentrated in the regional and local press. Like EMAP, the company appears to be entirely concerned with the business aspects of the press: acquisitions, advertising and manpower savings from new technology. The *Birmingham Daily News* was launched as an independent enterprise as the first daily free newspaper in the country. It met difficulties in competing with the existing Birmingham daily press, owned by BPM Holdings, a subsidiary of the US company Ingersoll Inc. of Princeton. In 1987 Reed took it over with the intention of starting similar free morning papers in ten cities during the 1990s. In 1989 the company reported that revenue 'was strong due to acquisitions, launches and buoyancy in both property and job advertising', and that the benefits of direct input technology had exceeded expectations. During 1988 alone the company acquired six regional newspaper companies including the Independent Group of free newspapers in north London, the *Wirral Globe* and the Citizen Group in Blackburn. At the same time they sold South-West Counties Newspapers, 'since its operations fell outside the division's main marketing areas'.[18]

This reflects a general tendency among the corporate owners of local newspapers to identify regions of the country which they wish to dominate by the establishment of territorial monopolies. This then provides them with cost and income advantages. They are able to set up, or acquire along with companies taken over, regional printing centres which will minimize production and distribution costs. They are also able to maximize the target area for advertisers and to streamline advertising for a region rather than for a small locality. For instance, by acquiring the Independent Group, Southern Counties Newspapers increased its circulation to 1.3 million free newspapers around London.

Reed's businesses are concentrated in three main areas: the North of England, an area from the West Midlands to the Welsh border and London. In Birmingham they publish the *Daily News*. Their largest single area of operations is in the North of England, where at the beginning of the 1990s they were publishing forty titles from Warrington in the south to Carlisle and Tyneside in the north. They operate there through Northern Counties Newspapers Ltd, whose head office is in Bolton, at the former head office of the *Bolton Evening News*.

The history of this paper is indicative of the general trend in the British regional press over the past three decades. It was owned from its origins until the beginning of the 1970s by the

a dynasty of Bolton Liberals. Tillotsons also
per manufacture, wharfage and the manufacture
kaging. The *Bolton Evening News* was the parent
series of weekly newspapers, the Journals, which
e south-east Lancashire area and used the firm's
presses Mealhouse Lane printing works above the head
office and editorial department in the centre of Bolton. Then the
family sold out to St Regis, a US paper-manufacturing conglomerate, who 'rationalized' the workforce, reduced the number of
titles, combined titles under single editors, reduced the pagination
of papers and eventually sold out to Reed. Under pressure from
the freesheets, particularly Eddie Shah's Messenger series, the
Journals in the Manchester area closed down, and those that
remained themselves became free. Eventually Reed also acquired
Shah's Messenger series, along with Academy Holdings Ltd, a
publisher of weeklies in the south-west Manchester area which
Shah himself had previously taken over.

INTERNATIONAL THOMSON

International Thomson are a Canadian-based multinational who
dominated the take-over of the local press in the UK in the 1960s
and 1970s, and pioneered a business approach to newspapers in
general and to the local press in particular. They were also the
first spectacularly conglomerate business to become involved in
newspaper ownership as a major business activity. The firm had
a wide variety of interests outside newspaper publishing, not least
a big involvement in oil production. Thomson's operations in the
UK include Thomson Holidays, Portland Holidays, Lunn Poly
and Britannia Airways, and they are involved in oil and gas
extraction throughout the UK offshore fields. Roy Thomson, the
multimillionaire proprietor, adopted a 'hands-off' approach to
editorial matters and affected only to be concerned that the papers
showed a profit. At the time this conflicted with the ethic of the
'normal' tradition of local newspaper proprietorship which had
envisaged the paper as part of the institutional make-up of 'the
local community'. As a consequence the proprietor would have
certain expectations of the editorial content of the paper and of
its political stance. Thomson also owned the *Sunday Times* and
took over *The Times*, before selling both to Rupert Murdoch after

a long and costly industrial dispute over new technology, which his Antipodean successor resolved with his now legendary tact.

The firm retained its interest in the regional press, however, and in the early 1980s International Thomson, through Thomson Regional Newspapers, was the most successful publisher of local newspapers, with an aggregate circulation of over 6 million copies. The company's circulation fell back in the mid-1980s, but it still claimed to be the largest regional newspaper publisher in the UK, with 33 paid-for and 37 free newspapers by 1988. Again the same pattern of growth and contraction by acquisition and concentration in certain regions can be seen. In 1987, for instance, Thomson made 'tactical acquisitions' in the form of the purchase of the Weekly Courier series in Morpeth and the move by the subsidiary Thames Valley Newspapers to complete ownership of a property newspaper in the region. Although the number of titles owned by Thomson is not so great as the number owned by the other leading corporate owners, they tend to own better 'quality' papers, in the sense that they include big-circulation, prestigious regional evening and morning papers such as the *Scotsman*, the *Belfast Telegraph* and the *South Wales Echo*.

Of the total of twelve regional dailies owned by the company, the remainder are the *Aberdeen Press and Journal*, the *Aberdeen Evening Express*, the Blackburn-based *Lancashire Evening Telegraph*, the Cardiff-based *Western Mail*, the *Cleveland Evening Gazette*, the *Edinburgh Evening News*, the *Newcastle Journal*, the *Newcastle Evening Chronicle* and the *Reading Evening Post*. These morning and evening papers are the focus of eight regional production centres in Belfast, Aberdeen, Edinburgh, Newcastle, Teeside, Blackburn, Reading and Cardiff. In addition there are two centres producing weekly series based on Celtic Newspapers at Merthyr Tydfil, and Chester and North Wales Newspapers Ltd at Chester.

Thomson are less likely to expand by acquisitions in the near future (the early 1990s) than by the expansion of existing business through innovation. Thomson have innovated in regional newspapers by opening a new Sunday paper, *Scotland on Sunday* and are planning the launch of a similar *Wales on Sunday*. They plan as a result to be able to cover 40 per cent of the UK population with the circulation of their titles. Significantly the 1988 annual report said:

In the near term, we shall be placing less emphasis on acquisitions, as we have been especially active in recent years and need time to assimilate the many businesses that have joined us. Furthermore, there has already been much consolidation in the publishing industry . . . reducing the number of attractive companies that remain independent at a time when competition for acquisitions has increased.[19]

This is a graphic illustration of how the market in stock and in competitors to be bought up concerns newspaper publishers as much as the market for their products.

Clearly, intense competition for acquisitions will be cyclic in that it will force up prices beyond what is justified by expected profit gains and avoidance of competitive disadvantage. Periods of consolidation will also be required by individual firms while they digest new enterprises and derive their expected advantages from them. There is no reason, however, to expect such slowdowns in the rate of take-over to be other than temporary so long as available firms exist to be acquired with the possibility of consolidating local territorial monopolies.

UNITED NEWSPAPERS

United Newspapers' company structure follows a similar pattern to that of Associated Newspapers. The main corporation, United Newspapers, is a holding company which owns six holding companies which in turn own the operating companies. The holding companies are the Extel Group Plc, Link House Publications Plc, United Newspapers Inc. USA, United Newspapers Publications Ltd, the owners of Express Newspapers, who publish the *Daily Express*, the *Sunday Express* and the *Star*, United Provincial Newspapers, who own the company's local papers, and United Publications Ltd. They also own 31 per cent of the Yellow Advertiser free newspaper group.

Apart from newspaper publishing, these companies own enterprises which operate in a variety of areas of activity. For instance, they are involved in the provision of information services through such companies as Extel Financial Ltd, The Exchange Telegraph Ltd and Dealers Digest Inc. USA. Similarly, they publish advertising periodicals and organize business exhibitions. One of their member companies undertakes contract printing of newspapers, and others undertake distribution of free newspapers and magazines. United Newspapers also owns a property company which owns the central London properties that Express Newspapers occupied before they moved away from Fleet Street.

Their regional newspaper operations are organized through fourteen publishing groups which produce 103 papers. Of these, eight are dailies: the *Yorkshire Post*, the *Yorkshire Evening Post*, the *Star* (Sheffield), the *Lancashire Evening Post* (Preston), the *West Lancashire Evening Post* (Blackpool), the *Chronicle & Echo* (Northampton), the *South Wales Argus* and the *Greenock Telegraph*. The remainder are 46 paid-for weeklies and 49 free weeklies.

United Newspapers moved into the ownership of national dailies and Sundays on the basis of its provincial newspaper and magazine ownership when it took over Express Newspapers. Extel was a further recent acquisition. In many respects United Provincial Newspapers form a secure basis for the rest of the empire. By 1989 United Newspapers had debts of £300 million incurred through investment in new technology consequent on the move from central London by Express Newspapers. These were not expected to be cleared until 1993. The success of the group in bearing this debt and making healthy profits was attributed by the *Financial Times* in early 1989 to their regional newspapers and in particular to their 'northern bias' which enabled them to avoid the slow-down then beginning to affect London and the South.[20]

Referring to the 'fine performance' by the company's regional newspapers, Lord Stevens of Ludgate, the company chairman, reported in 1988 that advertising was up by 21 per cent, with a 16 per cent increase in revenue for the year and a 32 per cent increase in profit over the previous two years. At the same time, costs were down by 19 per cent, and he was predicting greater benefits still to come as the result of new printing plant at Broughton, near Preston, which was opened in 1989.

It is interesting to note how an empire such as United Newspapers is built up, and an example may help to illustrate the process. The *Wigan Observer* is now a member of the United Newspapers empire. It was founded in the 1850s and survived for 120 years in the ownership of the Wall Brothers, a family of wealthy(ish) Wigan Liberals. During the 1960s the paper was particularly successful under the management of a man who had married into the family and had only a small shareholding in the firm. With a circulation of 47,000 it was the third biggest local weekly in the country. From accumulated profits the firm was able to buy a modern factory and, with a small loan, what was then a revolutionary new printing plant.

United Newspapers already owned the *Lancashire Evening Post*, which had an office in Wigan, and they approached the Wall family to take over the *Observer*. Against the opposition of the management the family sold out, and United Newspapers acquired a successful local weekly paper along with the most up-to-date plant in the region and a portfolio of real estate. United Newspapers also owned another weekly newspaper in nearby Chorley, the *Chorley Guardian*, and took advantage of the printing plant at Wigan by printing both papers on the same machinery, thus modernizing the appearance of the *Chorley Guardian* and maximizing the use of the investment made by Wall Brothers. Each paper was allocated a given number of hours' use of the printing facility, which, in turn, meant that a system of deadlines had to be introduced for copy to be ready for the machines, which imposed a new discipline on the reporters and sub-editors. These deadlines were imposed by the head office of United Newspapers, as were a new management structure and new rules of accounting for expenditure. Previously a successful independent family firm, the *Wigan Observer* became subsumed into the corporate bureaucracy, and the whole of that part of Lancashire became part of the United Newspapers fiefdom. If an extreme Labour government had taken over the paper in a programme of nationalization there would have been uproar. But no voice was raised against what did happen, partly because all the voices that might have been raised were owned by parties to the deal.

This is not particular to United Newspapers. All the big newspaper chains grow in the same way. In the case of United Newspapers a potentially more sinister trend in the development of such chains was the rumour in the late 1980s that the group might be taken over by the Canadian media conglomerate Hollinger Inc., which owns the *Daily Telegraph* and is owned by Conrad Black. The *Financial Times* reported that United's regional titles might be split between Hollinger and Ralph Ingersoll, the owner of the US Ingersoll Corporation which already owns the Birmingham Post and Mail series of newspapers, through the holding company BPM Holdings. This would have added a large portion of the British regional press to that already in North

American ownership. Any such move would be faced with examination by the Monopolies and Mergers Commission because it
would involve titles with a circulation in excess of 50,000. But,
as it is, Hollinger has built up a holding estimated at between 6
per cent and 8 per cent in United Newspapers.[21]

OTHER REGIONAL CORPORATE OWNERSHIP

The companies we have looked at so far have been large corporations which also own large proportions of the regional newspaper industry in the UK. There are three other kinds of large
corporate owner. The first are large corporations for whom their
holding of British regional newspapers does not constitute a major
element in their businesses; and the second are substantial British
regional newspapers which have expanded in chain operations to
provide themselves with a territorial buffer zone against encroach-
ment and sufficient critical mass to be able to survive in a market
dominated by a few large corporations with massive access to
capital. The third are the chains of local weekly and small evening
papers, which are small by comparison with the multinationals
and at the same time not concentrated around one big regional
daily.

The first approach is typified by Lonrho, which is the abstrac-
tion 'conglomerate' made flesh. Its diverse activities include manufacturing filing-cabinets, distributing cars, printing postage
stamps, managing hotels in Canada and mining copper, coal,
platinum and gold in Africa and around the world. It also owns
the *Observer* and twenty-six provincial papers in the UK. Through
George Outram Investments, Lonrho owns the *Glasgow Herald*,
the *Glasgow Evening Times*, the *Paisley Daily Express* and Scottish
and Universal Newspapers, who publish weekly papers in the
central industrial belt and the south-west of Scotland. Lonrho
also owns 14.96 per cent of Border TV, who in turn own 18.74
per cent of Cumbrian Newspapers. Another example is that of
the Ingersoll Corporation of Princeton, New Jersey, who own
BPM, the publishers of the *Birmingham Post*, the *Birmingham Evening Mail* and the *Dudley Evening Mail*. BPM in turn own the
Burton Daily Mail and Iliffe Newspapers, who publish the *Coventry Evening Telegraph*, which are both also the parent papers of
weekly series in their own regions. Ingersoll also own London
and Westminster Newspapers, who are publishers of paid-for and

free weekly newspapers. Lonhro and Ingersoll each account for about half the ownership of titles and levels of circulation of one of the big six owners.

The second sort of corporate owner is typified by The Guardian and Manchester Evening News Plc (referred to below as the MEN). The company has always published both the Manchester evening paper and the *Guardian*, previously the *Manchester Guardian*. Over the past two decades, however, as a strategy to protect its local base, the company has expanded into its own region – Manchester – and has taken over almost all of the potential opposition to the *Manchester Evening News*. Within the city area of its circulation there is effectively no opposition from the point of view of advertisements or readers.

The company produces a weekly free newspaper, *Metro News*, which distributes over 300,000 copies and carries a heavy weight of classified advertising. It is produced with a level of professionalism far beyond that achieved by any of its potential rivals and has a news section full of local news. In its style and substance it resembles a traditional paid-for newspaper. The local 'alternative' listings magazine, *City Life*, went bust and has now also been taken over by the MEN. The weekly series Lancashire and Cheshire Newspapers, which was centred on Stockport and was owned by Thomson Regional Newspapers, has been taken over by the MEN. G. & N. Scott Ltd, the publisher of the *Rochdale Observer* and associated paid-for and free weekly papers, is also part of the MEN group. They have also moved out of their own area and have acquired Surrey Advertiser Newspaper Holdings Ltd and Aldershot Newspaper Publishers. In addition to the *Manchester Evening News* the company publishes thirty-two provincial weeklies plus *City Life*.

Anyone inquiring why the company has been so determined to secure control of Manchester has only to examine the map of the area. To the south-west in Chester there are Thomson papers. To the south, in and around Stoke-on-Trent, the area is dominated by Reed. To the north the Bolton area is controlled by Reed. To the north-west Preston and Wigan are controlled by United Newspapers. Thomson own the Lancashire *Evening Telegraph* at Blackburn. To the east United Newspapers own the *Yorkshire Post* in Leeds and the *Star* in Sheffield. Only the *Oldham Chronicle* remains in independent ownership.

The *Liverpool Echo* and *Liverpool Post* have similarly developed a base in their region and in nearby North Wales of a number of weekly newspapers all held by the ultimate holding company Trinity International Holdings Ltd. The *Leicester Mercury* and the Midlands News Association, the owner of the *Wolverhampton Star*, have both adopted this strategy of territorial control through acquisition of the potential opposition.

The third form of corporate ownership is the number of smaller undertakings such as BET, who publish over fifty weekly paid-for and free newspapers concentrated around London and Reading and operating through seven subsidiaries. This is a business built on the basis of acquisitions in a region rather than based on a big regional evening paper. Such groups resemble nascent forms of EMAP. Other owners operating at a similar level are traditional owners of local newspapers such as Portsmouth and Sunderland Newspapers, which has been in the Storey family for generations.

Such groups become targets for take-overs, as we have seen in examining the large corporations; and each corporate owner faces the probability that, if it does not buy up an available group, another corporate shark will appear and devour it. Equally, corporate owners divest themselves of groups which do not fit in with their marketing strategies. Sometimes, when such a divestment takes place and there is a consequent acquisition by a competitor, agreements are made not to encroach on one another's circulation areas.

In the Lancashire–Yorkshire border area, for instance, Reed, Thomson and United Newspapers all occupy adjacent areas with the possibility of competition on the borders of territory. During 1989 the Thomson-owned Lancashire Evening Telegraph Group based at Blackburn acquired the South Yorkshire Times, a Wakefield weekly newspaper series, from Reed. Part of the deal was an agreement not to encroach on one another's circulation areas. Such arrangements in this type of deal are common. Thus the development of the local newspaper market as a system of agreed local monopolies based on territorial control is not always implicit or the unintended consequence of the market in ownership but is based on an implicit or explicit consensus between the 'competing' combines not to damage one another.

Such a consensus does not extend to the relations between the corporate owners of local newspapers and their employees. Indeed, the similarity of treatment handed out to workers would suggest, to a mind amiably disposed to conspiracy theories, a common purpose among employers. All the companies we have examined have been involved in equipping themselves with new technology and have in general done so by setting up or acquiring regional production centres to make the most efficient use of plant.

This process during the 1980s involved the signing of new technology agreements by the printing trades unions. Unions in the provinces never manifested the militancy which characterized Fleet Street industrial relations and in any event never possessed the same short-term power as their London national daily and Sunday comrades. The owners of the provincial press fairly easily achieved the re-equipment of their printing technology, with big reductions in costs and losses of print jobs. This is a process which never stops, and new systems based on direct typesetting and composing by journalists will virtually eliminate all printing jobs between the editorial department and the machine room.

From the point of view of the employer, the main stumbling-block was breaking down the traditional print union structure with new technology agreements. Once this was achieved, the process of continual reductions in personnel levels has become more and more of the same thing. But a new departure has been the attack on the trade union structure of the group of workers who, it was predicted, would benefit from the new technology – the journalists. Their union, the National Union of Journalists, has co-operated in arrangements following from the introduction of new technology. The new efficient technology was trumpeted as providing them with more work rather than less, since they would be able to originate their own material for printing. In the event, on the national dailies and Sundays it led to the disappearance of hundreds of journalistic jobs in their Manchester offices, which themselves virtually disappeared.

In the local press staffing levels have been reduced mainly through the advent of the freesheet and the asset-stripping mentality of the conglomerate owners. In one series taken over by Reed, two weekly papers each employing six reporters, an editor and a photographer first shed an editor, the remaining one editing both papers. They then combined to form one paper, with the closure of one paper. By now half the jobs were gone. This paper then combined with a third, so that two-thirds of the jobs went, and finally it has merged with a fourth. So now the outcome of twenty years of change is that one paper appears with four district

names attached to its masthead. It is now a freesheet with one
staff reporter. At the beginning of the 1970s the four papers
together employed twenty-five journalists.

The conglomerates are also beginning to impose individual
contracts of employment on journalistic employees. This involves
the unilateral abrogation of existing agreements with the NUJ
and their replacement with a contract between the individual
employee and, for instance, Reed International or International
Thomson. A letter from the Chorley Guardian Co. Ltd to its
staff in January 1990 is typical of this process. The computer
format reads:

GMJ/MG   12 January 1990

Dear

Any contracts that still exist between non-management
employees and the company are out of date and no longer
relevant to today's circumstances in staff relations.

Most of you have never been invited to sign a contract and I
feel that the time has come to take account of the changed
situation and set down mutually beneficial terms that reflect
the need for a better understanding that can only be in all our
interests.

Please read the contract carefully. Feel free to come and see me
to discuss any point that you may feel unhappy about or may
need clarification.

You will note that the salary review date changes to June 1st,
1990.

You are reminded that although under the terms of the contract, salaries will not be the subject of collective bargaining
you remain free to be a member of a trade union and the
contract does not affect your basic rights.

Yours sincerely

G. M. JOHNSTON
MANAGING EDITOR.

Despite its amiable tone, the letter makes it perfectly clear that
the journalist loses all collective rights. He or she will now have

to bargain as an individual with United Newspapers. The existing agreements are reneged on by the firm; the salary review date is unilaterally changed; and, despite the assurance that the contract 'does not affect your basic rights', the right to bargain collectively, the most basic means of redressing the inequality between the corporate strength of the employer and the individual weakness of the employee, is eliminated.

Any notion that trades union freedoms of the type advocated for Polish workers under communism are to be preserved, however, cannot survive perusal of the individual contract which the *Chorley Guardian* and other United Newspapers journalists are obliged to sign. The employee is allowed to be a member of a trade union – the employer would be breaking the law to deny such a right – but she or he is not entitled to take an active role in the union. The term of the contract entitled 'Personal Terms' declares:

> Under the terms of this contract of Employment your conditions of service are agreed between yourself and the Company and are completely delinked from any collective agreement which may be in force from time to time between the Company and a trade union representing employees in a broadly similar capacity to yourself, and you will not take an active role in any such trade union organisation.

This makes clear that any rights to be a member of a trade union are purely token, since the employee is not entitled to participate meaningfully in the union. Presumably a journalist attending a meeting, speaking or standing for office would be open to the possibility of being denounced and reported to management, who could then discipline him or her. It is clear that the relationship between the journalist and the employer is to be one of unquestioning feudal subservience.

The employee is also to be subject to a duty of blanket secrecy which is quite in keeping with the public information policy of the KGB under Brezhnev – an ironic indication of how deep United Newspapers' commitment to freedom of expression is. It declares:

> During the continuance of your employment with the Company or at any time after its termination, however arising, you will not use or disclose to any person or persons, except the

proper officers of the Company or under the authority of its Board of Directors, any confidential or secret information relating to the business or finances of the company, its parent, subsidiary or associated companies or any of their respective suppliers, agents, distributors or customers.

Under the heading 'Co-operation' the employee is informed:

As a key member of the company's staff you will require to co-operate in every way possible to ensure the continuity of the company's operations and its contractual commitments.

Clearly in the corporate tongue UnitedNewspaperspeak 'co-operation' means 'unquestioning and blind obedience'.

The final apotheosis of this definition of the relationship of the vassal to the employer is encapsulated in the clause absurdly titled 'Devotion to Duty'. It declares:

In accordance with the usual terms of our Contracts of Employment it is a requirement that your entire services are to be devoted to the interests of the Company, its Parent, subsidiary or associated companies and that on no account are you to engage in work outside unless special permission has first been obtained for you to do so.

Such contracts are now being forced on journalists throughout the industry. Journalists on local newspapers across the country are being asked to sign corporate versions of them, some written and distributed from head offices in North America. Because of the present government's industrial relations legislation, what can be enforced on a multinational-corporation-wide basis cannot be resisted on any basis other than that of the immediate employing company. Journalists in dispute with United Newspapers in the shape of the Chorley Guardian Ltd cannot picket the journalists working for United Newspapers at the nearby *Lancashire Evening News* because this would involve secondary picketing. No joint action between different subsidiary companies can be undertaken to prosecute a dispute at one constituent part of the conglomerate. The pay of senior qualified journalists working on weekly newspapers in the provinces in 1990 was between £8,000 and £9,000, about two-thirds of the average wage.

CONCLUSION

The local and regional press is only local and regional in that its markets are defined by locality and region. In terms of its ownership and its business strategy it is a massive corporate enterprise based on the elimination of territorial competition and a system of local regulated monopoly. In order to survive, local independent newspapers are forced defensively to adopt the policy of a corporate structure aimed at maximizing their control over their own and neighbouring circulation areas. Like The Guardian and Manchester Evening News they may move elsewhere in order to maintain the size necessary for survival. Distant acquisitions may also be subsequently used in a process of doing deals with other corporate owners as part of the process of territorial consolidation.

The drive for profit, which explains the desire of firms to eliminate competition through take-overs, also generates the constant drive for more and more low-cost production methods based on new technology and the lowest possible labour costs. This begins with new technology agreements with trades unions and ends with the banning of effective unions and the attempt to produce an entirely submissive workforce, taking no active part in trade union affairs, devoted to duty, 'co-operative' and bound by a contract where the only capital letters are accorded to the 'Company' and the 'Board of Directors'. What we see in the business strategy of the owners of the local press is the search for corporate power. What we see in the 'human resource management' policies towards employees is the search for corporate power. What we see behind the parish pump (now privatized) is corporate power.

Chapter 3

The traditional local press

The traditional local press in the UK is a phenomenon of the late nineteenth century, and is in part one of the outcomes of the process which culminated in the abolition of the 'taxes on knowledge' in the 1850s and 1860s. The focus of much that has been written about this period has been on the way in which the ending of the Stamp Duty, Paper Tax, Advertising Duty and compulsory security deposit led to the development of a mass-production and entertainment-based national press.[1] This development was exemplified by the so-called Northcliffe revolution which gave rise to the *Daily Mail* and was closely followed by the launching of other generally right-wing, sub-literate, populist news organs.

A counterpoint to this process was the demise of the radical press, which had been committed to propaganda on behalf of left-wing and working-class politics and had often been produced by voluntary labour on a co-operative basis. This press was local in the sense that it was bedded and read almost entirely in the area of its production.[2] Consequently a new, capitalist provincial press emerged which rapidly developed in embryo the economic characteristics of the modern local and regional press: industrialized production methods; dependence on advertising as the main source of income; and the growth of newspaper chains under the ownership of powerful individuals.[3] At the same time, the number of local newspapers sold exceeded that of nationals; they remained the prime source of information for the reading public – especially for working-class readers.

Two other developments which were closely related took place during the same period. First, the method of news production as an organized activity began to be formulated around the notion of the impartial recording of facts rather than as a means of party propaganda. Local newspapers founded in the latter half of the nineteenth century proudly announced that they would provide a reliable source of information for the local community, to which they pledged a commitment couched in terms of a parish-pump patriotism. Second, journalists organized themselves as a trade or profession (according to ideological self-image) based on the idea that they had a common set of skills, common interests and a common calling based on a professional duty to inform the community over and above any sectional or individual interests which might be the source of pressure on them in their work.[4]

This approach to news both as factual and as having a moral and societal value is one that has formed the basis of the ideology of news production in the traditional local press ever since. It combines the ideas that 'news' is empirically embedded in the event covered by a news story, that curiosity about such events is a normal and more or less universal human response, and that the reporting of them is part of the normative order on which communal life depends. The idea of the community has always formed an important element in the way the local press portrays itself. And this community has always been considered identical with the readership of the paper – the demand side of the market.

THE LOCAL PRESS AND THE TRADITIONAL VIEW OF NEWS GATHERING

This perception of the local press and the journalists' role in producing it is clearly expounded in the recent book *Writing for the Press* by James Aitchison, a senior lecturer and course co-ordinator in journalism studies at Napier College.[5] This revealing teaching book encapsulates the professional ethics of journalists in defining what they do and how this relates to the designated world they aim to describe. Dr Aitchison is a member of the training committee of the National Council for the Training of Journalists and a member of the council's Scottish committee. The book is approved by the National Council for the Training of Journalists in a laudatory foreword by the director, Keith Hall. The NCTJ is the body formed of representatives of both employers and employees which supervises the training of journalists and certificates them as competent professionals. As is clear from the content of the book, the audience aimed at is trainee journalists on local newspapers.

Dr Aitchison defines news in terms of the events of communal life and the 'natural' response, curiosity, by members of the community to such events: 'When our lives are touched by events then it is entirely normal that we should wish to know more about these events.'[6] He also stresses accuracy allied to the normative order as integral to the notion of news: 'When a newspaper keeps an accurate record of events then politicians, industrialists, sportsmen and criminals will receive their due recognition.' In this traditionalist, establishment view of the role of the journalist, then, accuracy is subsumed to a wider social purpose. A responsibility is being exercised; 'due recognition', whether the approval of sporting prowess or the public exposure of the criminal's guilt, is being dealt out by the dispassionate newspaper of record. 'Maintaining that record is a highly responsible and demanding task.'[7] This notion of the reporter as a dispassionate recorder of events who at the same time has a commitment to a higher purpose than merely to provide factual accounts of social life is made explicit: 'news values are not always the same as normal human values . . . in a factual and impartial news story there is no place for an account of the journalist's feelings'.[8] The reason for this imperative for factual and impartial news is a public responsibility: 'If facts are suppressed on the grounds that their publication could cause embarrassment to the subject of the story or to the reporter then this suppression will lead to a whimsical and erratic form of censorship.'[9]

There are two arguments against censorship put forward by Dr Aitchison. First, it would deny readers knowledge which might have an effect on their lives and would be of 'legitimate interest' to them; and second, 'this whimsical censorship would wrongly protect from public accountability those persons responsible for the actions and decisions' that effect people's lives. The particular example the author gives of a possible act of suppression is a young journalist not publishing a story about a schoolteacher, known to her, who was convicted of a drink-driving charge.[10] This role of the reporter and the local paper as part of the system of local social control is further reflected in sources and the news-gathering process, which he summarizes thus:

The reporter on a local newspaper must be aware of the main sources of news in his newspaper's circulation area. The reporter should identify reliable people who have access to those news sources and, where possible, establish a working relationship with these people.[11]

Built into this traditional view of news gathering by the local press which Dr Aitchison exemplifies is the idea of the coincidence of the newspaper's circulation area with that of the community: 'the main news sources of a local newspaper are of course the people and events that make up the life and identity of the community in which the newspaper circulates'.[12] But it is to the institutional establishment that he looks for the embodiment of this community and the source of information about communal events. The first source he quotes is the council, the second the local Member of Parliament and the third the court. 'Other important sources' are the police, the fire brigade, the ambulance service, the hospital, local industries and business and their representative bodies, the chamber of trade or commerce or a traders' association, trades unions and trades councils, and the local football club. 'Secondary sources' are schools and colleges, churches, local clubs and societies and local branches of national pressure groups and charities.[13] He also points the young journalist to documentary sources of news from the same institutional order.

This traditional view of the role of the local journalist bears a strong resemblance to the traditional functionalist approach to the social sciences. Central to it is the idea of a community, a social unit of indeterminate size united by some common set of interests and worldview which differentiate it from the wider social world which constitutes its environment. There is then a definitional equation between the life and events of the people in that community and its institutional structure, so that the versions of events promulgated by powerful individuals within this institutional order become the established truth of communal life. The market, in the form of the circulation area of the newspaper, is also identified with the community so that even if they are not definitionally identical the two are at least in a mutually supportive relationship. And the role of the journalist is formulated precisely in functionalist terms: to provide a record of the community; to make people publicly accountable who should be; to participate in the system of social control; and to do this in the context of a set of relationships, with 'contacts' chosen by their roles in the institutions which they themselves and the newspaper identify as the defining structure of the community.

This version of the role of the journalist as the slave of fact and truth is part of the occupational ideology expressed by journalists' professional organizations and by newspaper proprietors since the foundation of the modern commercial press. It conceptualizes news writing as reportage, where the journalist simply records the world as it is. It resembles the ethics of impartiality and balance which underlies the reporting of news by the BBC and ITN and was embodied in the charter of the BBC and in the legislation which established the IBA. We can also see in the attitudes of the local newspaper reporter the same sort of attitudes as those revealed by Philip Schlesinger in his study of BBC news,[14] in that the *idea* of impartiality and balance is part of the professional ideology of such workers and a way of their explaining their calling.

One editor we interviewed in our research referred to a similar case to that mentioned by Aitchison: a relative of his own who was found guilty of a minor criminal offence whose case he reported in the local weekly paper he edited because he felt that part of the punishment was the publicity, and that to suppress a report of a relative would be a corrupt act of the same order as a police officer's favouritism to a relative. Another editor took this further, and quoted the fact that he had complaints of anti-police bias from the local chief constable and of anti-left bias from the leader of the council Labour group as evidence of his own professional detachment. He stressed that he would not get into bed with any interest group and resisted all attempts to engage his loyalty by interested parties. Such a view is not necessarily an empirical description of what journalists and editors actually do, although it may be; but it is a prescriptive and ideological statement indicating both what journalists think they ought to do, and why this justifies for them the exercise of their professional competence.

DIVERSITY AND THE DEFINITION OF 'LOCAL' NEWS

In order to understand the way the traditional commercial local press operates it is necessary to bear in mind that it embraces a wide variety of types of newspaper, differentiated in terms of both the regularity of their publication and the size of their audience. Both of these factors affects the way journalists work, the content of the newspaper and the nature of the business. In general the larger the area of circulation and the more frequently the paper appears, the more the local paper includes national and regional as well as local news; the less frequently the paper appears and the smaller its circulation area, the more exclusively its news coverage is strictly local.

Evening papers in particular are often large undertakings with journalistic staffs of up to forty and circulations in the tens of thousands. They produce several editions a day, which change during the course of the day, and the speed at which reporters, sub-editors and editors work is greater than on national dailies. This is because the first editions are on the streets at lunchtime, which means that deadlines for copy have to be as early as eleven o'clock in the morning. As further editions come out during the day, stories, headlines, page layouts and the distribution of news between pages change as stories develop. Mostly any such changes will be minor. But on some occasions there will be major changes during the course of the day, and these will be normally be effected during the hectic two-hour period between eleven o'clock in the morning and one in the afternoon. This can have major effects on the way in which reality is constructed, as we shall see below.

In order to understand how the local press works, it is necessary to grasp how local news is defined. Stories are considered local when they apply specifically to some aspect of the area in which the newspaper circulates. A fire which happens in the area, a crime which is committed in the area, a decision by the local council and the death of a local worthy are the self-evidently local events which are the raw material of local news. Similarly, 'national' and international stories may have a local angle. National and international stories are those which originate as accounts of events in the national news media. This does not mean that there is some absolute transcendent reality which exists at the national or international level. News is not the outcome of 'real' events. It is the outcome of production processes and work routines of journalists who produce *accounts* of events. The events they construct as national or international reality may well originate in local accounts. The stories take on their transcendental character when they are shown to have some supra-local significance.

For instance, the existence of 'mad cow disease' became a national British story as a result of the incremental process of reporting lots of local cases of the disease. It became international when it affected the relationship between Britain and its European trading partners. Similarly, AIDS became a national and international story as a result of the accumulation of hundreds of thousands of cases throughout the world.

Each of these stories might then become a 'local' story when news producers show it to have a local angle. For instance, a paper with a rural circulation might check with the local branch of the National Farmers' Union whether their members have any cases of 'mad cow disease' or whether their livelihood has been affected. Any local paper might check with local meat traders to see if beef sales have been affected by the scare. In the case of the AIDS epidemic, a paper with an inner-city circulation area, particularly in a place such as Edinburgh with a major drugs problem, might follow up the story with angles on the difficulties for the local health service, or with news about campaigns by local social work agencies.

Sometimes national and international stories are capable of being made local by particular local connections. When a British businessman is shot dead by Iraqi troops, the paper serving the area he lives in will interview his family. When there is an earthquake in Armenia or Iran there is a Manchester angle, because the city's fire brigade and a local hospital have a specialist team for searching for and retrieving bodies and rescuing survivors of such disasters, so that on such occasions the 'mercy team' is said to be 'flying out' or 'standing by' to play its part in the international rescue effort.

A classic example of this process is the 'local man involved in international crisis' story which appeared in the *Manchester Evening News* of 15 August 1990. It was headlined 'John jets in from desert ordeal'. The fact that it was a locally focused story was signalled by the first three words, 'A Swinton man', which announced that the man's residence in the suburb of Salford was significant. The Swinton man 'who fled across the desert to escape Kuwait flew into Manchester and the arms of his wife and children today', the introduction declared. The rest of the article then went on to itemize his name, occupation and age, his words on arrival at Manchester airport, the few clothes he had on and the fact that he had nothing else. The report then described his reunion with his family and gave a brief account of his dramatic escape from Kuwait.[15]

THE LOCAL WEEKLY PRESS

The most local of local newspapers is the local weekly. These were usually founded and owned locally in the nineteenth century but gradually came to be dominated by regional chains, and eventually by national and multinational corporations (see Chapters 1 and 2). The news content of such papers relates entirely to the locality where they sell. Inasmuch as national stories are covered, this is only the case if there is a local 'angle'. No national stories appear purely in their own right.

A single edition of the *Stockport Express Advertiser* for 11 February 1988 illustrates the way in which stories which are 'national' or 'international' in origin or which refer to events outside the locality are made local and become 'Stockport' stories. The front-page lead story, 'Skier killed in avalanche: trip ends in tragedy after Paul switches his holidays', concerned a ski death in Italy in which the victim was a man from Stockport. The first words of the story again denote the local focus: 'A Heaton Moor man . . .' Heaton Moor is an area of Stockport.[16] Inside on page three was a story from a court in Tenerife entitled 'Tenerife brawler jailed', but again the first words explain why it is in a purely Stockport paper: 'A Stockport man was jailed in Tenerife after a violent street fight . . .'[17]

These reports are the result of a network of information available to the local press whereby events which involved locals away from home become part of the basis of news production. Freelance news reporters who cover court cases concerning individuals who are residents in other areas send copy to the newspaper in that area. This sort of 'local' news thus depends on the fact that people from the paper's circulation area are dying, committing crimes and experiencing adventures elsewhere in the world.

Another sort of local news is the result of the disaggregation of 'national' stories. The same copy of the *Stockport Express Advertiser* illustrates this process. 'Cuts may hit elderly' is the headline over a story whose introduction declares: 'Health care for the elderly could be earmarked for cuts in the latest round of NHS spending economies'; this is a story produced by the local journalist about the effect on the area of the national policy of health cuts.[18] This may come from a number of sources. Government information services may provide local figures and information to the press; journalists may check with the regional or district offices of national services such as the NHS or the Department of Employment for such information; or it may be volunteered officially or unofficially by sources such as members of health authorities or by pressure groups.

Local newspapers routinely look to the national press for the source of their stories. One of the authors of this book worked as a junior reporter in the early 1960s on a local weekly newspaper managed by an ex-editor of the *Stockport Advertiser*, a precursor of the *Stockport Express Advertiser*. Every morning this small plump man (who had fought in the First World War in the Artists' Rifles) would read through the morning copies of the national dailies looking for news which might become the basis for stories about the area. He would cut such items out and paste them on to pieces of paper on which he would write: 'Get local figures', or 'Is he a local man?' or 'Are any local men among the injured?' This frenzied attack on the national press involved him in perhaps an hour of intense activity at the beginning of the day. Sometimes reporters who had brought in a newspaper they had purchased on the way to work would find it hacked to pieces on the editor's desk. Two identical *Manchester Guardian* stories would then appear pasted to two separate pieces of copy paper each bearing the scrawled injunction to 'get local figures'. This habit earned him the sobriquet 'Slasher Wilson' among his staff. Not all local newspaper editors vandalize their colleagues' newspapers, but they do all operate some system of scrutinizing the national and regional media for items which may form the basis of local news.

The main sources of news, however, are those suggested by Dr Aitchison and are based in the circulation area of the paper. An analysis of the sources of 865 stories in fourteen British local weekly newspapers shows a widespread common reliance on five main sources of news. These are local and regional government, voluntary organizations, the courts, the police and business. Between them they accounted for 67.5 per cent of all the news stories we surveyed – see Table 3.1. Local and regional government, normally in the shape of the local council, is seen to be the modal source of news, accounting for 23 per cent of stories.

Table 3.1 Local press: sources of news

Source	Total	Percentage
Courts	105	12.0
Coroner	10	1.0
Police	98	11.5
Other emergency services (fire, ambulance)	11	1.5
Council (and regional authorities)	199	23.0
Business	73	8.5
Government	32	3.5
MPs	11	1.5
Schools/colleges	33	4.0
Clubs/voluntary sector	107	12.5
Charitable appeals	36	4.0
Political parties/pressure groups	13	1.5
Churches	25	3.0
Public protest	14	1.5
Investigations	9	1.0
Other	89	10.5
Total	865	100.5

Sources: Glossop Chronicle, Bury Times, Westmorland Gazette, Cumberland and Westmorland Herald, Burnley Express, Rochdale Observer, Rossendale Free Press, North Wales Weekly News, Wigan Observer, Lochaber News, Oban Times, Warrington Star, Stockport Express Advertiser, Lothian Courier.

It is important to understand that these data are concerned with the sources of stories and do not necessarily tell us the nature of the content or the amount of space taken up by items originating from the various sources. Police stories are often no more than 'fillers' – one-inch single-paragraph stories, under headlines as gripping as 'Video stolen', or the occasionally humorous 'Flasher sought by police', which only revealed that 'a man who exposed himself to a woman near Llandudno's Asda store on Sunday evening is being sought by police'.[19] Council and court stories are frequently longer and more prominently placed.

Equally, not all papers place the same reliance on the same sources. In the rural press there are invariably farming sections which involve news about auctions and farming economics, and about local shows. This is revealed in a greater reliance on the business and voluntary organizations of the area as sources of news than among the urban papers where the councils, the courts and the police emerge as the dominant sources of news. These variations do not detract from the central point about the sourcing of news: namely, that it is based on information from the formal organizations of an established local order.

The news sources subsumed under 'Other' are not unified by any common characteristic. Either they are too small in number to be worth counting or they are not possible to identify in terms of a general category. In some papers, for instance, deaths and wills are a source of news, whereas in most they do not figure at all. In general, the most significant source encompassed in 'other' is the direct link between the paper and the public. This stems from two sorts of activity: the journalist seeking information from individuals she or he knows in the community, which gives access to a gossip network; and individual readers coming to the paper with information which they think will form the basis of news. These stories are not numerous but they are often the most significant, in that they are often big in terms of space taken up and in the prominence given to them. This sort of story is exemplified by an item in the *North Wales Weekly News* of 16 August 1990. Headlined 'Mum fears the worst in bin mystery', it concerned a local woman whose 'globe-trotting' son's belongings had been found in a dustbin in Florida.[20]

A general type of story for mid–August 1990 was a variant of the international story made local, already discussed. This related to the Iraqi invasion of Kuwait. The *North Wales Weekly News* had 'Anxious wait for Gulf families'. The staff had managed to locate four families in the circulation area with members in Kuwait, but none had been given any information about their relatives, and in the sense that there was no specific occurrence which could be written as a gripping narrative it was a story with a weakness.[21]

The same work of locating local people with a Kuwait interest produced a dramatic result for the *Bury Times* staff. Under the headline 'Desert escape drama' the paper's page-one lead concerned the escape from Kuwait of a building manager. The problem was revealed in the subheading 'Ex-Bury man tells of Kuwait freedom dash', in that the subject of the drama had not lived in Bury for twelve years. A second incident concerned a current resident of the area working in Iraq who had phoned his family from Baghdad with the news that he was trapped in his hotel. A third story concerned a student who had cut short a holiday to Saudi Arabia and flown home.[22]

In the *Rossendale Free Press* a couple had heard from their son and daughter-in-law, both physiotherapists, that they were safe and intending to stay in Saudi Arabia. 'We won't quit Saudi war zone,' the headline declared, somewhat prematurely.[23] These stories all illustrate how national and international stories are *made* local by the ingenuity of the journalist and that this is possible only because of the contacts that exist between readers and the newspaper.

Another source of stories not identified as a separate heading in our table because of the small number of cases was bankruptcies of local firms. These tended to be presented as significant since they have implications for individuals and for the local economy. Such stories often involve a good deal of investigative work by the reporter. An attempt to rescue a shoe factory from bankruptcy was the main lead in the *Rossendale Free Press* – 'Shoe jobs toe-hold: managers set up rescue package for crash company'. The story was based on information from the company and the receivers, and its primary focus was on the 170 workers whose jobs were at risk.[24]

A *North Wales Weekly News* front-page lead headline, 'Big stores shut-down', referred to the sudden closure of a furniture shop and a carpet store in Llandudno which had left customers without the goods they had paid for and staff unemployed and without the wages due to them.[25] In the *Glossop Chronicle*, 'Metals firm to close' revealed that thirty people were to lose their jobs because of the failure of one multinational – Union Carbide – to agree the sale of Glossop Metals to another multinational, Realindus.[26] Each of these stories is presented as a local issue in terms of its effect on the local economy and is not located as part of a general economic decline or in terms of its relationship to international markets.

The overall nature of news coverage in the local weekly press is that it relies heavily on the organized output of symbolic events, decisions and official accounts produced by a local establishment in sectors of the state, business and the formal voluntary sector. The result of this is a depiction of a localized society unrelated to any world beyond except inasmuch as members of that society are affected by it or participate in it as members of that local society. It is also a depiction in which investigation by journalists and public protest originate few accounts.

As we show in Chapters 2 and 4, these traditional weekly papers are in decline in the face of a new phenomenon and an existing one growing ever more powerful: the local weekly free newspaper, and corporate ownership. Many which thrived twenty years ago no longer exist or have become free newspapers. Independents have been taken over by chains; small and medium-sized chains have been taken over by conglomerates.

THE LOCAL AND REGIONAL DAILY PRESS

The local and regional daily press, predominantly an evening press, is radically different from the weekly press, but manifests wide differences within itself. Evening and regional morning papers provide a news service which is an alternative to the national dailies. Indeed, for the early part of this century most working-class readers relied primarily on the local paper as a source of news.[27] As a consequence, national and international news has traditionally formed a major part of these newspapers' coverage in terms of news significance, although not necessarily in terms of the number of stories or the amount of space.

Local evening papers vary from those like the *Bolton Evening News* and the *Coventry Evening Telegraph*, with circulations measured in tens of thousands, to those such as the *Birmingham Evening Mail* and the *Manchester Evening News*, with circulations around a quarter of a million – in the same order of magnitude as that of *The Independent* or the *Guardian* and more than that of the *Financial Times*. These papers normally mix national, international and local news throughout their news sections, although world and national stories tend to be concentrated in the front of the paper. The parochially local is thus mixed with issues of national and international significance. The *Birmingham Evening Mail* of 18 December 1989, for instance, carried on page two stories dealing with the beginning of the Romanian revolution, with the return of the director of the Taganka Theatre five years after being removed for staging productions displeasing to the Kremlin and with the decision by the Labour Party to abandon support for the closed shop.[28] On the opposite page a human-interest story was based on two photographs, one reproduced as part of a celebration of 150 years of policing in Birmingham and showing a police officer leading four children across the road in 1946, the second showing the same policeman, now a 70-year-old retired chief superintendent posing with the same four people, now middle aged, traced by the *Evening Mail*.[29] Such an item could as easily be found in the pages of the *North Wales Weekly News* or the *Bury Times*.

In general, the local evening press rely on news agencies for their coverage of international stories, and although they may employ one or two staff in London who cover what are defined as the big national stories, they will also rely heavily on freelance copy for national coverage. This is not always the case, however. During the US–Iraqi confrontation of August 1990, for instance, the *Manchester Evening News* had their own man, Carl Johnston, in the Gulf with the British forces. The paper was chosen by the Ministry of Defence to be allowed an accredited correspondent with the task force, the only one from among the British provincial press. Johnston's copy was given the full treatment by the news editor. In the 21 August edition he was given most of page one and most of page three. On the latter page a white-on-black tag identified the story as 'Manchester Evening News reporter Carl Johnston from the Gulf', and the headline declared: 'We're set for war says Tornado Ted: warning of fighting by the weekend.'[30] Beneath these rumours of wars, Laurie Bullas was reporting, under the headline 'Golfers can stymie water company's business park', that Denton Golf Club were opposing the sale of land on which they had a 2,000-year lease by North-West Water for redevelopment as a business park.[31]

A staff member in the cockpit of a distant war, however, is not the norm for a local evening newspaper, even for the one with the biggest circulation in the country outside London. The strength of such a paper is in its coverage of what become major events in its own region. The *Sheffield Telegraph*'s coverage of the rhino whip case, when detectives were beating prisoners in the Sheffield police cells in the early 1960s, and the *Bradford Telegraph and Argus* investigation of the Poulson case exemplify this.[32] More recently, the Stalker affair showed how a local evening paper was able to use its local connections and reputation, along with the presence of a sufficient number of journalists on the ground, to dominate the reporting of a major local issue which became a national and international story.

During the three months from mid-1986 the mass media nationally attempted to discover the reason behind the removal from duty of the Deputy Chief Constable of Manchester, John Stalker. Stalker had been in the process of investigating fatal shootings of six unarmed Irish Roman Catholics at the hands of heavily armed groups of Royal Ulster Constabulary officers. From the outset the *Manchester Evening News* was able to float theories which were followed by other newspapers and which were often borne out by events. It was the first paper to identify the fact that Stalker had been in the process of demanding access to a transcript of a tape-recording made by British intelligence officers of the shooting in an Armagh hayshed of Michael Tighe, a 17-year-old with no paramilitary connections. And it was first to suggest that the Deputy Chief Constable was on the point of pressing charges of conspiracy to pervert the course of justice against senior RUC officers.

When Stalker was removed from duty it was announced that an investigation was to be held by the Chief Constable of West Yorkshire, Colin Sampson, into alleged disciplinary offences by the Manchester police chief. The *Evening News* was the first paper to identify the nature of the charges, namely that Stalker had been an associate of local businessman Kevin Taylor, who was the subject of police investigation. It gave Mr Taylor the opportunity to claim that the reason for this investigation was an attempt to 'get Stalker' by the government in order to stymie his investigation of the six killings in Ulster.

The *Evening News* was also the first paper to identify the source of the allegations against Stalker as David Burton, alias Bertlestein, who had been a police informer, had given information to the RUC, had associated with the IRA and been convicted for dishonesty, and whose allegations were not substantiated by any other witnesses. He was also dead by the time that John Stalker was suspended. The Tory MP for Barrow, a former Manchester Council Conservative Group leader, Cecil Franks was also frequently reported by the paper as attacking the good faith of the government in the actions taken against Stalker and the investigation of Taylor, as were local Labour politicians. When national newspaper reporters came to Manchester to report the case, the *Manchester Evening News* and its then crime reporter Paul Horrocks were one of their first ports of call for information. Papers such as the *Washington Post* were provided with news by the Manchester evening paper.

At the end of 1989 when Kevin Taylor came to trial on allegations of defrauding the Co-op Bank, only the *Manchester Evening News* covered the trial. The trial lasted sixteen weeks, during which evidence was given by prosecution witnesses under cross-examination that the bank had not lost money due to Mr Taylor's business with them, that witnesses had been questioned for hours on end by police who seemed concerned to 'get Stalker', and that witnesses had been obliged to change their statements until they were strong enough for the police. During the last week it was revealed that two filing-cabinet drawers full of police documents on the cases had gone missing, that other papers had been burnt, that police had committed contempt of court, and that they had earlier obtained order of access to Taylor's bank accounts by making statements to a judge which they admitted were not true. Until the day when the trial finally collapsed and Taylor was acquitted, no other newspaper had carried any coverage of the trial except for a single story in the *Guardian*.

This is not to argue that no other paper or other part of the media made any contribution to the investigation of this case. *Panorama*, *Granada News*, the *Guardian*, the *Observer* and the local alternative magazine *City Life* all moved the story along in a major way. But in terms of frequency, amount of coverage, origination of lines of inquiry and persistence, the *Manchester Evening News* dominated the investigation of the affair. This is the outcome of three factors which relate to the nature of the local evening press.

First, the editorial staff knew, or knew of, the main characters in the drama before it began. Paul Horrocks had been reporting police affairs in the area for the previous fifteen years, and was able to call on numerous police and other contacts with access to Greater Manchester Police and underworld rumours. The editor, Michael Unger, had an even more vital role in the coverage. He himself had written or helped to write a number of stories on the affair, and had an insight into what was happening to Stalker brought about by the fact that eighteen months before his removal from duty Stalker had first made contact with the editor about his investigations in Northern Ireland and about his worries concerning the inquiry. Unger himself revealed this in 1988 at the point when Stalker's own book on the affair was being published.

This caused a breach in relations between the two men. There is no doubt that this close knowledge of local events stemmed from the relationship between the local paper and the area it reports, which requires as a normal part of the production of news frequent interaction between journalists and spokespeople of the local establishment and informants in the rumour network.

Second, the other side of this relationship is that contacts and sources of news have their own reasons for dealing with the press. John Stalker's lawyer, Roger Pannone, mobilized a press campaign to get his client reinstated without recourse to a disciplinary tribunal. In order to do this, he organized press conferences and provided individual journalists with information. The audience he primarily wanted to influence was the Greater Manchester Police Authority, since they had to make the decision whether to send the Stalker case to a disciplinary tribunal or whether to return him to work without further action. For Pannone the main medium by which this propaganda war was to be fought in relation to this audience was the *Manchester Evening News*. This strategy by Pannone is merely a clarification of the nature of the normal relationship between news sources and journalists. Even if only implicitly, sources have reasons for talking to journalists, because the press is part of a complex process of interaction among actors. The local press is part of such an interaction process.

Third, the *Manchester Evening News* as a local newspaper was interested in the Stalker affair as a local story. Therefore, when the Taylor case came to court the paper automatically covered it. When the evidence was considered too technical to justify a full-time reporter's presence at the court, they kept a watching brief through retaining the local court-reporting freelance news agency. The national press showed an interest only when the outcome of the case showed that there seemed to be truth in the allegations that the government was out to discredit Stalker and that Taylor had merely been a means to do so.[33]

This coverage although exceptional can be seen as the outcome of normal activity of news production by the local press. A story in the Aberdeen-based regional morning paper the *Press and Journal* (now in its 244th year) illustrates this point. Its second lead on the front of 31 March 1990 concerned the death by shooting of an anti-nuclear campaigner, Willie MacRae. The article was headlined 'Two-shots claim in MacRae death riddle', and the reporter John Vass recounted the claim by a Grampian regional councillor and former SNP MP, Hamish Watt, that Mr MacRae had received a second bullet wound to his head.[34]

This claim was prompted by a series run during that week by the *Press and Journal* on the death of Mr McRae. Mr Watt claimed he had been given the information by a former nurse at the Aberdeen Royal Infirmary who had assisted in the operating theatre when medical staff tried to save the shot man's life. The significance of the second bullet wound was obviously that it precluded the 'suicide theory'. Mr Watt was quoted as saying that Willie MacRae had been assassinated for his 'too-extensive' study of NATO activities in Scotland.

> Willie knew too much for his own good and being a lawyer could present his knowledge of, and opinion on, the risks involved in the nuclear business in such a convincing way that someone somewhere was just not prepared to tolerate.

The report revealed that neither Mr MacRae's medical reports nor the post-mortem data have ever been revealed; nor was there ever a fatal accident inquiry.[35] The fact that the story was used so prominently and that the paper had run a series on the death, and the reference to the non-publication of the medical reports and the post-mortem data, along with the failure to hold a fatal accident inquiry, all indicate that the assassination theory is entertained by the paper as a serious explanation of events. Like the coverage of the Stalker affair in Manchester, it shows that at times the regional press is capable of presenting news which challenges the notion that society is universally harmonious and that government is necessarily benign.

The regional evening press needs to respond to the speed with which versions of events have to be interpreted and produced as news at times of emergency. A further example from the *Manchester Evening News* illustrates the speed and pressure of such processes. On 1 April 1990 Strangeways gaol in Manchester was the scene of what up until that point was the most spectacular riot ever to occur in a British prison. It started in the prison chapel and quickly spread throughout the gaol. The chapel seemed at first to be the birthplace of a national religious revival, since instead of the normal congregation of 100 over 300 men turned up apparently eager for a few words with the Lord. However, this impression was quickly dispelled when the prison chaplain had his eye blacked and the mob of enthusiastic converts attacked prison officers and the habitually religious prisoners. They then seized the main prison buildings, fired one of the wings and made their way via some convenient scaffolding to the roof, where they hurled slates and other building materials on to the warders below, stopping only to brutalize the Rule 43 prisoners (sex offenders, police informers and others kept separate for their protection) on the way.

By the following morning the *Evening News* had eight of their twenty-five reporters working on the story. The health service correspondent discovered that twenty body bags had been taken into the prison by ambulance men, one of whom told her that it was feared that twenty prisoners were dead. Many of the Rule 43 prisoners had been taken to hospital injured, and there were stories of drug-crazed prisoners roaming about inside the goal.

Presented with this information and the first deadline for news at 11 a.m., the editor decided to accept the story about the twenty dead as accurate. The first edition came out with its front page taken up almost entirely by a photograph of prisoners hurling slates from the prison roof. This was beneath a two-inch-deep headline which declared '20 DEAD?', while beneath it a caption read: 'ROOFTOP REVENGE – prisoners in stocking masks and stolen warders' caps hurl tiles into the courtyard below'. At the bottom of the page a secondary headline stated: 'Drug-crazed rioters "cut throats of sex offenders in prison bloodbath" '. In the second edition, when doubts were raised about the strength of the body bags evidence, the headline was changed by the addition of a question mark to the '20 DEAD?' claim. By the last edition the headline was changed to 'MAYHEM' as it became clear that the taking in of body bags was a normal precaution taken by the emergency services.[36] This was the outcome of the need at times for the editor of such a newspaper to make sense of the versions of events he or she is receiving at a speed which allows little time for reflection on the quality of the evidence available. This represents the opposite pole in the activities of the provincial daily press from the sort of campaign exemplified by the coverage of the Stalker affair, the shooting of Willie MacRae or the investigation of John Poulson, where events are interpreted and reinterpreted over a period of months or even years.

The great bulk of the local coverage in the provincial evening and morning press, however, does not come into either of these categories. It is like that of the local weeklies – the outcome of the sort of sources indicated by Aitchison, above. Equally, the reportage of national and international news generally derives from secondary news sources such as freelance correspondents and the major news agencies. The outcome is that such news coverage is generally bland and occurs under such attention-grabbing headlines as 'Job joy at supermarket' or 'Artist sues Leeds firm over its "vulgar" jigsaw'. The norm for leader comment in this sort of newspaper almost always leans towards the respectable, the acceptable and the non-controversial. The *Yorkshire Evening Post*, dedicated in its constitution to be conservative with a small 'c', begins a leader with the stout-hearted declaration: 'Let's face it, the transport system of this country – if it still can be called a system – is in an unparalleled state of chaos'; but after eight paragraphs of argument it ends with the somewhat underwhelming conclusion: 'Nothing less than an immediate edict from Downing Street to get the mess sorted out will do.'[37]

Only the *Manchester Evening News* appears ready to be rude to such local institutions as the police and to its Chief Constable James Anderton in particular. For instance, at the end of his year's office with Association of Chief Police Officers, Mr Anderton was embattled with the media. In a speech at Bolton he attacked the media as arrogant and guilty of 'blatant nosiness' in prying into domestic and private matters. He also objected to media comments on 'anything at all affecting the role and duties of the police'. In response, the Manchester paper referred to a claim made by the Chief Constable, on a radio programme earlier in the year, that he might be a 'prophet of God', in order to lampoon the police chief. 'Prophet Jim hath spoken again,' the leading article began. And in reference to his call for controls on the press it commented: 'It is not clear whether this is one of the Almighty's ideas or whether Mr. Anderton thought it up for himself, but it sounds remarkably like censorship to us.' The final sentence maintained the same combative and satirical pitch: 'Prophet Jim, who is not renowned for being averse to a spot of personal publicity, should practise what he preaches.'[38]

Despite these shafts of vigorous debate and investigative news coverage, the general disposition of the traditional local press, both weekly and evening, is towards news coverage which appears to uphold the local establishment and to celebrate the values of a stable, orderly and conflict-free local community. This is conveyed not so much as a desirable end-state but as an existing reality. Local papers often carry on their masthead the number of years they have been in existence – normally over a century, occasionally two. One of the most frequent features is photographs of the locality 25, 50 or 100 years ago. So are reprints of news items of the past. These all help to sustain a picture of a stable, continuous community.

But the reason for this is not necessarily or exclusively some deep commitment to functionalist, conservative ideas on the part of the producers of the local press, nor even necessarily that such views are forced on them by the owners. It is that the production of news requires a regular supply of validated and 'reliable' information, and this is produced through the local government bureaucracy, business public relations departments, the local law-enforcement agencies and the local establishment of amateur clubs and associations, who all have reasons for wanting their versions of events to be published as news. The fact that other sorts of news and non-conforming opinions do get published, however, shows that where the market for news or the particular interest of a local editor or reporter is strong enough, or where there are forces in the interplay of local politics which disrupt the normal tendency towards blandness, some elements in the traditional local press are capable of stepping outside the normal sheepfold that they inhabit.

Chapter 4

Free newspapers: some of the news that's fit to print – and much that isn't

Free newspapers undoubtedly represent the single most significant development in the structure of the local press since the 1960s. The spectacular and rapid growth of free newspapers, in terms of both number of published titles and aggregate distribution figures, has been described, in a style uncharacteristically bland for the *Guardian*, as 'the quiet revolution in newspapers'.[1] In an equally untypical but more euphuistic prose News International, referring to the ephemeral and short-lived character of some free newspapers in conditions of a volatile market, observed that 'free-sheets come and go like feathers in the breeze'.[2] Developments in the free press, however, have not always been heralded in such measured terms. An article in *AFN News* with the intriguing title 'Why do people on a diet read more free newspapers?' reported the major findings of a British market research survey on patterns of readership which discovered that '76.1% of men who use hair restorer also read free newspapers, while only 54.7% read paid-fors'.[3] Such apparently fatuous, if not bizarre, research emphasizes the need for free newspapers to identify for advertisers, as precisely as possible, their readership and its consumer preferences. The significance of advertisers to the free press cannot be overstated. Their influence is pervasive and central in determining the free newspaper's financial viability, the number of copies distributed, the distribution areas, the nature of the paper's readership, levels of staffing and, ultimately, the content of the newspaper. Free newspapers, above all other sectors of the local press, offer the clearest possible refutation of the suggestion that newspapers, left to the forces of the market, can be relied upon to produce a wide range of critical news and reporting of their community for their readers.

The emergence of the free press is an important phenomenon not merely in its own right but because of its implications for paid local newspapers. Free newspapers' substantial distribution figures, often achieved at the expense of the traditional paid-for weekly press; the advertising revenues they attract and their growing dominance in local advertising markets; their high levels of market penetration, readership figures and consequent importance to readers as a source of news about their local communities – each signals the substantial importance of free newspapers within the local press. To discuss 'free newspapers' as if they constituted a homogeneous entity, however, can be misleading. Variety is evident in many aspects of their production. Free papers come (literally) in all shapes and sizes and are distinguished not merely by technical matters such as pagination and their use (imaginative or otherwise) of layout and colour, but by journalistic considerations such as the ratio of editorial to advertising adopted by particular papers and, perhaps most significantly, the quality of the news and editorial they carry. It is not especially contentious to claim that the editorial quality of some free newspapers is very poor by comparison with their paid-for weekly equivalents. Indeed, the issue has been a major focus for discussion and debate within the free newspaper industry, with the pejorative term 'freesheet' reserved for those papers of particularly undistinguished editorial quality.[4] The marketing director of Reed Southern Newspapers, the single largest producer of free newspapers, claims that overall the quality of editorial is improving but concedes that

> free newspapers in the '70s varied enormously in quality. Some justifiably were called 'freesheets', keeping the ads apart with PR puffery and plugs for their advertisers. Some made circulation claims which were at best wishful thinking and at worst downright 'porkies'.[5]

The quality of a newspaper's editorial reflects, of course, the financial and journalistic resources it possesses, and these in turn are highly variable within the free press. Reed Regional Newspapers, for example, which is part of the larger Reed Group, publishes in excess of 100 free newspapers with a weekly aggregated circulation of 5,832,249. The company's flagship free newspaper, the *Daily News*, employs approximately forty journalists and publishes regular freelance columns by journalists such as Peter Jenkins, Claire Rayner and Barry Norman. At the opposite end of the resource spectrum is the *Cheshire and District Standard*, established in September 1986 and earning a place of dubious distinction in newspaper history by becoming the first newspaper to be launched without a single staff journalist, being instead wholly reliant for copy on a local news agency.[6]

The issue of editorial quality in part reflects this relative access to resources, but more critically it expresses the paradox implicit in the philosophy of the free press. Free newspapers are the most rapidly expanding element in the local press, but their accelerated development has been achieved by reversing the traditional 'logic' of newspaper production. The conventional wisdom of newspaper publication suggested that quality news reporting, across a wide range of issues, was the essential magnet necessary to attract readers, who, in their turn, would woo advertisers. In this way the newspaper was provided with its twin sources of income from advertising revenues and sales of the newspaper. For free newspapers, however, the quality of news and editorial is largely irrelevent, since free distribution means that newspapers need no longer 'win' a circulation on the merits of their news reporting. Copies distributed to selected geographical sites, where identified readers belonging to known socio-economic groups reside, ensure that free newspapers are able to guarantee to advertisers high levels of reach or penetration of carefully targeted readers (consumers).

In the free newspaper market, the traditional designations of buyers, sellers, readers and commodities have been thrown into the air and returned to the ground in something of a jumble. The 'buyers' are no longer readers trying to buy a commodity called 'news'. The demands of the market have metamorphosed 'buyer' (readers) into the commodity for sale by free newspapers to advertisers – if the price is right! News still has a role, if somewhat compromised, to play in this new order of things. It must straddle the difficult divide between being sufficiently interesting to engage readers' attention, but never so interesting that it might detract from the content of the advertisements.

Newspapers, of course, have always been dependent to some degree, and often in large part, on advertising revenues to provide a proportion of their income (the 'qualities', for example, derive up to 70 per cent of their income from advertising). What sets free newspapers apart from their traditional paid-for equivalents, however, is their total reliance on advertising to the exclusion of all other revenues. A number of significant consequences for the organization of free newspapers, their staffing structures, their news-gathering routines and related matters stem from this fundamental difference in their economic structure and organization.

First, a greater proportion of space allocated to advertising over editorial is evident when free newspapers are compared to their typical paid-for equivalents. Second, their economic organization makes them more susceptible to the influence of advertising interests at points where potentially they might conflict with policy concerning editorial content. The director of the Yellow Advertiser Group, for example, claimed his newspapers had dropped their sports pages not because of any lack of reader interest but because they were failing to attract advertising.[7] An editorial in *UK Press Gazette*, adopting the language of the tabloids, spoke of 'the officially sanctioned tyranny of the advertising department whose ability to sell any space in any position mugged the editorial pages'.[8] Third, they possess smaller journalistic staffs since their reliance on news gathering is less acute than in the paid-for local press. Fourth, free newspapers are less accountable to their readers since the papers are distributed free, with financial viability being markedly less dependent on retaining or enhancing readership than is the case with paid-for papers. Good, bad or indifferent in terms of editorial content, whether desired or detested by the public, the paper is posted routinely through the selected doors in its distribution area. Fifth, to keep advertising rates to a minimum, free newspapers have attempted to minimize their news-gathering costs in ways which, for various reasons, have not been available to, or considered desirable by, the paid-for press, generating further differences between the two types of newspaper.

As well as employing fewer journalists, free newspapers operate in a climate which places less emphasis on the professional training of staff. Editorial staff are, quite simply, less significant than the telephone sales staff who sell space by the column inch. It is perhaps unsurprising, given the relative downgrading of the journalistic role, that trades unions in general, but the NUJ in particular, have been less effective in securing members in the free newspaper setting. Free newspapers have consequently been less constrained than the paid-for weekly press in their efforts to introduce flexible ways of working, breaking down traditional divisions of labour between production and editorial staffs. The unions' difficulties spring from the problems they encountered in trying to secure negotiating rights with some of the anti-union entrepreneurs like Shah who were pervasive in the early days of the free press. A direct consequence of low trades union membership has been the ability of the free press to introduce new printing technology, with its potential for low-cost/small-run production, which has given the free press a further competitive edge over its paid-for rivals.

The most effective way to reduce the costs associated with news gathering, of course, is to abandon any pretensions to being an investigative news-gathering and -reporting organization. Alternatively, news can be 'bought' from the Press Association or a local news agency or, better still, can be provided for free by courtesy of the press releases issued by 'non-news' organizations such as the public relations departments of central and local government, various regional authorities, local business, local political party organizations, pressure groups and a host of other local organizations. This is a strategy which many free papers have adopted, and the acceptance and incorporation of these 'information subsidies' explains how the free press is able to carry a considerable amount of local government/political news with substantially fewer journalists than the paid-for papers. The role which information subsidies play in the free press's reporting of local government is considered in more detail below. We begin by examining the reasons underlying the growth of free newspapers, followed by an assessment of the current state of the industry and the recent developments of the daily 'metro' concept for free newspapers.

FREE NEWSPAPERS: THE IMPETUS FOR GROWTH

In broad-brush terms, free newspapers are the progeny of market forces and market demand. The managing director of the Yellow Advertiser Group described free newspapers as 'a response to the needs of the marketplace'.[9] The period of their most rapid growth coincided with the sea-change in British political attitudes which prompted the election of the Thatcher administration and witnessed the elevation and celebration of the simple idea of the market as a panacea for the resolution of problems in economy, polity and society. Free newspapers seemed to exemplify the Thatcherite dream. They were given away and yet still generated money and profits.

In truth, the development and growth of the free press reflect a fortuitous convergence of three factors: the relatively poor and declining circumstances of the traditional local press; the consumer boom of the 1960s and 1970s and the expanding advertising industry's need for new and local media outlets; and finally, developments in printing technology and associated changes in staffing levels and the traditional organization of production.

The extant local press acted as a spur to the development of free newspapers in two apparently contradictory ways. First, its long-term decline provided a gap in the local newspaper market for potential rivals; but second, the strategies adopted by some local papers to survive the challenge of the free press also contributed to the latter's expansion. Throughout the 1960s and 1970s the paid-for local press constituted a series of local monopolies with small-circulation newspapers servicing discrete and carefully defined areas. The 1977 Royal Commission on the Press, rarely considered to be over-critical in its appraisal of the local press, confirmed that 'competition between daily provincial newspapers has almost entirely disappeared'.[10] For evening papers there was competition 'only in one area',[11] with 'very little competition between weeklies'.[12] Circulations and numbers of published titles were declining,[13] reflecting in some cases bland and parochial editorial content in tandem with an unimaginative and dated layout; paradoxically, overstaffing and understaffing were both common criticisms. Lionel Pickering, who established the Derby Trader Group of free newspapers, dispelled some of the romantic mythologies which have subsequently come to obscure the real character of these papers. 'I know we get accused of closing down good paid-for newspapers,' he claimed,

> but in 1966 there were so many ancient, ailing, weekly paid-for papers. We've all worked for them, each one run by one man and a boy, with loads of correspondents sending in antiquated copy from village fêtes about Mrs Jones' home-made jam. They were started in 1750, they were not professional and quite frankly the people who were running them didn't know a thing about newspapers. They were in it for the advertising

with circulations of 4–5,000 and they were ripe for the taking, quite frankly.[14]

The paid-for local press, therefore, because of its inefficiencies and shortcomings, created a gap in the local newspaper market which the free press promptly filled. But traditional papers fostered the growth of free papers directly. A popular defensive strategy for the paid-for press, if threatened by a free newspaper, was to establish its own free newspaper. In the process, the intruder is denied both potential advertising revenues and a *raison d'être*. The editor of an evening paper circulating in a West Yorkshire town confided in interview that free newspapers were

> an absolute menace. They're a big threat. They come and take your advertising revenues. We had one here but we've seen it off. . . . We ended up buying it but we also set up our own weekly free as a defensive measure.

Establishing a free newspaper can be achieved via two quite distinct routes. Some firms which own weekly newspapers have simply 'gone free'. This has typically involved amalgamating two or more different titles in neighbouring circulation areas, with consequent savings deriving from cuts in staff members and costs of premises. Evening papers, on the other hand, as noted above, when faced with competition for cheap advertising from free weeklies, have established their own weeklies as junior partners with the express intention of demolishing the opposition. Utilizing plant and office space at times when it would otherwise be relatively under-used, and pasting up the free weekly using stories culled from the evening paper, keeps production and journalistic costs for such publications very low, enabling them to offer cut-price advertising rates while still breaking even. Some of the firms producing paid-for weeklies which have gone over to free distribution are also producers of evening papers, and managements in these enterprises face a poignant problem. They have to make sure that their free newspapers are attractive enough to smother the opposition but, at the same time, ensure they are not so good as purveyors of news – or so cheap as advertising media – that they compete with the main title, the traditional evening paper.

A second factor prompting the burgeoning of the free press was the aspirations of the expanding advertising industry for new media outlets. Advertisers were also becoming increasingly frustrated by the power of monopolistic local publishers and concerned by their ability to charge ever-higher advertising rates in return for annually declining ABC figures. Consequently, the competition which free newspapers brought to the local press market was welcomed by advertisers. But there were three other reasons why free newspapers began to attract advertising revenue. First, there was the influence of what might be termed the 'Heineken factor'. Because they are distributed, free newspapers reach those readers which other newspapers cannot reach. They bring into the market, for example, people who have stopped buying newspapers. Second, free newspapers offered advertisers guaranteed delivery of their message to a clearly identified readership and promised to reach more of the prestigious, high-consuming A and B socio-economic groups. Third, advertising costs per thousand reached are typically one-third of those for paid-for weeklies, reflecting the low production costs of free distributions – see Table 4.1.

Table 4.1 Advertising cost per 1,000 (square column cm) in the regional press

	Titles	Circ'n	Total advertising cost (£000)	Cost per thousand
Free newspapers in Association of Free Newspapers	477	23,391,153	1,467.62	6.28p
Paid-for weeklies	570	7,567,627	1,453.50	19.20p
Evenings	79	5,472,679	469.42	8.58p
Morning	17	1,452,260	159.67	10.99p
Sunday	8	1,947,761	101.90	5.23p

Source: A–Z of Britain's Free Newspapers and Magazines, Gloucester, AFN, 1990.

In combination, these advantages proved a powerful enticement to advertisers.

Third, free newspapers harnessed the advantages to be won from new typesetting and printing technology to great effect. New technology offered not only a technically superior end product, but opportunities for lowering production costs by employing fewer journalists and operating more flexible production routines which blurred the division of labour between production and editorial; typesetting skills were acquired more readily using new technology. Free newspapers were able to introduce new technology into their operations precisely because they were new and, initially, small-scale and non-unionized enterprises. In the traditional press sector, established trades unions representing print workers and journalists saw new technology as a potential threat to jobs and resisted its introduction. Eddie Shah judges the activities of trades unions as the crucial factor distinguishing the free from the paid-for sector. 'The regional press', claims Shah,

> is forced to sell itself for a price because they can't get rid of the old trade unionism and the restrictive labour practices the trades unions impose as quickly as the regional press would like. When you go free like we did you can be bolder in your logic.[15]

In combination, the decline of the paid-for local press, the needs of the advertising industry and the introduction of new technology provided a substantial impetus to the free press.

THE FREE NEWSPAPER INDUSTRY

The history and recent development of the free press have been characterized both by the enormous success and rapid growth of the industry, in terms of number of published titles and advertising revenues, combined somewhat paradoxically with an apparent inferiority complex and evident desire to gain credibility and respectability for the new industry, measured by the conventional yardstick of journalistic integrity and quality. In this section we explore both aspects of this development by reviewing briefly the expansion of the free press; the mushrooming of its advertising income; changing patterns of free press ownership; the nature of its readership; and finally, the establishment of the Association of Free Newspapers as part of the industry's attempt to gain respectability.

Free newspapers first began to be published in the early 1960s. Initially, they were devoted almost wholly to advertisements, reported very little news and displayed little identification with the communities in which they were distributed. These early 'freesheets' posed little threat to the established newspapers. By the mid-1970s, however, the expansion of journalistic staff and the deployment of new technology were producing a new generation of free newspapers which, in appearance at least, closely resembled their paid-for counterparts. After a slow start, in which the fledgling industry suffered the ridicule of journalists and editors in the paid-for press, free newspapers began to take off.

The growth in published titles and circulation figures throughout the 1980s has been breathtaking. Since 1980 the number of free newspaper titles has grown from 325 to 1,156, with a certified distribution of 43.5 million copies.[16] The free press phenomenon, moreover, is European-wide, with Germany, France, Belgium and Great Britain publishing more than 4,000 titles with a distribution approaching 200 million each week and employing 150,000 people, with a further 500,000 employed part-time on distribution.[17]

More significantly, advertising revenues have grown commensurately with these figures. In 1980 advertising revenues for free newspapers were approximately £84 million but by 1989 they had grown sevenfold to reach almost £600 million. Job recruitment and property advertising have been especially vigorous and extremely important areas of growth, with the former expanding by 269 per cent and the latter by 546 per cent between 1982 and 1986.[18] More generally, free newspapers have achieved steady progress throughout the 1980s, establishing their growing predominance in the local press market. In 1984, with an annual income of £224 million representing 24.7 per cent of the local press advertising market, free newspapers overtook the market share enjoyed by their paid-for weekly counterparts. The subsequent market shares for both weekly and daily paid-for papers have declined, but the bullish expansion of free newspapers resulted in 1986 in the total weekly newspaper market share becoming greater than that of daily local papers.[19]

Table 4.2 confirms the financial success of free newspapers as a marketing phenomenon.

Three aspects of the economic expansion of free newspapers are especially noteworthy. First, as Table 4.2 confirms, advertising income more than doubled between 1984 and 1988. Second, the market share of free newspapers has increased considerably over the same period, while that of paid-for weeklies (–3.4 per cent) and regional dailies (–6.1 per cent) has continued to fall. Third, speculations concerning the future fortunes of free newspapers look promising. A report by Zenith Media Buying Services, a division of the Saatchi empire, predicted that by 1992 free newspapers' market share will surpass the position held by regional dailies and that advertising revenue will undergo a further fourfold increase to £2.1 billion by 1992; the remainder of the regional press will share a mere £1.9 billion. Zenith also forecast that the current 33.8 per cent market share will exceed 52 per cent by the turn of the century.[20]

Table 4.2 Advertising expenditure (£m.) and market share in the regional press

	Free	Paid-for weeklies	Paid-for dailies	Total regional press
1984	£224 (24.3%)	£223 (24.2%)	£474 (51.5%)	£921
1985	£262 (26.1%)	£234 (23.3%)	£507 (50.5%)	£1,003
1986	£314 (28.5%)	£242 (22.0%)	£544 (49.4%)	£1,100
1987	£405 (31.6%)	£270 (21.1%)	£605 (47.3%)	£1,280
1988	£522 (33.8%)	£320 (20.8%)	£701 (45.4%)	£1,543

Source: Advertising Association; reprinted in *AFN News*, October 1989, p. 21.

Patterns of ownership of the free press have changed rapidly during the 1980s reflecting these high financial incentives which have attracted buyers into the market. As we noted in Chapter 1, free newspapers were typically established by individual entrepreneurs rather than companies or the traditional newspaper chains. They were often judged as interlopers who had little experience of the newspaper industry, but seemed attracted by the possibility of profits at a time when publishing free newspapers promised more lucrative rewards than selling scrap metal or second-hand cars. Individuals made small fortunes as the growth of their publishing concerns spiralled. In the late 1980s the majority of these entrepreneurs opted for the philosophy of 'take the money and run'. The processes of competition and monopolistic accumulation of smaller companies by the larger conglomerates, which worked through the commercial local press during the previous eighty years, worked through the free newspaper market in a fraction of the time. The mid- to late 1980s witnessed a number of sales of free newspaper companies to older, more traditional newspaper publishers. In 1985, for example, Paul Morgan sold Morgan Communications to Reed International for £9.7 million.[21] The success of the independently owned free newspapers resulted in the traditional major publishers effectively monopolizing the free market by the onset of the 1990s. Many of the publishers of paid-for papers, who had previously ridiculed free newspapers or considered them as defence mechanisms with which to protect their paid-for titles, came to embrace free newspapers as part of a segmentation philosophy designed to expand their revenue and fill the market-place. This change in publisher attitude, and the increasing attempt to secure monopolistic control of the market, is exemplified by Thomson Regional Newspapers (TRN). In the late 1980s TRN was allegedly in 'an expansionist and acquisitive mood, encouraged from the top'.[22] This mood has seen TRN free newspapers grow from 13 titles distributing 786,000 copies in 1983 to more than 100 titles distributing more than 5 million copies by summer 1989. Other companies which have developed considerable free newspaper interests include EMAP (1.45 million copies), Eastern Counties (1.03 million), United Provincial (2.05 million), Northcliffe (1.5 million) and The Guardian and Manchester Evening News (1.4 million) while Reed Regional Newspapers remain the undisputed largest publisher of only free newspapers, with almost 6 million copies distributed each week.

The effect of these developments is that the market in free newspapers is currently characterized by monopoly to the degree where the leading ten companies publish more than half of the free titles published, with the twenty-two largest companies distributing in excess of 70 per cent of all free newspapers. The major players in the free newspaper market are no longer 'gung-ho' entrepreneurs personified by Eddie Shah. Recent shifting patterns of ownership have culminated quite quickly in a situation where 'free publishing has come to be dominated by older established companies'.[23] The decision by Lionel Pickering to sell his Derby Trader Group to TRN in June 1989 for a figure reputed to be £25 million was heralded in the UK Press Gazette as 'the end of the era of the self made free newspaper entrepreneur'.[24]

A key component in the success of free newspapers has been publishers' ability to convince advertisers that their newspapers are not merely distributed but actually read. Free newspapers' advantage over their paid-for rivals resides precisely in meeting advertisers' requirements that information about their product reaches a very high proportion of readers in a particular area: in brief, a newspaper through every letter-box – guaranteed. But it soon became clear to advertisers that such guarantees were of little value if the newspaper wasn't read. In the 1970s doubts about the editorial quality and news content of free papers led to a widespread scepticism that, once delivered, free newspapers were dispatched promptly to the rubbish bin. The industry needed to establish its credibility with advertisers as producers of free newspapers rather than freesheets. Consequently, the free newspaper industry has conducted a good deal of research in an effort to establish the facts of newspaper readership.

The most recent survey conducted by Target Group Index in late 1989 reviewed readership patterns across forty-two areas of Britain in which 134 free weeklies and 61 paid-for weeklies circulated. Perhaps the major finding is that more people read free newspapers than any alternative; 76.6 per cent of adults read free newspapers, compared to 73 per cent who read national Sundays, 67 per cent national morning papers, 43 per cent local paid-for weeklies, 29.5 per cent local evening papers and 13.2 per cent regional morning papers. The results are impressive if unsurprising given free distribution.

The amount of time spent reading a free newspaper, however, varied between 12.2 and 39.4 minutes, averaging 22.5 minutes over the sample. Sixty-one per cent claimed to read more than half of the paper, with 39 per cent stating that they read 'all or most' of the paper. Free newspapers (6.57 days) are retained in the house almost as long as paid-for (7.09 days) but are referred to only twice during the course of the week compared to three times for the paid-for paper. Free newspapers are read across all age groups, ranging from 73 per cent of people aged 20–24 to 80 per cent of people 65 and over; equivalent figures for paid-for papers are 40 per cent and 42 per cent. Very significantly, free newspapers score exceptionally well among the higher socio-economic groups: 67.5 per cent of As and 76.1 per cent of Bs; paid-for equivalent figures are 38 per cent and 43 per cent.[25]

The summary conclusion of the research is that 'free newspaper advertising is the most cost-efficient way of using the regional media',[26] perhaps underscoring an important purpose of the enquiry: to consolidate free newspapers' credibility with the advertising profession. It appears to have worked. The media director of Saatchi & Saatchi claimed: 'I do not regard that something which is free is inherently inferior to a paid for publication. We judge papers on their merits' (fine meritocratic sentiments indeed, but he continued in more pragmatic vein), 'who it reaches and how.'[27]

A major element in free newspapers' attempts to gain acceptance with advertisers, the public and the broader newspaper industry has been the establishment of the Association of Free Newspapers (AFN) in 1980. The association allegedly began life in a stationery cupboard at the Yellow Advertiser Group, but celebrated its tenth anniversary at a House of Commons reception with Michael Heseltine as speaker.[28] AFN's objectives are hard-headed. It is the representative organization and official voice of publishers of free newspapers and magazines in the UK, 'created with the aim to give the industry respectability and credibility'.[29] The officially stated purpose of the association is 'to uphold and promote the highest standards and interests of free newspapers and their proprietors'.[30]

By the mid 1980s AFN had 128 member organizations and 19 associate members who jointly publish 552 titles distributing some 27 million copies weekly. Membership embraces some of the largest traditional chain publishers including Reed Regional Newspapers, Thomson Regional Newspapers, Northcliffe, Ingersoll and Westminster Press.[31] AFN's success in attracting the more powerful forces in publishing into its fold has proved a problem. Initially, AFN acted as an umbrella grouping linking and promoting large numbers of individual enterprises, but the majority of free newspapers are now owned by major groups who have their own marketing operation and their own public relations, promotion and research departments. AFN's need to define a new role for itself in order to survive was left too late. In late 1990 TRN and Reed left the Association, claiming that the Newspaper Society is the appropriate body to represent all newspapers – paid-for or free. In February 1991 the Association changed its name to the Association of Free and Weekly Newspapers to reflect the change in membership and its intention to embrace paid-for and free weekly papers.

But for more than a decade AFN has worked well as an information exchange and co-ordinator of common interests within the free newspaper industry. Its overriding concern has been to promote a favourable image for free newspapers and to establish the credibility and respectability of the fledgling industry. It has sought to achieve these agitprop objectives via four principal mechanisms.

One of the association's earliest concerns, perhaps unsurprisingly given the economic structure of free newspapers, was to enhance the credibility of the industry with advertisers. To this end, AFN members worked closely with the Audit Bureau of

Circulation (ABC) to form VFD (Verified Free Distribution). In brief, this is a system which certifies and guarantees free distribution claims of newspapers. The VFD figure published by the newspaper masthead signals the average minimum number of copies of each issue of the paper distributed in a defined area in a period of not less than six months and not more than twelve months.

Second, AFN adopted a code of publishing practice to which members must agree to conform. The code's ten rather timorous articles could hardly be considered restrictive. For example, members must publish VFD figures prominently in each edition of the newspaper (article 4) and must 'agree to make every effort to ensure that distribution of free newspapers . . . is carried out to the highest standards. Delivery agents will at all times be instructed to ensure that they do not leave matter protruding from letterboxes.'[32] This last seems a rather demanding request to make of the army of underpaid schoolchildren and housewives who typically constitute the 'delivery agents'. Article 7 suggests that members should merely 'endeavour to abide by the British Code of Advertising Practice', while a more rigorous code of publishing practice might reasonably have replaced 'endeavour to' by 'must'. Some voices in the industry have argued that the code should be 'beefed up' to try to tackle, from a different angle, the problems relating to editorial quality. A delegate to the 1987 AFN conference argued that 'AFN should introduce basic staffing levels. There is such a wide variation in the quality of newspers which I am bound to think is linked to the number of people employed.'[33] To date no such proposal has been introduced into the code, although AFN does have a working group examining issues of staffing, training and editorial quality. Despite the obvious shortcomings of the code, membership of AFN signals a commitment to some minimum standards, although the primary objective once again seems to be the offering of guarantees concerning distribution and quality to advertisers rather than readers.

Third, the association organizes an annual conference which claims to be an international gathering of members, but, much like the World Snooker Championships, British names seem to dominate the delegate list. Like many conferences it is a mixture of PR exercise, uncritical celebration of the industry's achievements and social gathering, rather than a forum where formal business is conducted; the conference typically begins with a golf tournament. A roll call of recent keynote speakers signals the political climate of the assembly: in 1989 Conservative minister David Trippier; in 1990 Peter Morgan, director-general of the Institute of Directors, the economist Professor Patrick Minford and Conservative politician Edwina Currie. In 1986 Jeffrey Archer was greeted warmly by delegates, but vocal rumblings marked the arrival of the NUJ's Harry Conroy at the lecturn.

Finally, the association produces a monthly newspaper, *AFN News*, which is mailed directly to advertising and marketing agencies. A tabloid format, with pagination varying between 20 and 32, *AFN News* has used full colour since October 1989. The paper devotes a considerable amount of space to advertising, while the remainder is unashamed 'puffery' and self-promotion for both AFN and individual member newspapers – a freesheet in the classic mould. Story headlines in the May and June 1990 issues include 'It's official! Frees really do need the Association', 'AFN in healthy form', 'Frees campaign is great success' and finally a special feature, 'Frees a market force for all'.

In summary, the free newspaper business is currently booming in terms of numbers of published papers and economic rewards. Doubts remain, however, both inside and without the free newspaper industry concerning the quality of some free newspapers in what is acknowledged to be a 'mixed bag' of highly varied publications. The establishment of AFN has undoubtedly boosted self-confidence within the industry and enhanced its respectability and public image beyond. The industry is changing rapidly. Shifting patterns of ownership have seen the supersession of individual entrepreneurs by the larger publishing companies. Newspapers themselves are also changing in an effort to establish new or as yet untapped markets. A daily free newspaper, the *Daily News*, is regarded by some as the flagship of free newspapers' achievements as well as a portent of future developments. Curiously, it seems at first glance to be the mirror inversion of many free newspapers. To date, it has failed to make a profit, but it is widely acknowledged to be a newspaper of quality and editorial merit. It is worthy of closer examination.

THE 'METRO' CONCEPT AND THE *DAILY NEWS*

The *Daily News*, launched in Birmingham on 2 October 1984, was heralded as the first of a new type of free newspaper: the 'metro' free. The paper's title is a misnomer, since the *Daily News* makes only four appearances each week, missing publication on Saturday, Sunday and Monday. It distributes 276,000 copies daily, claims 427,000 readers and takes 25 per cent of the total newspaper advertising revenue market in Birmingham.[34]

The 'metro' newspaper concept and its particular embodiment in the *Daily News* are both the idea of Chris Bullivant, a free newspaper entrepreneur who became convinced that the successful formula of his weekly papers – low cost base, low advertising rates and high penetration – could be replicated for a daily. The 'metro' is a free morning paper distributed in major metropolitan centres within the space of one hour each morning. The key idea is to provide advertisers with massive penetration of households in a metropolitan area over an extremely short time span – a readership reach which cannot be rivalled by television or radio.

The *Daily News* was envisaged as the forerunner of a network of free daily newspapers in the major cities, with the greatest prize being a successful free newspaper in London. The idea is a source of constant speculation within the free newspaper industry. In 1987 Robert Maxwell was printing dummies of a 48-page 'metro' entitled the *Londoner* and was contemplating a spring launch, although the paper never appeared.[35] Perhaps his painful involvement in London's paid paper market dulled his enthusiasm.

The 'metro' concept, however, seems fatally flawed. The experience of the *Daily News* suggests that free newspapers can be financially viable only if published as weeklies. Two major problems confront a daily free: first, the relatively large scale of the operation needed to break even; and second, the problem of distribution which requires considerable expenditure to resolve. A free weekly can be viable covering a relatively small geographical area and, since its news content is not especially topical, it can be distributed at almost any time of day across a two- or three-day period. A free daily, however, needs a large catchment area and to meet the needs of its advertisers, as well as its readers, has to reach its audience at a specified time on the day of issue.

But it is a third problem which presents perhaps the most substantial obstacle to the development of the daily free newspaper: namely, the opposition of the existing daily paid-for paper which enjoys a monopoly of both readers and advertisers. Events in Manchester are illustrative of the difficulties. In 1987 both Maxwell and Bullivant were reputedly investigating Manchester as a possible site for a second 'metro' newspaper. The Guardian and Manchester Evening News Group (MEN) responded promptly by producing the Manchester *Metro News*, a weekly free published for the first time on 5 June 1987 with an initial distribution of 319,000 (now 600,000). MEN management claimed that, by using Press Association copy, the paper could move quickly to daily publication if any predators moved in. An invasion would be unlikely, however, since advertisements placed in the existing *Manchester Evening News* are published in the *Metro News* for free, offering advertisers a low-cost and guaranteed distribution which would be difficult for any rival newspaper to equal, especially as a newcomer to the market. Tony Boore, MEN managing director, made explicit the defensive function of the *Metro News*. 'I think we will get our market so tightly sewn up', he claimed, 'that no one will be able to come in and steal our business. What we are saying to Cap'n Bob, Chris Bullivant, Northern Counties Newspapers and Eddie Shah is "beat that".'[36] If this analysis is correct, the *Daily News* looks set to remain the sole 'metro' daily for a good while.

The *Daily News* was launched in a mood of considerable optimism. David Scott, its launch editor and later the paper's chief executive, devoted a year to researching the enterprise. He judged that there was a substantial gap which a free newspaper could fill. Traditional provincial dailies were typically in decline, but additionally 43 per cent of households in Birmingham did not regularly take a national newspaper. Evening papers seemed to suffer particular hardship because of the expansion of television ownership, which became the prime news source between 5.30 p.m. and 10.30 p.m.[37]

Despite this early optimism and the subsequent annual predictions that the paper is about to move into profit, the *Daily News* has not been a commercial success. It has yet to break even, and its future is now discussed in less sanguine terms. Media pundits believe that the only way the paper can survive is to become weekly or bi-weekly. The *Daily News* which is currently hitting the streets, however, is almost unrecognizable from the paper launched in 1984 amid speculations of a newspaper revolution. It has a new masthead, new typeface, new market position, new owners, new distribution areas, a new management structure and a radically revamped content. Its launch also announced the outbreak of a newspaper war in the Birmingham area which has proved to be protracted and expensive to all combatants. The battle in Birmingham seems to have assumed a symbolic significance, beyond the immediate concerns of two rival newspaper groups, reflecting the long-running war between the free and paid-for sectors of the local press. Both sides of the free/paid-for divide are keeping a watchful eye on the continuing struggle and routinely claim victory to be theirs.

The short history of the *Daily News* has been characterized by change. Developments in the economic and organizational structures reflect the continuing attempts by management to set the paper on course for profit. The *Daily News* was established in October 1984 by Chris Bullivant, a 'non-aligned' entrepreneur with financial backing from Reed; the first editor was David Scott. By January 1986 a new editor, Malcolm Ward, had been appointed, and in 1987 Bullivant sold a 51 per cent stake in the company to Reed. The *Daily News* was merged with the Reed Group's weeklies in neighbouring Solihull, Bromsgrove and Redditch, with the aim of converting each of the weeklies into a daily. The scheme was tested only in Solihull, but failed. The *Solihull Times*, returned to weekly publication, but the *Daily News* extended its distribution area to include the town. In October 1988 Reed International merged the *Daily News* with the Worcester-based Berrows Newspaper Group which publishes fifteen paid-for and free weekly papers in an area stretching from Stafford in the north to Hereford and Gloucester in the south. The purpose behind the merger seems clear. It created for the new company a single market for advertising of 950,000 copies with a combined readership of 2.25 million. The chief executive of Reed Regional Newspapers observed:

> The *Daily News* is now established as a powerful medium in its own right. By adding it to the stable of Berrows thorough-bred free and paid publications, we can offer local, regional and national advertisers a wide range of quality products in flexible packages.[38]

The financial prospects of the paper are undoubtedly enhanced for being part of a £32 million group, rather than remaining a single newspaper with a turnover of £8 million per annum, but continue none the less to be a mixed bag. Production costs are high. Each 32-page paper costs 12.3p to produce and deliver. Revenues remain wholly dependent on advertising. In 1988–9 revenue grew by 30 per cent and market share by 7 per cent, but the paper's primary competitors, the *Birmingham Post* and the *Birmingham Evening Mail*, still dominate in the key advertising market of 'situations vacant'. The Thursday issue of the *Evening Mail* is crammed with jobs advertising which attracts many extra buyers as well as additional advertising revenue. The *Daily News* argues that, by relying on 'sits vac' advertising for 46 per cent of its revenues (the *Daily News* receives only 4 per cent of its own income from this source), the *Evening Mail* is 'unbalanced' and vulnerable to changes in the economy.[39]

The distribution areas identified by the *Daily News* have changed considerably, but its basic distribution arrangements have been judged a success from the outset. This is crucial to the overall success of the enterprise, since advertisers must be convinced that their message is getting into every home. Despite the use of cheap labour, this is an expensive business, with printing and distribution accounting for 70 per cent of costs.

A military metaphor is appropriate in discussing distribution. A small army of 3,000 children and young people deliver the 300,000 newspapers in an operation which starts at 4.30 a.m. when twenty-five area agents receive bundles from the printers. There are 100 adults on stand-by each morning to cover for absenteeism. Distributors are subject to a code of discipline for laxity and are rewarded, in addition to wages, with video recorders and televisions for outstanding effort. Low wages, the average age of the workers and the absence of trades unions make the operation a Dickensian employer's dream.

But while the basic system of distribution has been effective, the areas targeted for distribution have shifted radically. Initially, the distribution system was based on the principle that everyone resident in a particular local government area should receive a paper, but distribution is now aligned with the sixteen catchment areas covered by the major stores and shopping centres. This latter is undoubtedly a less democratic principle of distribution, but, as the editor readily admits, 'to ensure success, distribution must be organized to meet the needs of advertisers'.[40] Indeed, the reason why the *Daily News* is not published on Saturdays and Mondays is not, as the chief executive rationalizes, because they are poor days for news, or because readers do not want a paper on those days; it is because advertisers are unwilling to support a newspaper on those days.

These changes in management and distribution have been mirrored by changes in the paper's editorial style, prompted by a desire to change market position. Early editions of the newspaper reflected the belief that the natural market for a free newspaper was at the bottom end of the market. Pre-publication research revealed that 90 per cent of Birmingham people buying a morning paper took the *Star*, *Mirror* or *Sun*. Consequently, the editor felt that 'bright, breezy and brash were the buzz words'.[41] The same research had revealed, however, that almost 50 per cent of those surveyed did not read a morning newspaper and were critical of many aspects of tabloid newspapers. It was decided, in the light of experience and re-evaluation of the initial research, to reposition the *Daily News* in the middle of the market traditionally occupied by papers like the *Daily Mail* and *Daily Express*. Malcolm Ward, the editor newly appointed in 1986, was given a revised brief to create 'a more upmarket local/national paper' which would be an acceptable substitute for a morning national paper. Ward believes that the *Daily News* is now 'firmly in the middle market', offering as evidence the fact that 'sales of the *Daily Mail* and *Daily Express* have gone down in the city'.[42]

The paper has now adopted a new format. Page one features the best news story of the day, whether national or local. Page two carries international news, page three local and page five national. The overall aim of the paper is to be 60 per cent local, 30 per cent national and 10 per cent international. All advertising has been removed from the front page and page three, with the volume of advertising on the early pages being reduced. The paper's reliance on 'showbiz features' and a page-three pin-up has given way to more local news. The paper claims that the strength of its editorial policy is reflected in a growing readership, from 376,000 to 453,000 during the period January to December 1989; equivalent figures for the *Evening Mail* show a decline from 429,000 to 374,000.[43] Indeed, a mark of its success is the fact that 17,000 readers outside the free zones are prepared to pay for their copy. But the quality of editorial in the *Daily News* in untypical of the free press and is matched only by the Manchester *Metro News*, voted free newspaper of the year in 1989 by the Newspaper Society. In terms of the sheer quantity and range of news reported, as well as the quality of its in-house editorial team and its celebrity freelance writers, the *Daily News* outstrips many of the national tabloids circulating in Britain. So it is hardly surprising that some national papers have witnessed a decline in readership in the Birmingham area by up to 50 per cent.[44] Yet, as noted above, the *Daily News* has also had dramatic consequences for local competitors. Its publication marked the outbreak of a newspaper war.

The first casualty of the *Daily News* was the circulation figures for the *Birmingham Post* and its sister paper the *Evening Mail*. By 1986 the Birmingham Post and Mail Group's difficulties had become so severe that the company offered to sell its four titles – the *Birmingham Post*, the *Evening Mail*, the *Sports Argus* and the *Sunday Mercury* – to the *Daily News*, but Reed were not interested; Bullivant claims it was a crucial error.[45] In 1987 the US company Ingersoll took a £60 million major shareholding in the Birmingham newspaper group in what was judged by some to be the first stages in its plans to establish itself as a major force in British publishing. In October 1988 the advertising advantages deriving from the *Daily News*'s merger with the Berrows Group, combined with the revamped editorial policy, gave the paper a further edge over its local rivals. Ingersoll's response has been twofold and dramatic on both counts.

First, Ingersoll appointed Chris Oakley, the highly successful editor of the *Liverpool Echo*, to the post of assistant managing director and editor in chief of the Birmingham Post and Mail Group. A number of major innovations stem from his arrival. He has ordered new presses from Germany and plans to introduce full colour in each of the group's four titles, beginning in late 1990. The *Post* and *Mail* joint editorial desk has been scrapped, with twenty-seven extra journalists appointed for the two papers. Major changes in editorial policy are planned for each of the titles. The *Evening Mail* has already moved to a downmarket position and adopted a tabloid style, running high-profile campaigns against 'crack' and changes in the National Health Service. The morning paper, the *Birmingham Post*, has returned to broadsheet format and, although well read by the business community, is seeking to widen its appeal as a quality paper, competing for readers with the *Guardian*, *The Independent* and *The Times*; it is also actively seeking more women readers. Change is also planned for the *Sunday Mercury*, although the *Sports Argus* will remain substantively the same.

Second, in September 1988 an Ingersoll subsidiary, New Enterprise Publications (NEP), moved to the offensive by announcing radical plans for a network of community newspapers in thirty-nine areas of Birmingham with a combined distribution approaching 500,000. Intended to be 'as local as your corner shop', the community papers, each with a distribution of 12,000, derived from a philosophy of 'small is beautiful'.[46] Each paper carries the name 'Focus', and at least half of the editorial content is local. The project plans, including the recruitment of thirty journalists, were a well-kept secret. Ingersoll's inspiration for the 'Focus' network comes from experience in the USA, where, in Long Island, the company has nearly eighty community papers with a combined circulation approaching one million. The project seems to be faltering, however. Within four months of launch, *UK Press Gazette* reported that the new titles were making 'heavy losses'. Nineteen of the titles were axed, and staff reductions and other cost savings were made; the editor of the 'Focus' titles was moved to another NEP paper.[47] The entrails do not read optimistically for the future of the titles.

Other, less significant combatants are entering the fray. The Wolverhampton Express and Star Group plans to launch two new free papers in Birmingham, in retaliation for Reed's take-over of the Wolverhampton-based Lendon Group of free newspapers which brings competition to the heartland of the *Express and Star*'s circulation area. In 1989 Bullivant launched a new paper in Redditch, where both Reed and Ingersoll have titles.

The outcome of this war seems uncertain, since both of the major protagonists enjoy the support of powerful backers. More appears to be at stake in Birmingham than money, with Reed and Ingersoll apparently prepared to sustain unprofitable enterprises, at least in the short run. But the beneficiaries of the skirmishes to date have undoubtedly been the readers. The *Daily News* has been obliged to relocate itself upmarket from its initial launch position and shift its editorial policy to emphasize more news reporting, especially local news. The papers in the Post and Mail Group have been revamped editorially and revitalized with additional journalistic staff.

The quality of the *Daily News* and the *Birmingham Post* is beyond dispute, but neither is currently financially viable and each relies on the 'deep pockets' of its respective patron. Perhaps daily papers can survive and flourish only in conditions of local monopoly, and the market in Birmingham is overcrowded. Certainly the experience of the *Daily News* seems to underscore the view that aspirations for the content of free newspapers are radically contrained by the papers' basic economic structure and reliance on advertisers; profitability can be achieved only at the expense of editorial quality. The relationship between editorial content, news–gathering routines and reliance on advertising revenues is considered in the final section.

FREE NEWSPAPERS AND THE REPORTING OF LOCAL POLITICS

Assessments of the editorial quality of free newspapers vary considerably, reflecting a genuine diversity evident across different newspapers. Journalists working in the paid-for papers, however, express scepticism about the quality of reporting of local affairs in free newspapers, identifying their reliance on advertising revenues and independence of their readership as significant causes of poor coverage. The economic 'logic' of free newspaper production – which identifies readers, rather than news, as the 'commodity' to be sold – generates an ethos in which editorial is necessarily subordinate to the requirements of advertising. Free distribution, moreover, places free newspapers beyond public criticism and accountability. Free newspapers do not have to earn the respect of their readers; they are merely pushed through the letter-box. Free newspapers 'are a very light read', observed an editor of a West Yorkshire evening paper:

> they make no serious attempt to cover local or community affairs at all. They're not interested in that sort of thing. That's the big bonus they have. There's no come-back on them except from the advertisers, so they can cover what they like. The readers don't have any come-back.

Harry Conroy, general secretary of the NUJ, is in broad agreement, imputing a direct connection between free newspapers' dependence on advertising and the low quality of editorial. 'There's nothing wrong with free newspapers', he claims, 'as long as they remain free newspapers. Unfortunately, market forces mean that when things are bad the first thing that will be cut is journalistic standards, because it's the adverts they live on and not the circulation income'.[48] An inevitable consequence of this 'logic' is that free newspapers will employ less journalists than paid-for newspapers. Many journalists in the local press tend to be young, relatively inexperienced professionally, and rarely possess a degree or relevant training. But lack of journalistic training seems to be a particular issue for free newspapers, where 'a lot of people are training on the job and are just cheap labour'.[49]

Free newspapers' independence of their readers, combined with their scarce journalistic resources and their desire to minimize news-gathering costs, may dispose some papers to fill their editorial columns by 'buying in' editorial copy at a lower cost than it could be produced for by an in-house journalistic team. It is common practice for newspapers, especially local papers, to buy copy from organizations such as the Press Association or a local press agency to supplement the work of resident journalists. But free newspapers' requirements for cheap copy seem to have prompted a related development. Free newspapers have become reliant on the news output (press releases, news statements, press conferences and hand-outs) emanating from non-news organizations, including the public relations departments of the local authority, various regional organizations, local political parties and a wide range of pressure and interest groups. These press releases are perhaps best characterized as 'information subsidies', since the staffing and monetary costs associated with gathering and distributing the information are borne by the organization issuing the press release and not by the newspaper. This constitutes an in-built subsidy from the public purse for the local press.

Free newspapers' dependence on these 'subsidies' seems to have become particularly acute in the reporting of local government, typically an important area of coverage for local newspapers. A local government public relations officer claimed: 'it's clear that many frees rely heavily on handouts from the public services to fill editorial columns'.[50] This development reflects the mutually beneficial relationship which has developed between PROs and free newspapers in recent years. The viability of free newspapers depends on a 'mini-max' philosophy: their ability to combine maximum advertising revenues with minimal news-gathering costs. This latter aspect of the financial balancing act can be readily achieved if free papers are willing to publish the well-written press releases of PROs, but give them a new identity as 'a story of local relevence' attributed to 'our local government reporter'. For their part, local government PROs have come to regard free newspapers as ready outlets for publishing stories which paid-for newspapers may find unattractive, which tend to ignore criticism of the local authority and stress the positive aspects of local government administration. PROs have come to feel fairly confident that their press releases are unlikely to be rewritten but will be published virtually verbatim, because free newspapers are so editorially understaffed.[51]

The logic of competition between papers in the local market obliges paid-for weeklies, and to some extent even daily papers, to resort to these low-cost news-gathering strategies. One PRO expressed misgivings about this new role as 'local government correspondent' for the local paper. 'It is perhaps flattering', he claimed,

> to have one's press release appear as the front page lead in a widely distributed free, but I'm always left with the uneasy feeling that I'm the main arbiter of County Council news for a substantial section of the public. That should not be my job but, alas, increasingly it is.[52]

If this analysis of developments is correct, the notion of the local press as some pluralist breed of watchdog, guarding the public interest by making local politicians and government accountable, is effectively redundant.

There are clear evidential signs suggesting that the press watch-dog, perhaps having swallowed too many public relations bones, is taking an ill-deserved after-dinner nap. Two pieces of evidence are especially noteworthy.

First, research conducted by the Society of County and Regional Public Relations Officers indicated that free newspapers are reluctant to report council affairs directly and rarely send reporters to meetings of a council or its various committees. The survey of forty county areas reported a 'substantial decline in direct coverage of local affairs'; 334 free newspaper titles distribute in the survey area, but only 8 newspapers sent reporters to council meetings.[53]

Second, free newspapers are less interested in local government affairs than other local newspapers. In a survey of local government PROs, only 8 per cent cited free newspapers as the local paper 'most interested' in local politics, compared to equivalent figures of 51.2 per cent for paid weeklies, 38.4 per cent for evening papers and 14 per cent for local morning papers; local radio and regional television lagged far behind at 1.7 per cent and 1.2 per cent respectively.[54]

The suggested importance of public relations officers and the press releases they issue for the editorial content of free newspapers has been assessed at least in a preliminary way by examining the success of PROs in stimulating stories in the local press. Press releases issued by the public relations department of Northumberland County Council, between 13 September and 15 November 1985, were compared with local press coverage of local politics across the same period, to establish the take-up rate of stories and to assess the extent of any journalistic editing of the press release to enhance the story. There are, of course, many factors which decide which events are reported in a newspaper, and relations between politicians and journalists are subject to radical variations in different settings, but the results suggest that in this particular political and geographic locale PROs were influential in prompting stories in the free press.[55]

The success rate for publication of stories based on the press releases was nearly 100 per cent. The 25 press releases issued between 15 October and 15 November each prompted stories in the local press. The success rate for the previous month was not quite so high, but 19 of the 21 releases were sources of stories in the local press. Across the two months of the study, 96 per cent of releases were published in the local press. This is a very high strike rate. A study of local newspapers in Louisiana, for example, revealed that only 48 per cent of releases issued over a four-week period resulted in stories in the local press.[56] These figures may, at first glance, seem surprisingly high; but analysis of the newspapers showed that it was probable that many other local government stories featured in the papers had similarly originated from other public relations departments in the proximate Tyne and Wear County Council and Newcastle upon Tyne City Council, and from public relations centres in neighbouring authorities, suggesting an even greater receptivity to information subsidies for free newspapers; it also signals a significant agenda-setting potential for public relations officers in the region.

Most press releases stimulated stories in more than one paper. One release issued on 9 October, focusing on high levels of local unemployment, appeared in seven papers (*Northumberland Gazette*, 11 October; *Morpeth Gazette*, 11 October; *Hexham Courant*, 11 October; *Berwick Advertiser*, 17 October; *New Post Leader*, 17 October; *Cramlington, Blyth, Whitley Bay and North Shields Courier*, 17 October; *Morpeth, Ashington and Bedlington Weekly Courier*,

17 October), and it was commonplace for press releases to be published in three or four papers. Only 11 of the 44 releases forming stories in the press made a single appearance, while 19 were published in three or more newspapers. The local press seemed to be recycling the same news around the county.

Most press releases were picked up fairly quickly. Dailies, predictably, tended to cover the story within one or two days of the release, with weeklies proving slower but not tardy, with a time lag of about four to six days. These results are perhaps not so surprising when it is remembered that the majority of PROs are ex-journalists who know the local newspapers, their deadlines and the type of story they like to report; they are able to target both content and timing of the release with considerable accuracy. There were, however, some remarkable time lags, with the longest being twenty-four days.

The two daily papers, the *Newcastle Journal* and the *Newcastle Evening Chronicle*, were much less reliant on the press releases as news sources, although 22 of the 44 releases did prompt stories in the two papers. But when press releases were used they were always substantially edited. This was not simply a matter of cutting a word here and there or lopping the last paragraph, but usually involved a complete rewrite of the information contained in the release. This editing of the release contrasted sharply with practice on the free weeklies, where editing was rare. In the two-month sample period, weeklies either reproduced the press release verbatim and in full or simply removed whole paragraphs or changed their order.

What is important to note is that, over the sample period, none of the stories were enhanced by the free press; they contained no information additional to that contained in the release, and the bulk of these releases were swallowed whole by a copy-hungry free press. Even though releases always end with a contact name, address and telephone number, there was no evidence that any journalist made contact to obtain a supportive quote.

These findings, which suggest that in one particular area the local press was highly responsive to information subsidies emanating from a local authority public relations department, have subsequently received a more generalized confirmation. A survey of local government PROs, conducted in each of the 540 UK local authorities, revealed that 82 per cent of respondents claimed that more than three-quarters of press releases issued resulted in stories in the local press, with respondents frequently writing comments such as 'nearly 100%' or 'almost always' on the questionnaire.[57]

The willingness of free newspapers to accept these public information subsidies reflects, at least in part, a special skill among local government PROs to offer newspapers what they want in the way of news materials. But, more importantly, it directly reflects newspapers' resources, of which staff resources are clearly the most significant. Most daily papers employ a 'municipal', a journalist specializing solely in local government affairs, whereas on weekly paid-for papers local government is merely one aspect of a broader journalistic brief, perhaps including courts, industrial affairs and business. The economics of free newspaper production require even leaner editorial staffs, with a specialist local government correspondent being a very rare breed. The logic of these varying staffing levels suggests that daily, weekly paid-for and weekly free newspapers might form a descending hierarchy of receptivity towards, and dependence on, information subsidies. This pattern of reliance is confirmed by the available research findings. When asked which local newspaper is 'most likely to use a press release', 42 per cent of PROs identified free newspapers, compared with 30 per cent paid-for weeklies, 22 per cent evening papers and 5 per cent dailies.[58]

The importance of information subsidies to the local, especially the free, press is occasionally illustrated quite dramatically. The abolition of the Greater London Council, for example, with the consequent closure of its thirty-strong press department which had been handling 200 press inquiries daily and issuing 1,200 press releases annually, created great difficulties for local media. A meeting of London media staff, convened to discuss this 'information vacuum', concluded that the demise of the GLC press office meant that 'there was likely to be a shortage of London news stories'.[59]

It should be noted that, even though they are heavy users of information subsidies, free newspapers occasionally object that government bodies are using them as 'notice-boards'. One free newspaper editor complained that the Department of Energy was giving advertising revenues to radio, television and the paid-for press, but was exploiting free newspapers' needs for information subsidies, expecting them to carry details of energy campaigns for free. 'Free newspapers', the editor claimed, 'are probably the most powerful media tool for PR people. But they will not be used as a soft touch.'[60] Free newspapers' objections here are typically financial rather than editorial. They object, it seems, not to being used as a notice-board so much as being used as a free notice-board.

SUMMARY

In the past three decades, the achievements of free newspapers have been considerable. They are no longer ridiculed as mere advertising 'freesheets', since, in some instances, these publications have matured into interesting, well-produced, local newspapers not readily distinguished from their paid-for counterparts. Their growth has been prompted by the difficulties facing the traditional local weekly papers during the 1960s and 1970s, the aspirations of an expanding advertising industry and the development of new print technology. The financial success of free newspapers is beyond question, while business forecasts suggest that by the end of the 1990s free newspapers will enjoy substantially increased advertising revenues and a larger market share, and will constitute an even more significant sector within the local press than currently. The success enjoyed by weekly free newspapers, however, has not transferred readily to the daily market; and distribution problems, combined with the scale of advertising revenues required to sustain them, may militate against establishing a network of 'metro' daily papers.

But while the financial success of free newspapers is uncontested, there is less consensus concerning the quality and range of their editorial content. We have argued that the economic 'logic' of free newspapers prioritizes advertising above editorial interests, obliges free newspapers to minimize their costs of news gathering and may, consequently, require them to employ few journalists and become reliant on external sources for copy. In these constrained circumstances, free newspapers are unlikely to follow the laudable if ambitious example of the *New York Times* and publish 'all the news that's fit to print'. Their adherence to a more humble maxim seems probable; 'all the news that's readily available to print'.

Chapter 5

The alternative local press

The history of the alternative local press over the past two decades illustrates, perhaps more poignantly than any other aspect of the local media, the power of the market in marginalizing ideological debate. As we have indicated earlier, the proposition which underlies the business-based corporate press is that the free market in the production, distribution and ownership of the news media necessarily leads to freedom of thought and expression and an 'open society'. The fallacy of this general dispensation has often been laid bare elsewhere. James Curran, for example, has shown how newspapers with large circulations have been unable to survive because the relative poverty of their readers has prevented them from attracting sufficient advertising revenue to meet production and distribution costs.[1] Murphy has indicated that the pressures on the processes of producing news, in both the traditional and the alternative local press, militate against news coverage which does not reinforce versions of reality promulgated by actors in positions of power in established authority systems.[2] In the development of the radical alternative press, both of these processes have been at work.

Journalism of the left has had two major concerns: first, the propagation of left-wing views which would otherwise receive no exposure, except for mockery in the established press; second, the production of revelatory news, discussing aspects of society and politics which conventional news outlets cannot or will not report. The major problem which both of these aspects of the radical press present is that of finding sufficient income to sustain publication of papers dedicated to such a project. Newspapers' normal survival strategy in a market environment is for their readership to constitute the demand for identifiable goods or services for which the press then becomes the vehicle for advertisements. A second option, that favoured by the 'pauper press' of the early nineteenth century, is to use free labour or cheap labour in the production of such publications. The problem with revelatory news journalism is that it is a labour-intensive activity – as we shall show below – and this means that a lot of skilled labour has to be employed for a relatively small news output. It also provokes other potential costs in the form of possible libel actions and the legal advice necessary to avoid them. But the effects of the market in its many forms work their way through in the operation of the radical press with great complexity. In order to examine these processes, we will examine the radical press over the past two decades, looking at those magazines and newspapers whose main ideological thrust was revelatory rather than propagandistic, and whose primary concern was to develop an ideology of radical journalism.

THE RADICAL NEWS ALTERNATIVE

Format and content

In the early 1970s local 'alternative' magazines sprang up throughout the country. They were nearly always co-operatively owned and run and dedicated, to a greater or lesser extent, to the promulgation of radical political views. They were usually based on an editorial format which combined news coverage, features and a review section focused on rock music and similar arts and entertainment features. The crucial element distinguishing those that survived from those which failed was in most cases the 'what's on' section.

The papers were based on a clear commitment to articulating a left-wing radical analysis of politics and to news coverage based on exposure of what was normally hidden from view. The politics of the papers were reflected in the structure of their organization and in their style of writing and production. Typically they were co-operatively owned; open debate and open editorial meetings with egalitarian decision-making were the norm. They were generally foolscap- or A4-sized magazines with a different headline and story format from the local newspaper. But they also employed a different form of language and mode of story-telling, which instead of conforming to the authority structures of local communities challenged them through narratives in which the truth behind the appearance was revealed or in which figures usually ignored or presented as victims or problems became the central characters. In their attempt to challenge conventional ways of constructing social and political reality, these publications resembled the 'pauper press' of the early nineteenth century – a similarity underlined by a journalist who worked on such a paper and who was the loving owner of a set of bound copies of the *Poor Man's Guardian*. But in important ways they were different. The old pauper press succeeded in bucking the market by use of volunteer labour and cheap technology to reach a readership with which the journalists were organically connected through common participation in a political and economic struggle for citizens' rights. The alternative press has never been in this relationship to its readers. It succeeded by exploiting the market in advertising to subsidize its radical journalism. The readership was always being sought by the producers of the press – this press did not arise from its readership.

In most of the alternative press of the 1970s and 1980s there was always an unresolved conflict between the need to survive in the market and the desire to produce a journalistic challenge to established society. There were broadly two ways in which this tension could be addressed. The first was to produce extremely cheap papers using the most basic technology so that costs were kept low, and thus obviate any reliance on advertising – a strategy which might be expected to guarantee greater editorial independence. The other was to produce a more ambitious publication using sophisticated layout techniques, aimed at a broader market, distributed more widely and sustained by advertising based around a 'what's on' section.

These two approaches could be identified by their characteristic cover designs which signalled much of the content. The minimum-cost approach was exemplified by the *Manchester Free Press*, which was originally produced by professional journalists in the city during a newspaper strike and was continued by them subsequently, as a spare-time operation. Its cover was black and white and news-based. Its masthead declared its purpose: 'Manchester Free Press. The news you're not supposed to know'. Each issue would carry a cover story such as 'Equal pay fraud'[3] or 'Health report shock'.[4] A column headed 'Inside stories' trailed the contents, which revealed that the thrust of the paper was revelatory stories, agitprop and a strip cartoon entitled 'Alf and Ada' which was a highly entertaining and unrestrained account of inner-city Manchester in the 1970s.

Such a cover left the prospective purchaser in no doubt about the nature and purpose of the magazine. It was set on exposure of the political system by revealing those facts which would otherwise never be revealed. There was clearly someone who was attempting to keep such information from the public, and the *FREEP*, as the paper was known, was going to thwart such establishment secrecy. Whereas the pauper press of the 1820s to the 1840s had been primarily dedicated to the propagation of ideas and opinions, the local alternative press of the 1970s and 1980s was more concerned with investigation and revelation. A paper such as the *FREEP* was one of the more single-minded and purist examples of such publications in that its predominant style and substance were news of this revelatory type.

The *FREEP* was founded in the early 1970s and survived for four years into the middle of the decade. The *New Manchester Review* was founded at the end of this period, in 1975, and adopted a different approach to the balance between the market and ideology. Its cover was based on a pictorial design, with references to the contents as explanatory captions. While the *FREEP* boasted its intention to publish 'the news you're not supposed to know', the early issues of the *NMR* genteelly described itself as 'the fortnightly review of entertainment, politics and current affairs in Greater Manchester'. Its content was always more geared to the coverage of arts and in particular rock music and film in the city than was the *FREEP*'s. As it developed, the fortnightly *New Manchester Review* appeared in a glossy cover with sophisticated colour graphic design and carried a flash in its right-hand top corner 'Plus what's on guide'.

Such covers would feature, for instance, a photograph of the football club manager Malcolm Allison headlined in orange type 'BIG MAL', while trailing references to inside features – '*Rock:* Jimmy Pursey', '*Food:* The Chinese syndrome' – and, along the bottom, the advertising back-up: 'FREE! Kentucky Fried movie tickets *WIN!* The new Police album'. News stories inside the magazine dealt with issues such as 'School may close to save cash on toilets' and a revelation that a firm which had been awarded £2 million in government grants was to cut 360 jobs in Manchester. This display of the consumerist side of the alternative press at the expense of news stories which depict the bleak side of capitalism is one way of dealing with the market-based difficulties faced by all such magazines, but it is not the only one. Nor is it uniquely successful.

The co-operatively run radical weekly publication *Leeds Other Paper* has now survived for more than a decade, from the 1970s to the 1990s, on the iron rations of hard news about Thatcherism in the North combined with a satirical contempt for the system. For more than ten years the paper remained austerely black and white – its only concession to post-Fordism its pink masthead 'Leeds Other Paper with what's on'. The front page carried on the tradition of papers such as the early *Manchester Free Press* with the lead news story dominating, and the 'what's on' trailer discreetly placed at the foot of the page. In 1990 *LOP* adopted a colour-printed cover, but continued to reject the glossy paper of its more overtly consumerist alternative alternatives. It became the *Leeds and Bradford Other Paper*, flagging itself 'The independent voice of the region' and then, in January 1991 assumed the name of the Chartist paper, *Northern Star*, to signal its continuing commitment to radical journalism as well as its intention to expand its circulation area into the West Yorkshire region. The cover is still used to indicate contents mainly focused on current affairs and news, with legends such as 'Ambulance service under workers' control'.[5]

The covers, then, indicate the dilemma facing the radical alternative press; the papers were generally founded in order to promulgate a certain type of news and to espouse a coverage of the arts both of which would be truly alternative to the established commercial local press. The people who would identify with rock, reggae, jazz and folk music would also be young and radically minded. This was the notion of radical chic: that the desire for sexual liberation, gender equality, personal freedom, guiltless hedonism and left politics would be unified in a single seamless set of the optimistic young and some middle-aged and elderly gurus from the beatnik era still sustained by monkey-gland extracts and evening primrose oil. But, though the music and hedonism might be youth-oriented and iconoclastic, this did not mean that they were the same thing as left politics; and magazines were generally driven to search primarily for one or the other. In order to examine this further, we will look at the content of such publications, focusing on the distinctions which these publications make themselves between their news sections and the sections dealing with entertainment, the arts and what has increasingly become identified as 'style', which is a euphemism for buying things or rampant consumerism.

Alternative magazines identify their news sections as 'news' or 'reports'. They frequently also run news features on issues of politics or current affairs. We have lumped together both news and news features of this type, as distinct from the review and consumerist part of the publications, in order to begin to build up a picture of the nature of the phenomenon. This exercise is not meant to provide anything more than a preliminary outline.

The more news-oriented examples of the radical alternative press of the mid-1970s manifested a preponderance of news and news features. Their business was serious politics and current affairs. The editorial content of the *Manchester Free Press* of the period was 70 per cent news and news features, with the rest devoted to the arts. *Rochdale Alternative Paper*, *RAP*, devoted over 90 per cent of its editorial space to news and news features.

Purely commercial advertising commanded little space according to the degree to which the publication was systematically produced and distributed and the regularity with which it appeared. The quarterly *Mole Express* carried less than 10 per cent. The fortnightly *FREEP* carried up to 25 per cent. Classified advertisements for groups to do with health, housing or legal advice and other 'progressive' causes could typically obtain free space in such publications. Such advertisements were an information source for readers and would therefore increase sales.

Northern Star continues to provide content which is news dominated. Although less than half the editorial content is either news or news feature – usually between 30 per cent and 40 per cent – it appears at the front end of the magazine and constitutes the biggest single coherent section. Paid advertising space continues to constitute about 25 per cent of the total space.

The other model of the radical alternative magazine, based on the glossy-coloured-covered, listings-dominated format, carried a much smaller news and news-feature component. Of the editorial content of the *New Manchester Review*, an average of 16 per cent came into this category. The remainder of the paper was made up of such material as reviews of rock and other music, art exhibitions, 'fun', sport, theatre, film, television, 'good food' and pub guidance. Advertising accounted for between 30 per cent and 40 per cent of the content. In its early days, however, this magazine's editorial content had been predominantly news and current events – between 60 per cent and 70 per cent, with the remainder given over to reviews and 'what's on'. It also carried a smaller amount of advertising, something less than 25 per cent.

Such crude distinctions do not in themselves constitute an explanation of what was happening to the radical alternative press, but they do pose questions which require explanations. The relatively small amount of news coverage in the glossies does not reveal what significance this news may have had for those who produced it, or for particular groups of readers. The large amount of coverage given to consumerist topics equally does not mean that such material was necessarily an abject surrender to the values of the market – the content may well have expressed a system of values based on a rejection of acquisitiveness. In order to understand the phenomenon of the radical local press and its development more fully, it is necessary to examine the qualitative nature of the content. But it is necessary first to see how this sector of the local press stands currently.

Two local alternative magazines bestride this sector of the local press like colossuses (or colossi). These are the original London listings magazine, *Time Out*, and its junior competitor, *City Limits*, both weekly magazines. *Time Out* is over twenty years old, and *City Limits* has now survived its first decade. It could be argued that they have now ceased to be part of the local press, since they are circulated nationally; but they remain locally, or at least regionally, identified. *Time Out* describes itself as 'London's weekly guide', and *City Limits* is flagged as 'London's guide'.

News and strictly current-affairs-based news features vary from issue to issue, but in each case the regular input news is less than 5 per cent of the total columnage of the publications, and less than 10 per cent of total editorial material. *Time Out* is about 44 per cent advertisements, and *City Limits* carries around 30 per cent. A sample of similar listings magazines from around the country suggest that these represent typical values. Some listings magazines carry around 33 per cent advertising, others around 42 per cent. The distribution is bi-modal around those two values. Some deviant cases exist of magazines running on less than 20 per cent advertising.

Such magazines, as the use in their mastheads of words such

as 'what's on guide' and 'listings' suggests, rely for their sales on lists of events and their venues. (The title of the Bristol and Bath 'what's on' guide is *Venue*.) Such lists are a source of information for readers and a marketing ploy. They also constitute a free advertisement for the events and venues in the listing. Although the hope is that such entries will elicit advertisement from some of the beneficiaries, this is only the case on a minority of occasions.

Such listings sometimes merge into the review sections of such publications or are interspersed with them. Sometimes they are clearly demarcated. The London magazines *Time Out* and *City Limits* are heavy with such sections. In each case they occupy more than half of the magazine's pages. These are also the sections which carry the heaviest load of advertising. Obviously, entertainments advertisers wish their entries to be among pages where their target audience will be reading. In general for such magazines, the normal proportion of actual listings in relation to editorial material is around 50 per cent, while the 'listings' section may occupy three-quarters or more of the total pagination. This section will then carry, in addition to advertisements, introductory articles for each different subsection of the listings section, reviews and advertising back-up articles.

Breaking the silence

The original 1970s-style alternative press concentrated on a number of themes in its news coverage and even in its 'what's on' guide. We will begin with an examination of the news. The whole thrust of such news coverage was that it would tell stories that other papers, and in particular the traditional local papers, did not tell. In this it was breaking two sorts of silence. The first was that imposed by the secrecy of local government, the police and business. The second sort of silence reflects the local press's neglect of a range of topics from the coverage of trade disputes from the workers' point of view to issues to do with poverty and news of interest to male homosexuals and lesbians. In order to comprehend this type of news coverage, we will examine the nature of such stories and then consider how they are produced.

The local authority and the police force have always been the focus of much of this sort of news coverage. One of the original defining characteristics of the alternative press, which marked it out from the traditional commercial local press, was its willingness to publish stories about the alleged corrupt or suspect activities of public figures who appeared as pillars of society or authoritative sources of truth in the traditional coverage of news. This sort of news is exemplified in a trial on page one of an issue of the *Manchester Free Press* from the mid-1970s – 'Which Tory alderman is getting £158,000 from the council to do nothing?' The same issue contained another recurrent theme of such news: the examination of right-wing organizations with anti-trades-union objectives. Entitled 'Murphy chips in', this article examined an organization known as Truemid which was receiving a lot of publicity at the time as a 'moderate' organization of trades union members who were combating 'extremism' in trades unions. The article traced the background of some of the leading lights in the organization, including Brendan Murphy – he of the headline – who was at the time public relations officer of Stockport Council, which was Conservative controlled. It dealt in some detail with Murphy's role as a council spokesman during a binmen's strike. His press statements about the strikers had so enraged Labour members of the council that they had threatened to produce their own press hand-outs about the dispute.[6]

Investigative journalism: the Fieldhouse affair

The *New Manchester Review* produced a series of analyses of the activities of Conservative members of Manchester City Council in the areas of housing association developments and planning applications. During 1978 they carried a number of articles referring to the complex relationship between the various business and voluntary-sector activities of the council's Conservative group leader, Alderman Arnold Fieldhouse. The journalist who wrote the articles, Andrew Jennings, also researched Alderman Fieldhouse's business dealings for the BBC TV programme *Tonight*.

The focus of the story was the relationship between Fieldhouse's profitable property business, Slade Property Management Ltd, and a number of housing associations partly funded by government money to provide subsidized housing for special-needs groups of tenants. A particular story involved the way in which planning permission for redevelopment was obtained on a plot of land which was owned by a Fieldhouse company before being sold on at a profit to one of the housing associations he managed.

The *Tonight* programme investigated the deal and confronted Fieldhouse with evidence they had about the way in which planning permission had been obtained. Jennings had been the source of the information and had done much of the investigation for the programme. A transcript of the interview was then used by the magazine as the basis for a news item. This was one in a long line of pieces on this particular Tory alderman. The headline, which clearly relied on this previous coverage to engender reader familiarity with a character in a long-running saga, was simply made up of the words 'Fieldhouse Inc.' across the columns which made up one and a half pages of the issue. Above it, a strap-line declared: 'Andrew Jennings examines the allegations against GMC leader Arnold Fieldhouse and uncovers another row involving Trafford's new mayor'.[7]

The introduction read:

> For a few amazing moments millions of TV viewers saw Arnold Fieldhouse crack up. From being cocky and confident he crumbled into stutters and confusion. And whatever his defenders are claiming now, he admitted knowing that a bogus planning application had been made – in a deal that made him a personal profit of £2,850.[8]

The transcript of the interview was reproduced unedited as dialogue. The TV interview concerned the way in which Fieldhouse bought a site on Slade Lane in Longsight, Manchester, on which a housing association managed by Slade Property Management had subsequently built a block of flats named Harper House. The interviewer, Mike Walsh, confronted Fieldhouse with an allegation that the planning application for the redevelopment of the site was made by Montford Estates as owners of the land, while in fact Fieldhouse himself owned the land. During the course of the interview Walsh revealed that the BBC had seen a copy of the planning application document in which Montford Estates wrongly claimed ownership.

At first Fieldhouse denied that they had claimed ownership, but then in the face of the reference to the planning application form he retreated and offered an explanation of why the application had been made in the name of the company and not in his own:

> Let me be very honest and very frank with you why that

application was made in Montford's name. Because of the wrangling that was going on and the utter unfairness in connection with applications being made by politicians of another political party, it was prudent to do it this way.[9]

Walsh then went on to explain that when a planning application is made part of the application form is two certificates. The first, certificate A, is to be filled in by an owner making an application. The second, certificate B, is to be filled in by the owner when someone other than the owner is making the application. Walsh explained that a false claim to ownership by a non-owner filling in a certificate is a criminal offence under section 29, subsection 27, of the Town and Country Planning Act.

The response was reported by Jennings:

> F: Well, I did not complete the certificate – I do not know what Montford did when they made the application or whether they used form A or B. But let's be very honest about all this. I mean, do not let's start splitting hairs, er, if it is an offence – I do not know even if it is, er, er. You know, lying . . . underlying all these things that, er, are introduced under our laws and regulations is to stop wrong practices that are going to hurt anybody. Was anybody ever hurt at all by that?
> W: You are saying that some laws can be broken.
> F: No, I did not say that at all. I said laws were introduced very often to protect in the extreme and not in trivial cases where obviously no harm was being done to anybody.[10]

Jennings's article went on:

> One explanation for why Fieldhouse disguised his application was because of the detestation felt for him and his operations by the Labour controlled council.
>
> The reason? During the late 60s when the Tories last controlled Manchester, Fieldhouse was chairman of the city Finance Committee. At that time, loans to housing associations were made direct from local authorities.
>
> At that time Fieldhouse's major housing association, the Manchester and District, won over £2.5 million (in the days before inflation!) for 12 flats projects. Each time an application came before the Finance Committee, Fieldhouse quite properly

declared his interest and did not vote. But his loyal Tory colleagues did and he got the money.[11]

The journalists who write such stories regard it as their job to investigate the nature of power, wealth and authority. The author Jennings, now a journalist on Granada TV's *World in Action*, would often give voice, only partly in self-mockery, to his favourite motto: 'They're all in it together.' This story is not simply about the land dealings of one particular property developer. It has a meaning beyond its own narrative structure. This derives from the fact that the developer in question had been a major power-broker in the city when Manchester City Council was run by the Tories and continued to be a leading figure in the Tory Party. The meaning of such stories is that the system of rules and regulations which legitimizes the exercise of power in the existing authority structure can be subverted by those in authority. This is shown to be a characteristic of the system – not the fault of some individual who happens to be venal.

In this approach to news production, the normal means by which 'truth' is established in the traditional manufacture of news is overturned. Those official spokespeople who are normally quoted in order to verify the truth of a version of events themselves become the objects of scrutiny. So do the versions of events which they promulgate. Instead of the reporter constructing reality by reproducing a construction of the world emanating from those in established positions of authority, other forms of validating information have to be used.

Evidence for this sort of story comes from three sources: informants whose occupation or social position gives access to knowledge of the affairs of those under scrutiny; documents produced by the system, preferably confidential ones obtained from 'moles', because the fact that they are hidden can in itself be seen as significant; and 'confession' by those involved.

In the case of the Fieldhouse enquiry, all three kinds of evidence were sought. Numerous individuals had been complaining at a variety of levels over a period of a decade. These included some tenants of the flats owned by the housing associations who did not wish the property they were in to be managed by Slade Property Management; Labour members of the city council who did not like the fact that Fieldhouse was able to raise so much money for projects through the public purse which seemed to end

up entirely legally in the coffers of Slade Property or Fieldhouse
& Ross Builders; officials at the town hall and at the Housing
Corporation, the national organization in London which adminis-
tered housing associations for the country as a whole.[12]

Documents, mainly from public records, were used to establish
the membership of housing association management committees
and of company boards of directors. But copies of private documents relating to ownership and sales of land were acquired from
individuals who had properly acquired them during previous business dealings and subsequently wanted them made public.

Finally, because the story had been aired on television, the
words of the man in question could be quoted directly as he
acknowledged at least some of the facts referred to in the story
– his ownership of the land, for instance. His words could also
be quoted in a passage which could be interpreted as a defence
of breaking laws if this did not involve hurting anybody.

These sources of evidence are the means by which such stories
can be made to stand up. But this does not tell us about the
means by which journalists 'find' the raw material for such stories
in the first place, or how they decide whether the material can
be shown to be significant. Probably the most common means
of 'finding' news is through contacts. The radical alternative press
relies on contacts whom the traditional local press ignores: people
with axes to grind, people with low status who wish to complain
about the powerful. Sometimes individuals in positions of authority have stories they wish to tell which they have to tell without
identifying themselves. Sometimes they write for the alternative
press under *noms de plume*. In the case of the Fieldhouse investigation, it was the complaints of tenants and those who had been
involved in business with the alderman which directed the attention of a number of reporters from the *NMR*, *FREEP* and Granada TV towards his business activities over a number of years.

But reporters also usually live in the area which they cover.
Where the alternative press relies on voluntary labour for its
journalistic output, the reporters also probably work in the area.
They are frequently active members of the local Labour Party,
CND or the green movement. This means that they constitute
sources of their own news.

INVESTIGATIVE JOURNALISM: WHISKY GALORE

An example of the process of finding and checking a story and forcing a 'confession' from those in authority was provided by another *NMR* investigation. On this occasion an investigation into one of the other favourite targets of the radical alternative press – the police – formed the focus. One of the contacts of the *NMR* was a police officer who gave information to other newspapers when things happened in the Greater Manchester Police which he believed to breach laws or regulations and upon which he was not able to obtain redress from normal police channels. He had phoned the magazine from a public phone booth and had then met Jennings in a public house. Jennings was most concerned not to be 'set up' and had been circumspect in his dealings with the police officer at first. But after a series of stories with such timeless titles as 'Costly tune from boys in blue'[13] and 'Jim Anderton, the secret Tory',[14] the officer became one of the prized contacts of the magazine.

In early 1979 he asked to see Jennings and told him of an unsolicited gift made by the then Iranian chargé d'affaires in Manchester, Dr Ebrahim Jahannema, to a number of senior officers in the Greater Manchester Police. It happened the previous Christmas when the consular limousine, complete with CD plates, had drawn up outside Manchester Central Police Station in Bootle Street in the city centre. A flunkey bore a number of crates of Crawford's three-star de luxe Scotch into the building, with individual bottles labelled as gifts to named officers. The police contact explained that the significance of this was that the police disciplinary code includes a rule prohibiting an officer receiving a gift from a member of the public or being in a relation which might create an obligation on behalf of the officer to a member of the public. This was highlighted in the case of the GMP by the high-profile public attitude of the Chief Constable towards morality, which included an implicit portrait of himself as a man of unimpeachable rectitude. It was further underlined by a strict adherence to such rules for junior officers exemplified by the case of a sergeant who had reputedly lost his stripes for 'nipping out of the station with his mac over his uniform for a quick glass of Guinness'.

For Jennings the context was made yet more appropriate by a recent police incursion into the Iranian consulate at the request of the consul in order to arrest students who were protesting against the fascistic excesses of the late Shah of Iran. The students were subsequently charged with public order offences. Were the bottles of whisky gifts in return for services rendered?

These factors gave the story a clear ideological significance by challenging the probity of the police hierarchy in relation precisely to the system of rules by which the police are legitimized and through which senior officers discipline their juniors. The only question was whether it was accurate and if so whether it could be shown to be true in a public way.

Jennings believed the story because the police source was established by then as a 'magic contact'. The reporter's job was then to make the story 'stand up'. The way he chose to do this was a frontal attack on the consul. He determined to interview the diplomat and to broach the subject of the whisky at an unguarded moment. He hoped that Dr Jahannema might not be sufficiently aware of British rules of police conduct as to realize that the receipt of such a gift by a senior police officer might constitute any problem. Jennings also hoped that the consul would not know the reputation of the *NMR* as a left-wing 'muck-raking' magazine. The first gap in his knowledge meant that he might unwittingly provide the requisite 'confession'; the second that he might agree to an interview.

Fortunately for Jennings, global history was intervening on his side. It was about the time when the Shah was packing his bags for his final long holiday away from Iran, while that pillar of wisdom and broad-mindedness, the Ayatollah Khomeini, stood ready to take over the reins of power and organize a complete change-over of the political prisoners.

Cashing in on the crisis, Jennings telephoned to ask for a meeting with the consul so that the *NMR* could find out the feelings of the Iranian population of north-west England about the crisis in their country. The consul agreed to see him and expressed delight at the prospect. In planning the interview, Jennings intended to gain the Iranian's confidence by talking about the problems of the Shah and their repercussions for Iranians abroad and then nonchalantly pop the question about the whisky. A companion local newspaper journalist, I was to provide the grovelling flannel to make the adversary feel confident, while Jennings the former *Daily Express* man would 'do the business'.

On the morning of the appointed day it was announced from

Iran that the Shah had made an excuse and left. When the journalists arrived at the consulate, a suite of offices in a modern con-
crete-and-glass block, all seemed deserted except for a lone policeman who stood guard outside. Behind the glass doors at the front
was a wooden barricade, and where a glass panel had been
smashed a small wooden panel had been fixed in its place. A
small notice instructed callers to use the rear door.

The journalists entered through a back room which was equip-
ped as a kitchen, apparently for making drinks and lunches for
guests. They passed through the foyer, where the walls were
decorated with spray-painted legends in what seemed to be Per-
sian and which we took to mean something broadly uncompli-
mentary to the government of which the Iranian host was up
until that time a more or less loyal servant.

The consul was a small dapper man in a pin-striped suit, who
revealed that his father was a journalist and that he was keen to
meet the press. He stressed, however, that the journalists must
not publish anything about his attitude to political events in Iran.
This was a major concern of his, but it was an easy matter for
the journalists to concede; they could state with total candour
that their concerns were purely with events in Manchester. The
reporters moved on to his social contacts in the locality. He
volunteered that he got on especially well with the police.

Jennings pounced on the opportunity: 'Yes, I was down at
Bootle Street the other day, talking to the lads there. They really
appreciated the whisky you sent them for Christmas.'

The consul did not acknowledge the remark as having any
conversational significance. Perhaps he did not understand the
idiomatic phraseology, or was ignorant of the fact that Bootle
Street was the central police station. Perhaps it was strategic
incomprehension. The interview became increasingly direction-
less. But Jennings still had to obtain the confession and continued
doggedly with the observation that the officers at the city police
headquarters had commented how generous the consul had been
in sending them whisky for Christmas. This time the consul
acknowledged the remark, but asked: 'What whisky?' Jennings
said he had heard that a number of officers had received presents
of whisky from Dr Jahannema at Christmas. Oh no, the consul
assured us, that was simply the officers who had come to the
consulate 'when we had the slight disturbance here' and were
given glasses of whisky.

Still smiling amiably, Jennings pressed on: 'Oh, that's funny. I'd heard that two crates of Crawford's three-star de luxe whisky were delivered to Bootle Street police station in the consular car.'

'Oh, of course,' the diplomat responded equally amicably; 'we sent out bottles of whisky, about 200, to many people in Manchester: banks, businesses. We sent about five to the police.' The reporters exchanged a glance in acknowledgement that they had got 'a result', as the consul went on: 'But you don't want to publish that. It's not important.'

They left as quickly as possible, shaking hands without embarrassment, assuring him once more that they would not publish any of his comments on the high politics of Iran.

The 'confession' by the consul was not enough in itself to 'prove' that the story had both significance and substance. Unlike the Fieldhouse story, the words spoken were not uttered in front of a television camera. Jennings was only going to use the 'result' with the consul to try to make the system confess. He was going to challenge the police with his knowledge of the whisky, and with the fact that he knew it through the consul, so that they would not be able to deny it. He rang up the Greater Manchester Police press office and explained:

We were down at the Iranian Consulate this morning, interviewing the consul about how Iranians are feeling about the crisis in Iran, and during the course of the interview he happened to mention that he had given some whisky to police officers at Bootle as a present.

A day later the press officer phoned back with the official statement:

It appears that unknown to the Chief Constable of Greater Manchester a parcel allegedly containing intoxicating liquor from the Iranian Consulate in Manchester may have been delivered to a Manchester police station before Christmas.

The matter is now being investigated.

Another parcel addressed to the Chief Constable and Mrs Anderton from the Consul-General of Iran in Manchester and his wife was delivered at the same time to the Chief Constable's office.

The benefit of this gift was passed on to the Northern Police

Convalescent Home at Harrogate since it is the Chief Constable's policy that personal gifts should not be retained.

This statement was the system confessing. It was a factual acknowledgement that the whisky gift had been made and that this constituted a sufficiently serious issue that it required an internal police disciplinary enquiry. Intense journalistic work had produced a story that would be both validated factually and significant in the sense that official action was going to be taken to investigate a possible breach of the rules constituting the legitimacy of the police.

The story 'Police probe case for prosecution' appeared under a provocative strap-line, 'Corruption', and was illustrated by a photograph of the police station which was captioned 'Bootle Street Police Station: whisky galore?'[15] The story related the gifts of the expensive Caledonian spirits to the prosecution of the students who had invaded the legation. It began:

'An internal police probe has begun following investigations by the Review which revealed that gifts have been accepted by some senior officers.' It then related the case of whisky to the case concerning the students. 'No one', wrote Jennings, 'could suggest that individually gift-wrapped bottles of Crawford's three-star de luxe Scotch would in any way influence the outcome of the case.' There followed a summary of how the ten Iranian students had entered the consulate, had torn up pictures of the Shah and had sprayed slogans on the wall.[16]

The next day, the report went on, the police applied for the ten to be remanded in custody pending charges of conspiracy and burglary as well as those already made of criminal damage. 'Creditably, stipendiary magistrate John Coffey refused, despite police claims. . . . But after the arrest and before Christmas, a consular car drew up at the nick and bottles of Crawford's were distributed to named officers.'[17]

The article then quoted Dr Jahannema:

'I sent out about 200 bottles of whisky at Christmas. Only about five or six went to policemen. I would rather you forgot about this whisky business, don't publish that.

'Mr Anderton is a very nice man, very serious, very religious. In London and other countries it is normal to give presents. But I know your police cannot be bought and I wouldn't even dream of trying. I wouldn't want to. But we did have some trouble here and, yes, we did give some drinks of whisky to the police officers who were very helpful.'[18]

The rest of the story was made up of the references already quoted above to the consulate, Dr Jahannema's worsteds and a full quotation of the police press statement.

After publication the story was taken up by the *Manchester Evening News* and the national press, focusing on the police decision to hold an internal disciplinary enquiry and on James Anderton's gift of the money value of the whisky to a charity. The alternative press had created an event in the shape of an official enquiry which the traditional press then covered as the normal process of reporting the actions of the authority system. Further examples of the sort of news coverage of the radical alternative press of the same period can be found in *News Limited: Why You Can't Read All about It*, by Brian Whitaker.[19] A section entitled 'Extracts from the free press' contains twenty-eight pages of extracts from the *Liverpool Free Press*, which lasted from 1971 to 1976 – more or less contemporaneous with the *Manchester Free Press*.[20]

Activists from the era of the original development of the alternative local radical news bemoan the spread of consumerism among the modern listings magazines. But although this is generally true of the present listings magazines it is by no means universally the case. It is still possible to find the same approach to journalism in the modern manifestations of this type of local media. Apart from the redoubtable *Northern Star*, there are glossy listings-based magazines which can still demonstrate the same commitment to investigation. *Venue*, for instance, which describes itself as Bristol and Bath's biggest 'what's on' guide, runs exactly the same sort of investigation into local crookery as the *New Manchester Review* did in the 1970s. In 1987 its reporters Robin Askew and James Garrett investigated the affairs of the Bristol 1000 and KWEV job agencies which had been the beneficiaries of large amounts of public money. They examined what had happened and the activities of named public figures.[21] This was a long-running story which the magazine pursued into the next year with stories such as 'More questions than answers' which pursued the issues of the debts and the nine secret bank accounts of KWEV and an attempt to sweep under the carpet the difficulties of the Bristol 1000 jobs agency.[22]

It is important to understand that the stories referred to in the old *NMR* and in *Venue* were published in the glossy-style listings magazines which in purely content terms are dominated by listings. Yet in both magazines news is seen to be important. This is reflected both in the time and effort spent in producing it and in its positioning at the front of the magazine. *Venue* in particular has a section with page headings 'NEWS' in large block capitals. It is clear also that these stories are seen by those who write the magazines as revealing things about the nature of the system and consequently as a sort of political action. This is not to say that they are part of a programme of political action, but rather that revelation itself is seen as an action on the political system.

This sort of silence-breaking involves breaking open the system to show its inner working, to the embarrassment of those who run it. The sources of the information on which such revelation is based have to be individuals who work within the system and have the knowledge required to expose what is hidden. The second sort of silence-breaking simply involves reporting the activities of those groups who might be seen by the conventional traditional press as deviant, beyond the pale or simply involved in irrelevant minority activities not worth the notice of the main communal news organ.

Such news coverage does not require investigation of the activities of rich or powerful individuals, nor courting the libel laws. It simply means using as contacts the representatives of such groups and giving them a voice as news spokespeople in the same way that the traditional press does with the officials of local government, state agencies, formal communal bodies and business. Stories from conventional sources are also used when they refer to the interests of such groups. *Northern Star* provides a number of examples of this sort of story.

'Rape in marriage law must be seen to work for women' and 'Women step up security measures' are both stories in which the sources are women's groups. 'Black man awarded £6,000 damages for police assault' is based on a report of a court case. 'Emergency workers' control' is a story about ambulance workers in dispute running their own emergency service and relies on shop stewards' and workers' accounts as the sources.[23]

This sort of news coverage, then, marks out the radical alternative press as different from the traditional commercial press in that it challenges the conventional 'spokespeople' of authority and holds up to critical scrutiny the spokespeople as individuals, their activities and the system for which they speak. It does so by reference to the system of rules by which such a structure is legitimated. Second, it uses as primary sources the contacts who are marginalized by the usual process of news production, and it gives coverage to the news for which these contacts provide the raw material.

To identify those parts of the magazines which are occupied by arts reviews, listings and advertisements indicates something about the nature of these publications; but before we come to examine what this is, it is necessary to clarify the sort of review and advertisement which the magazines carry. To begin with, the sort of entertainment they deal with is more likely to be 'ideologically sound' (to adopt an imprecise term). During a country-wide tour the popular comedian Ben Elton, for instance, was interviewed at the end of 1988 both by *Venue*, to coincide with his performance in Bristol, and by the successor to *NMR* in Manchester, *City Life*. In each magazine the whole article was written within the framework of the question of how genuinely left-wing or idealistic Ben Elton really is, and more particularly addressing the issue of how the payment of large fees for his work might call into question his commitment to radical, left-wing or environmentalist causes. Both seem to acquit him of a sell-out or hypocrisy – the Manchester magazine with rather fewer reservations.[24]

There are also reviews which are purely to do with entertainment and show no overt signs of ideological commitment other than to pleasing oneself. Film is clearly one of the favourite leisure activities promoted by such magazines. Clint Eastwood or Cary Grant is more likely to be reviewed than the more politically radical Jean Luc Godard or Bertolucci. Rock reviews, sections to do with 'style', eating-out guides and sometimes sections headed 'Beer' appear to be written clearly for that section of the audience which buys the magazine purely as a guide to where to be in order to be in the right place in Manchester, Bath, Bristol, Leeds, London or Norwich – or for that part of the radical consciousness which takes time off from ideology to refresh itself in bourgeois self-indulgence.

But events listed also include political meetings of green and socialist groups, and meetings of women's groups and black groups. The classified advertising columns frequently include

AIDS help-lines or counselling services for young gay people. Some magazines accept such advertisements for free. Left-wing political parties and protest groups advertise in such publications. Manchester City Council used to advertise appointments through *City Life*. The doomed GLC advertised prominently in *Time Out* and *City Limits*.

THE ALTERNATIVE PRESS AND THE MARKET

It is, however, the case that the physical preponderance of listings material and the presence of advertising which the listings generate is a characteristic of such magazines because of their relationship to the market. This also helps to explain why so many of them have such short lives – why so few break the four-year life-expectancy barrier.

Such magazines are usually co-operatively owned and run. The co-operative will sometimes have some paid working members and others who are volunteers. They sometimes have employees who are non-members. At times an inner group of the co-operative take most of the decisions, do most of the work and sometimes save the co-op from its frequent brushes with terminal insolvency by mortgaging their homes. This often creates a two-or-more-class co-operative, with an inner circle of those whose commitment to the undertaking is much greater in all senses than those not so centrally involved.

Such magazines are rarely able to survive non-problematically on the proceeds of sales of radical news, views and investigation to an eager revolutionary public. They are confronted by the exigencies of the market in a number of ways. In order to survive they have to gear their editorial coverage to readers' leisure interests, which means that the magazine will be bought by people seeking a reference guide for where to go. It also means that the owners of cinemas, theatres and galleries, restaurateurs and the promoters of entertainment and events will have a motive for advertising in such magazines. Some of the editorial material – say, a special clutch of articles on health clubs – will originate from the urgings of the advertising representative as a means of whipping up advertising for a particular issue.

In this sense, magazines with a broadly radical-left interpretation of society, the economy and journalism are driven to use the currency of consumerism and the 'new times' to survive. This position may lead to forms of political dependence. *City Wise*, the Norwich magazine, is aided by the City of Norwich. The current Manchester alternative magazine *City Life* was for a time the recipient of council advertising of various kinds, including appointments advertisements. This stopped during a period of municipal cut-backs and during a row between a member of the co-operative and some members of the council. There is always the danger that the adoption of such stratagems as a bulwark against the hardships of survival in the market will blunt the independence of such magazines.

Such publications, if they live up to the expectations of their own staff, face a constant danger of ruin because of the cost of a single libel action; and because of their low incomes they cannot afford expensive legal advice. They must therefore rely on friendly and committed lawyers knowledgeable in the field who will work for nothing, or just take the risk of committing libel and hope for the best.

City Life, which took an active part in investigating and exposing a number of aspects of the Stalker affair, made reference to some of the less appetizing aspects of life in the Manchester Conservative Association which were associated with the case. In fact, the local association was in such a parlous state that Central Office closed it down after receiving complaints from local party members. A series of articles on this affair resulted in one of the leading characters in the Stalker affair feeling that he had been libelled, and the magazine was faced with either the expense of a court case or an out-of-court settlement. Eventually it went into receivership with the matter still unresolved, and it is now under new ownership with the matter still pending. The *NMR* was the target of a number of flying writs. One was from a candidate in a local election about whom the magazine made claims as to the source and extent of his election expenditure. When the writ arrived at the office the staff resorted to an old legal device, running upstairs to the attic, locking themselves in and giggling until the writ server had left. This is not always successful but is much cheaper than the cost of a counsel.

In order to increase the size of circulation or improve the quality of the publication, co-operatives constantly face the need to raise more capital. They do so by a number of means. Friendly bands and promoters run 'gigs'. Sometimes the co-operative itself enters into the promotion of events. When this happens there is always the temptation for the individuals involved, if they become successful, to go into such a business on their own account for their own profit rather than for the benefit of the co-op. Alternatively, members may borrow money against their own homes or other personal security.

A further strategy is the development of a secondary business activity. Typically, in doing its own layout and origination work the co-operative may develop the skills of the layout studio, especially if it employs a graphic designer. This area of activity is always likely to become more profitable as a business than publishing the magazine. This seems to provide an ideal solution, a milch cow to subsidize the magazine. But when crises arise and debts become too large for the bank to extend credit, or young enthusiastic co-op members become less young, less enthusiastic, more married and more parental, the idea of working for a profitable co-operative venture seems more attractive than attempting to shore up a constantly indebted magazine.

The *NMR* ceased publication under a weight of debt in 1979, for instance, and the co-operative went entirely into graphic work, paid off their debts and joined the old *FREEP* co-operative which had also previously gone through the same process of moving from magazine production to layout. They now operate successfully as a business under the title of Manchester Free Press. Their successors *City Life* developed layout facilities and used to lay out other magazines, such as *Gay Life*. But when they went bust they did not opt for the production option as a way of saving jobs or prolonging the co-op. The title was taken over by the *Manchester Evening News* and *Guardian*, and a number of the workers continue to produce it now as part of this newspaper group which has an almost complete monopoly of local newspaper sales in the Manchester area.

A final way in which the market penetrates the radical free press is probably the most important – through the operation of the labour market. The success of such magazines, when they do succeed, depends on the enthusiasm of individuals who are prepared to work for less than they might earn elsewhere. At times they work on mainstream newspapers or in the broadcast media and subsidize the alternative press from their own income. Those whose only work is with the co-op eventually succumb to the pressures outlined above and also to the desire to achieve a wider audience for their work. A number of investigative reporters in television and in the national press began their careers or spent some part of them working for such local investigative magazines.

But there is a secular tendency which dominates all such publications, and which only the *Northern Star* seems to have been able to buck in the long term. They either go under after a number of hectic and entertaining years, which is the most common fate, or they become increasingly dominated by business demands and thrive, as the two London listings magazines have, primarily as purveyors of 'style'. The alternative radical press do not provide an example of the free market creating choice and variety. Quite the reverse: they show it consuming them.

Chapter 6

The municipal free press

The growth of municipal newspapers since the early 1980s represents a significant development for the local press. It signals, moreover, the possibilities for creating a greater pluralism in local newspapers in terms of their ownership and organizational forms, their staffing and journalistic resources, but, perhaps most significantly, the ideological posture inherent in much of their editorial content.

The emergence of the municipal press, however, has proved highly contentious. Newspapers written, produced and published by local authorities, and distributed freely to each household in the authorities' boundaries, quickly became the subject of allegations of political bias by Conservative politicians in both central and local government. Their claim was that certain 'hard-left' Labour authorities were misusing their legitimate powers to engage in public relations activities by using public funds to publish municipal newspapers which were little more than vehicles for partisan propaganda. Some local authorities were allegedly orchestrating campaigns against central government policies, especially in areas such as the economy, job creation and social and welfare services, and were encouraging, through their municipal papers, support for highly politicized views concerning defence, unilateral nuclear disarmament, nuclear-free zones and civil rights in South Africa. Conservatives argued that these issues were unrelated to local affairs and that the provision of information about civic matters had been superseded by the dissemination of political propaganda – a practice which the tabloid press, with its sub-editorial obsession with the trite phrase, dubbed 'propaganda on the rates'.

In the national context, the Conservatives introduced the Local
Government Acts of 1986 and 1988 which placed severe restrictions on local authorities' publicity powers and limited their
ability to publish materials in municipal papers which statute
defined as 'political'. The strength of Conservative feeling about
the newspapers was evident during the Bill's passage through the
House. The then MP for Leicester South claimed:

> Propaganda is rife in Leicester. . . . The council is wasting
> money with the latest edition of *Leicester Link* promoting
> Labour Party propaganda . . . about Nelson Mandela. . . . Why
> should we have to pay to have such propaganda shoved up our
> noses? I object to it.[1]

His views were echoed by Nicholas Ridley, who addressed the
Conservative Party conference in 1986 and spoke against these
allegedly propagandist activities in unconciliatory terms. 'Some
local authorities', he claimed, 'spend their time and your money
pumping out vile political propaganda.'[2]

In the local context, Conservative politicians were and continue
to be critical of the municipal press. In Leeds, the Conservative
group has minuted its intention to abolish both the municipal
newspaper and the public relations department which produces
it, when the group retains control of the council. In Manchester,
the manifesto of a Conservative candidate for the local elections
in May 1986 promised to 'stop Labour's spending spree and
propaganda with your money' by abolishing *Manchester Magazine*,
the local authority free newspaper; the magazine has subsequently
ceased publication.

Labour authorities, for their part, refute the allegations of bias
and propaganda by asserting that municipal newspapers simply
express council policy and that such exposition is legitimate. A
newspaper editor is worth quoting at some length because she
expresses the local government position with great clarity.

> The primary role of the paper has always been to inform the
> public about the council's policies. . . . There is a very thin
> line between speaking for the council and speaking for the
> Labour Party when the latter hold 90% of total council seats.
> As far as I'm concerned the civic newspaper speaks for the
> council and by extension the Labour group since that group
> dominates the council. Similarly council policy is by that same

extension Labour Party policy and therefore it will appear predominantly in the magazine.[3]

In the House of Commons debate about municipal newspapers, Labour politicians spoke forcefully against the need for statutory controls of local government information and publicity services. Legislative controls are undemocratic, they suggested, since they restrict local government's right to offer local citizens information about political matters which may have consequences for them, as well as denying local government a right to reply to the various measures of central government designed to undermine and centralize powers currently possessed by local authorities. Statutory controls, moreover, reverse earlier government policy to expand local authority public relations and, perhaps most significantly, are hypocritical when newspapers such as *Ratepayer Reporter*, produced by Conservative authorities such as Westminster, are similarly partisan.

Liberal members Alan Beith and Simon Hughes suggested that the minister should 'not criticize one party without admitting his own party is equally guilty'.[4] Government hypocrisy was compounded by a central government which has spent unprecedentedly high publicity budgets to promote Conservative policies. This point was well made by Tony Banks MP, when he attacked

> the total hypocrisy of the government position. . . . If it is put out by the Conservative Party in government, by definition, it is information. If it is put out by Labour-controlled authorities, it is, according to the government, propaganda. . . . The government now spends many millions on publicity. We would call it propaganda, for that is what it is.[5]

It has been suggested that, if local authorities have been guilty of using municipal papers to disseminate 'propaganda on the rates', then arguably the Conservative government has displayed an increasing tendency to use television and national newspaper advertising for 'propaganda on the taxes'. But the issue is too serious to caricature in this way. The function of municipal newspapers in the network of local political communication, and their uses as vehicles for either propaganda or citizen information, requires serious assessment.

The quotations cited above, however, reveal that political

debate concerning the municipal press has itself been high in
doctrinal and rhetorical content, but has rarely offered more than
a paucity of empirical evidence to substantiate its claims. This is
perhaps not surprising. Municipal papers are a relatively new
component within the local media and have grown rapidly since
the 1977 Royal Commission on the Press dismissed their existence
in a mere two lines of its report.[6] The discussion here therefore
attempts a novel comparison of the controversial case concerning
'propaganda on the rates' with empirical evidence about the
municipal press. The data for the comparison are derived from
the responses to a detailed questionnaire distributed to local
authorities in England, Scotland and Wales, enquiring about
municipal newspapers;[7] a content analysis of newspapers published by both Conservative- and Labour-controlled local authorities; and finally, interviews conducted with public relations officers with responsibilities for producing municipal newspapers.

THE DEVELOPMENT OF THE MUNICIPAL PRESS

Perceptions of municipal papers tend in the direction of the anach-
ronistic. They are no longer the poorly produced single sheet of
paper which merely lists the place and dates of local councillors'
surgeries and the opening times of the local library and swimming
baths. Local authority newspapers have increased rapidly in
number, circulation and sophistication of editorial content and
style, and many are now indistinguishable, in form if not in
content, from their commercially produced counterparts.

Free distribution to all residents within the authority's boundaries guarantees that circulation figures are high and commonly
in excess of 100,000, sometimes 300,000, copies per issue. Strathclyde Regional Council, which is the most prolific of local
authority publishers, produces free newspapers for both 'in-house'
and public consumption. The 24-page tabloid *Strathclyde Report*
is published bi-monthly, is self-financing because it attracts an
average of £52,000 advertising revenues per issue and has a circulation of 935,000, which is larger than that of the *Observer* or the
combined circulation of the *Guardian* and *The Times*.

Readership figures for the municipal press are also high. An
unpublished survey about *Sheffield News* revealed that 50 per cent
of those who received the newspaper usually read it, and a further
34 per cent read it occasionally. Forty-nine per cent of readers

found it 'informative'; 48 per cent felt it was 'interesting'; but only 3 per cent considered it politically biased (the direction of bias being unspecified), and only a further 3 per cent considered the paper a waste of money.[8]

The reasons for the growth of municipal papers are fivefold and reflect changes in both media and political environments. First, many public relations officers report a decline in the coverage of council and committee meetings by the local media, especially the paid-for weekly papers, and the municipal press provides a substitute forum for the presentation of these affairs.[9] Second, local authority newspapers provide an outlet for important stories which are not considered sufficiently newsworthy by the paid-for or commercial free weekly press.[10] Third, the municipal newspaper can provide a counterbalance to negative coverage of local government in the national and local media. A recent study of the national tabloid press has revealed how coverage by some newspapers persistently discredited local government by labelling its councillors as the 'loony left' and presenting its activities and policies as ridiculous, anti-democratic and threatening to the general democratic consensus. The report suggested that, in this process, editors and journalists had promoted bias, omitted key facts from stories while fabricating others, and published lies.[11] Local newspapers can also be critical in their coverage of local authorities, and the editor of one municipal newspaper claimed that 'Our free newspaper helps us fight an uphill battle against press hostilities.' The editorial in the May issue of *Manchester Magazine* was less equivocal. 'Manchester City Council', it claimed, 'is increasingly on the receiving end not only of bias in the media but downright lies.'[12]

Fourth, municipal newspapers are a useful vehicle for conveying information from the authority to its public about a range of matters, including the provision of services, an explanation of how the figure for the local rate or, now, the community charge is calculated or the availability of grants for home improvements.[13] Finally, if Conservative allegations are correct, municipal newspapers have served as an effective weapon in a propaganda war against the direction of central government policy at a time of increasing tension and schism between the central and local aspects of the state. But these five factors explain only the demand for municipal newspapers; they do not account for local authorities' ability to produce them. Two additional factors have been critical here. First, the growth in public relations departments since the mid-1970s means that local authorities not only have staff with the journalistic expertise necessary to produce newspapers, but also have a heightened awareness of the public relations and communication benefits to be derived from their production.[14] Second, the availability of new printing technology and the practice of contracting out jobs to private printers have brought cheap printing, of a high technical quality, within the reach of most local government public relations budgets.

The questionnaire distributed to local authorities in England, Scotland and Wales revealed that ninety-seven authorities produced a newspaper for free distribution to residents or a selected target readership such as employees, council-housing tenants, community groups or voluntary organizations. The data presented in this section are in two parts. The first deals with information relating to numbers of papers produced, their size, format, length and frequency of publication. If local authorities are disseminating 'propaganda on the rates', it is important to establish the dimensions of their offence. The second deals with the economics of municipal newspaper production, the percentage of editorial space devoted to advertising, average costs of production and distribution, and local authority policy about whether the newspaper should be self-financing. Throughout both sections differences in practice between Labour- and Conservative-controlled authorities will be highlighted.

Seventy-four of the ninety-seven newspapers produced are for general distribution to local residents (see Appendix I). When publication of newspapers is correlated with type of authority, districts emerge as the most likely to produce a newspaper (43 or 12.9 per cent of all district councils), but a higher proportion of metropolitan districts (30.6 per cent) and London boroughs (24.2 per cent) publish newspapers compared to other authorities.

The political control of local authorities producing municipal newspapers reveals a more striking correlation, with Labour local authorities (72.0 per cent) nearly three times as likely to produce a newspaper as their Conservative counterparts (27.0 per cent). These figures compare interestingly with newspapers produced for limited distribution within the local authority; 57 per cent of such papers are produced by Conservative-controlled authorities but only 39 per cent by Labour.

Aggregate circulation figures are extremely high. Since distribution is free to local residents, circulation figures reflect population size and in turn the type of local authority. Consequently, it is unsurprising to find the largest circulations in the county areas (average 200,000 per issue), followed by the metropolitan districts (169,000) and London boroughs (107,250), with the smallest circulation in districts (77,722). There is a considerable variation in circulation across all types of authority, which in the district authorities, for example, ranges from 119,000 per issue in Nottingham to 28,000 copies per issue in East Kilbride. In the metropolitan districts the two largest circulations are for the *Sheffield News* and the *Manchester Magazine*, which both produce 220,000 copies monthly; both these latter papers feature in the content analysis below.

Municipal newspapers are a well-established aspect of public relations activities in some authorities, with the oldest paper, the *Harlow News*, boasting a pedigree of some twenty-four years. They have, however, undergone a period of rapid growth, with 47 per cent of all newspapers being less than five years old. The political control of the council seems again to be an important variable, with 80 per cent of newspapers established in the last five years being published by Labour authorities. A second period of growth for municipal newspapers dates from the reorganization of local government in 1974, when the new authorities were eager to establish a corporate identity and rapport with their local publics. A quarter of civic newspapers were established at the time of reorganization and during the subsequent three years.

Municipal newspapers vary considerably in their frequency of publication. Those published annually (16 per cent), usually at the end of the financial year, tend to focus on explanations of the new rate or community charge and a breakdown of the costs of service provision. These publications can be called newspapers on only the most liberal interpretation of that term. Quarterly (27 per cent) and monthly (24 per cent) publication were the most popular frequencies, and these more regularly produced newspapers begin to look less like news sheets and more credibly like newspapers in terms of their size, editorial style, layout and general appearance. Newspapers produced by Labour authorities tend to predominate among these more regularly published papers. Seventy-three per cent of quarterly papers, 100 per cent of bi-monthly papers and 88 per cent of monthly municipal papers are produced by Labour authorities, suggesting that they place a much higher value on the municipal press as a public relations vehicle for communication with their local publics. This presumption is supported by other survey findings. Labour authorities, for example, are seven times more likely than Conservatives to incur the costs of full colour printing for a newspaper and they also tend to produce much larger papers, with more than 90 per cent of newspapers containing between 9 and 16 pages being produced by Labour authorities, and 70 per cent of those papers printing between 17 and 24 pages.

The hub of Conservative allegations against municipal newspapers seems to be that they are produced with public funds, so it is important to have a detailed picture of their production and distribution costs.

Very few local authorities (4 per cent) have the facilities to print newspapers 'in house', and the majority (68 per cent) prefer to contract the work to a private printer; almost a third (27 per cent) use the printing facilities offered by the local commercial newspaper. Authorities reveal a similar reluctance to handle distribution, with the single most favoured option being to contract the task to a private company (47 per cent). The local newspaper provides a ready distribution network, and nearly a quarter (23.5 per cent) of responding authorities use it for their newspapers; an additional quarter (22.0 per cent) use the Post Office.

This diversity of production and distribution methods inevitably generates a considerable range of costs. Differences in unit costs, moreover, reflect and express the diversity of possible formats evident across the range of newspapers. Obvious candidates here are the number of pages and whether or not the paper uses full colour, spot colour or a simple black-and-white format. The London Borough of Barnet, for example, pays £16,000 for 119,000 copies of the *Barnet Borough News*, a unit cost of 13.4 pence. The paper, however, uses full colour and has forty-eight pages per issue. Two-thirds of its total space, moreover, is devoted to advertising, and it is intended that the paper should be self-financing. At the bottom end of the unit costs scale is Durham County, which produces 245,000 copies of the *Durham County Reporter* for £8,219, giving a unit cost of 3.35 pence. The paper is small with only four pages and prints in black and white. At the other end of the scale, Hertsmere pays £9,600 for 37,000 copies of the *Hertsmere Connection*. This generates a unit cost figure of 25.9 pence, which, after the deduction of £3,000 advertis-

ing revenues, remains high at 17.8 p. The average unit cost of
the seventy-four newspapers in the sample is 8.2 pence, which
suggests a highly cost-effective operation in all authorities.

Production and distribution costs per issue vary across different
authorities, in part reflecting respective populations and hence
circulation sizes: from £12,379 in counties to £1,932 in the Scottish
districts. Metropolitan districts, however, have larger circulations
than London boroughs, and the higher costs in the latter (£8,967
compared to £5,695) signal higher unit costs. The total cost per
annum for the different types of authorities suggests two important conclusions. First, London boroughs (£90,185) and metropolitan districts (£57,207) emerge as the largest-spending authorities; 75 per cent of the former and 83 per cent of the latter who
responded to the questionnaire are in Labour control. Second, the
sums of money involved are trivial as proportions of the different
authorities' total budgets. The figure of £535,525, for example,
which is allocated for the total public relations budget in Strathclyde, represented a mere 0.04 per cent of the regional council's
total estimated expenditure for 1986–7.[15]

Local authorities none the less try to offset these costs in a
number of ways. Maidstone's weekly paper, the *Borough News*,
for example, is produced for the authority by a local firm of
public relations consultants, one of whose partners is a former
editor of the local newspaper. The consultancy takes any profits
and equally bears any losses. Some authorities like Hull City,
perhaps for financial reasons, possibly because they lack adequate
in-house public relations resources, contract the task to an agency
for an agreed fee.

Most authorities try to offset costs by generating advertising
revenues, and 70 per cent of municipal newspapers sell advertising
space. Buyers may be in-house departments, other local authorities or commercial companies, with the proportion of total space
devoted to advertising varying substantially. Newspapers produced by Conservative authorities are disproportionately over-
represented among those papers carrying high levels of advertising. Conservative authorities produce only 28 per cent of newspapers; but 58 per cent of papers carrying between 41 per cent
and 50 per cent advertising, and 50 per cent of papers carrying
between 51 per cent and 60 per cent advertising, are produced
by Conservative authorities; the single paper devoting more than
60 per cent to advertising is also Conservative. It was a stated

objective, moreover, in 35 per cent of Conservative authorities that their municipal newspaper should be self-financing, whereas only 19 per cent of their Labour counterparts were set this goal. This is not to deny, of course, that papers like *Strathclyde Reporter* (published by a Labour-controlled authority) are largely self-sufficient because of advertising revenues, but simply to suggest that Conservative authorities seem more enthusiastic that papers should cover costs via advertising and accordingly allocate greater space to that end.

Three substantive findings emerge from the foregoing data. First, Labour-controlled authorities produce more newspapers, which are larger and more colourful and have a higher proportion of editorial to advertising. They publish them more frequently, and spend more on their production and distribution than Conservative councils. The Labour Party, moreover, tends to predominate among newspapers with larger circulations, and four-fifths of newspapers which began publication between 1982 and 1986 are located in Labour authorities. Second, the production of municipal papers across all types of authority, and without regard to their political control, is a highly cost-effective exercise, and the sums of money involved are extremely small in the context of the total budget of the authority. Third, Conservative councils are twice as likely as Labour to require their newspapers to be self-financing and, to that end, devote a higher proportion of space to advertising. This perhaps is not surprising, given Conservative commitments to the market.

THE CONTENT OF CIVIC NEWSPAPERS

Serious assessment of Conservative allegations concerning 'propaganda on the rates' requires some familiarity with the editorial content of the municipal press. Newspapers produced by Labour and Conservative authorities were analysed, and the percentage of total editorial which each newspaper devoted to specific policy or service provision areas was calculated. On those occasions where a particular story straddled two or more policy areas, as for example in the story about part-time adult education classes for unemployed people, the content was divided equally between the different policy areas; in this particular example, 50 per cent was allocated to education and 50 per cent to unemployment.

A brief point of methodological reservation should be noted.

Only a single issue of each of the six newspapers has been analysed, and an examination of earlier or later issues of the same
newspaper might have revealed slightly different content; to this
extent the analysis is indicative rather than substantive. The results
of the analysis, however, are consistent across the three Labour
and three Conservative papers and signal a discrete set of concerns
in the two groups of papers. Moreover, back copies of each of

Table 6.1 Labour civic newspapers

Subject-matter	Manchester Magazine	Sheffield News	Strathclyde Report	Average across 3 newspapers
		(% of total paper content)		
Gays	2.0	—	—	0.73
Women	—	—	—	—
Black/immigration	3.2	—	0.8	1.3
Disability	—	0.5	1.0	0.5
Social services	—	1.0	7.0	2.7
Conservation	2.0	—	—	0.7
Charities	2.6	2.9	—	1.8
Education	4.9	7.0	8.0	6.6
Waste collection	1.6	—	—	0.5
Unemployment	18.6	9.0	16.0	14.5
Economic development	2.5	10.5	4.0	5.7
Leisure	5.5	5.0	8.3	6.3
Health	1.6	4.0	—	1.9
Peace/nuclear	—	—	—	—
Welfare rights	1.2	—	4.3	1.8
International issues	0.5	—	—	0.2
Rates	5.0	—	—	1.7
Council/elections	5.0	15.0[a]	14.5[b]	11.5
Editorial comment	3.3	—	—	1.1
Advertising	22.0	24.5	25.5	24.0
Letters	5.0	—	—	1.7
General features	10.0	—	—	3.3
Housing	—	14.0	1.0	5.0
Transport	—	5.0	5.0	3.3
Trading standards	—	—	0.8	0.3
Law and order	—	—	—	—

Columns do not total to 100 because of rounding of figures.

[a] This fairly high figure represents a lengthy explanation of proxy voting.
[b] This figure reflects a long item detailing times and locations of councillors'
surgeries.

the seventy-four civic newspapers currently published have been read, and the six selected for analysis are unexceptional. Tables 6.1 and 6.2 set out the percentage of editorial devoted to the coverage of certain policy issues in Labour and Conservative papers respectively.

Table 6.2 Conservative civic newspapers

Subject-matter	Southend on Sea News	Rochford News	Here and Now	Average across 3 newspapers
			(% of total paper content)	
Gays	—	—	—	—
Women	—	—	—	—
Black/immigration	—	—	—	—
Disability	—	—	0.5	0.2
Social services	—	—	—	—
Conservation	2.0	1.0	0.5	1.2
Charities	1.8	—	—	0.6
Education	—	—	—	—
Waste collection	—	3.0	—	1.0
Unemployment	3.0	—	—	1.0
Economic development	—	—	4.3	1.4
Leisure	26.8	10.0	15.0	17.3
Health	—	—	2.5	0.8
Peace/nuclear	—	2.0	—	0.7
Welfare rights	—	—	—	—
International issues	—	—	0.5	0.2
Rates	—	—	0.5	0.2
Council/elections	2.2	6.5	3.7	4.1
Editorial	—	—	—	—
Advertising	46.8	50.0	53.0	49.9
Letters	1.5	—	—	0.5
General features	1.5	8.0	7.5	5.7
Housing	2.0	1.0	5.0	2.7
Transport	4.0	12.0[a]	1.5	5.8
Trading standards	3.0	—	1.0	1.3
Law and order	1.5	1.0	1.0	1.2

Columns do not total to 100 because of rounding of figures.

[a]This was a special photographic-based item on heavy snowfalls and the implications for transport.

Three observations emerge from a comparison of the two tables. First, and this is indicated by the gaps in Table 6.2, the

Conservative papers report a narrower range of issues. The Labour newspapers cover 23 issues, and 14 of these are reported in at least 2 of the 3 newspapers analysed. The Conservative papers, by contrast, range across 19 issues, but only 9 of these are reported in 2 or more of the newspapers.

Second, and more strikingly, the political control of the authority producing the civic newspaper seems to have important implications for content. Unemployment is a prominent issue in each of the three Labour newspapers analysed and accounts for an average of 14.5 per cent of total editorial. Unemployment is covered in only one Conservative newspaper and forms an average 1 per cent of total editorial. An examination of the treatment of the issues of education and economic development reveals similar disparities. Education issues are reported in all three Labour papers and constitute 6.6 per cent of editorial; the subject is not discussed in any of the three Conservative newspapers. Economic development is reported in all three Labour papers and forms an average 5.7 per cent of content; the issue is raised in only a single Conservative paper, amounting to an average 1.4 per cent of editorial.

Third, Labour papers seem more likely to give sustained treatment to a wider range of subjects than Conservative newspapers; in the latter, discussion of issues, with a few exceptions, is brief and truncated. Apart from advertising and items relating to leisure (which jointly account for almost 70 per cent of Conservative newspaper content), only four issues – general features (which is an aggregate category), transport, council/elections and housing – receive more than 2 per cent of total editorial. The reporting of other issue areas consequently has a 'bitty' feel. By contrast, in Labour papers eleven issues received more than 2 per cent editorial, and a range of topics are discussed in a more systematic and sustained way.

When the contents of the two groups of newspapers are rank-ordered according to the percentage of editorial devoted to a particular topic, the different issues preferences of the newspapers becomes apparent – see Table 6.3.

The Labour newspaper discussions of social services, education, gay people, black people and welfare rights have no counterpart in the Conservative papers. Similarly, the discussions of law and order (ninth in Conservative editorial priorities) and emergency

Table 6.3 Rank order of content/issues in Conservative and Labour papers

	Conservative			Labour	
Issue ranking		*Percentage of total editorial*			*Issue ranking*
1	Advertising	49.9	24.0	Advertising	1
2	Leisure/entertainment	17.3	14.5	Unemployment	2
3	Transport/road safety	5.8	11.5	Council/elections	3
4	General features	5.7	6.6	Education/nursery	4
5	Council/committees	4.1	6.3	Leisure/entertainment	5
6	Housing	2.7	5.7	Economic development	6
7	Economic development/job creation	1.4	5.0	Housing	7
8	Trading standards	1.3	3.3	Transport	8
9	Law and order	1.2	3.3	General features	9
10	Conservation	1.2	2.7	Social services	10
11	Waste collection	1.0	1.9	Health	11
12	Unemployment	1.0	1.8	Welfare rights	12
13	Health	0.8	1.8	Charity/fund-raising	13
14	Emergency planning	0.7	1.7	Letters	14
15	Charity/fund-raising	0.6	1.7	Rates and general service	15
16	Letters	0.5	1.3	Black/immigration	16
17	International	0.2	1.1	Editorial comment	17
18	Rates	0.2	0.7	Gays	18
19	Disability	0.2	0.7	Conservation	19
			0.5	Waste collection	20
			0.5	Disability	21
			0.3	Trading standards	22
			0.2	International issues	23

planning in Conservative papers have no Labour newspaper equivalents. It is perhaps worth noting, however, both because of the Labour Party's professed commitment to equal opportunities and because equal opportunities policy has been the focus of many Conservative allegations about 'propaganda on the rates', the paucity of discussion in Labour newspapers of women's issues (which are not raised in any of the three newspapers analysed), and the low salience of race issues and themes of disability and gay rights in editorial priorities.

The differences between the two sets of newspapers are in reality greater than Table 6.3 suggests. One of the difficulties with content analysis is that the categories identified for analysis – for example, leisure, law and order, unemployment – can on occasion create an impression of apparent similarity between the two bodies of content. Advertising is a good example here. Conservative and Labour newspapers both accept advertising, but the advertisements are quite different. Conservative newspapers tend to sell advertising space to private commercial companies who use it to promote a range of products from cars to electrical goods. In the Labour newspapers, however, advertisements are more likely to originate from departments within the publishing authority, and often their purpose is not to promote goods but to offer information about policies and services, especially in the area of welfare rights and benefits. *Manchester Magazine*, for example, carries advertisements for 'Hands across Britain', a concert to celebrate international nuclear-free zones, information relating to new grants for disabled people, Manchester's information centre, the housing benefits advice centre, Manchester AIDS line, the housing aids centre and Manchester benefits service, as well as a full-page advertisement against smoking. Conservative politicians in Manchester obviously consider much of this advertising to be propaganda, hence their election manifesto commitment to the abolition of the magazine, but the Labour argument seems both obvious and credible; to hear it is to feel its force. These are a range of information centres offering advice and detailed information about specific areas of council service provision or policy; to advertise such service provision is a legitimate activity and not an exercise in propaganda. What should be remembered amid the flurry of allegations is that advertisements can fulfil a range of purposes which may be rooted in the aesthetic as much as the economic or ideological. The editor of one municipal paper stated:

> Initially the purpose of the adverts was not to generate money but to make the newspaper look more like a newspaper. The adverts were used as page breaks to make the whole paper look busier and livelier than it does with just blocks of print and photos.

In summary, the content of municipal newspapers differs according to the political control of the authority producing the newspaper. Conservative newspapers carry a higher proportion of advertising than Labour, and this item combined with leisure accounts for almost 70 per cent of content. A narrower range of issues are discussed; fewer issues are subject to any sustained discussion; and unemployment and other welfare and social policy issues are either totally or effectively ignored in Conservative civic newspapers.

The content analysis above is essentially quantitative and deliberately avoids qualitative judgements about whether a particular item is partisan, ideologically biased or 'propagandist' in intention. Any such qualitative assessment would signal little more than a subjective judgement which would itself be vulnerable to allegations of partisanship. What constitutes propaganda is a complex issue, and the attempt to designate a certain item 'partisan' or 'biased' is fraught with difficulties; this point is central, although ignored by Conservative critics. An example will help illustrate the point.

In *Manchester Magazine* (May 1987, p. 8) a sixth of a page was allocated to detailing the revised schedule for dustbin collection in the Manchester area because of delay caused by the two public holidays in May. This was an unequivocally factual piece of reporting of information useful to local residents, and it is hard to imagine that anyone might find such editorial contentious, much less partisan in motivation. The reporting of waste disposal in the *Rochford News*, however, is more problematic. In the issue dated spring 1987, the lead article, which fills the top half of the front page, reports the council's intention to privatize waste collection and street cleaning for the next five years and to issue a contract to the value of £500,000 per annum to a private company. This appears to be a prima-facie case of partisan reporting since the preference of the Conservative Party for private contractors to provide services, with contracts allocated on a competitive tendering basis, rather than local authorities providing services directly, is well established. It therefore seems possible to distinguish the ideological from the merely factual. *Manchester Magazine*'s provision of a timetable for waste collection, it could be argued, is legitimate information, whereas the *Rochford News*'s celebration of the privatization of its waste collection services is 'propaganda on the rates'. Conservative councils like Rochford, however, have a forceful rebuttal to such claims. They are a democratically elected council, and the privatization policy is a democratically agreed policy of council. In publishing information in its civic newspaper, Rochford Council is undertaking no more heinous an enterprise than informing the public about the implementation of council policy. While this reasoning may be persuasive in removing the label 'propaganda on the rates' from such reporting, there can be little dispute that the report in the *Rochford News* was 'more partisan' than the item in *Manchester Magazine*. Judgemental categories such as 'more partisan' are, however, vague and insufficiently precise to allow helpful discriminations to be made between items of editorial in a civic newspaper. This is surely the hub of the issue. At the risk of quoting a cliché, one person's information is another person's propaganda. More substantively, there are no agreed, mutually uncontentious criteria which allow the separation of propaganda from information. The Conservative central government, however, by its advocacy of the Local Government Acts of 1986 and 1988, suggested that it felt able to do precisely this. For government to assume a lofty and censorial position above this inherent relativism displays at best an unjustified and cocky arrogance, at worst an inflexible authoritarianism.

EDITORIAL CONTROL

A final question, but one which is central to the allegation concerning 'propaganda on the rates', is the issue of editorial control. There are really two questions of importance here. Who writes copy for the newspaper? And who decides what will be in the newspaper? Inevitably answers to these questions reveal a range of practices across different authorities, but the questionnaire survey can provide some data to inform discussion and help make some preliminary clarifications about editorial procedures.

In 62 per cent of cases the editorial for municipal newspapers is written by public relations officers, and in a further 26 per cent of newspapers chief executives produce the copy. Forty-eight of the seventy-four newspapers (65 per cent) are written by members of the National Union of Journalists who are current or ex-journalists. Since the craft values of British journalism stress independence and place a high value on the watchdog role for journalism, it is not surprising that these professionals firmly reject allegations that their work is mere propaganda.

So far as editorial control in civic newspapers is concerned, data reveal that public relations and press officers figure predominantly (77 per cent) as occupants of the editorial chair; chief executives assume editorial responsibility for a further 12 per cent of newspapers. The remaining 10 per cent are edited by freelance journalists, a PR consultancy or a local authority public relations subcommittee. The important conclusion to be drawn is that the vast majority of newspapers are produced and edited by non-partisan officers of council and not by elected members attached to a political party. Consequently, allegations of partisanship or 'propaganda on the rates' are presumably similarly directed at officials and not at the elected members.

This outline of editorial control is, of course, simply a snapshot of an institutional structure which ignores possible complexities. The editor may be formally in charge of this structure, but what are the constraints on editorial control? Put slightly differently, may members or officers exert influence upon the editor and thereby editorial content? And, if so, to what degree? It emerged in interview with editors of such newspapers that members and/or officers might influence editorial content in broadly one of three ways. First, they might suggest or initiate stories; second, they might remind the editor of areas of council policy neglected in the newspaper's coverage; and finally, they might have the negative power of veto. Each of these three methods of editorial involvement is discussed below. It is, however, important not to forget a fourth and commonplace possibility, which can be dealt with briefly.

Some public relations officers suggested that editorial autonomy was simply not a problem. The major difficulty about editing a municipal newspaper is not editorial interference, but the reverse: namely, coaxing people to become involved. The problem often quoted was the difficulty in generating copy and getting information from departments. As one PRO suggested, employing a musical metaphor: 'While a one-man band might play a reliable little tune, a duo or quartet would improve the performance.' A different public relations officer claimed: 'It's a long and slow process trying to convince officers that what is a normal day's work for them can be good publicity for the county council.'

The first way in which members/officers may try to influence content of municipal newspapers is by initiating stories. One editor explained that senior politicians or directors often brought copy to the editorial office with a request that 'I would like you to promote issue X, Y or Z.' When asked what sort of weight such a request would carry, the editor replied that often it would guarantee the item's publication. 'Senior politicians, directors of service, senior officers, can apply a lot of pressure,' she confided; 'they have strong claims to space.' Two factors, however, mitigate against a member trying to promote their particular interest. Paramount among these is the independence of the editor. In any month there might be twenty such 'compelling requests', which clearly could not all be met, and the editor would adjudicate between them. One criterion guiding selection would obviously be newsworthiness within the constraints of the newspaper's production schedule. Articles would have a high priority if they would not be newsworthy in the next issue.

Second, competition between members guarantees a limited role for any individual. Councillors will 'jostle among themselves for space', and 'committee chairs will discuss among themselves those issues which they think should be included, prioritize them and pass them down to me. But ultimately I decide.' Editors are the final arbiter of content, but their options are to some degree constrained by the political composition of the council. Inevitably the chairs of major committees are held by members of the controlling group on the council, and this has implications for the frequency with which the three major political groupings are reported in the newspaper. News values, therefore, partly explain the exclusion of the two opposition groups. As an editor explained: 'If we want a spokesperson, we always want a Labour spokesperson because they are the holders of office within the council, they run the committees, they run the council.'

Members or officers may also try to influence the content of newspapers by reminding the editor of areas of council policy which have been neglected in recent issues. Judgements concerning material to be included in civic newspapers, to a much greater degree than their commercial counterparts, are informed by considerations other than news values. A newspaper should, of course, be entertaining and of interest to its readers, but that is not its sole purpose. A local authority newspaper is intended to inform the public about council policy and should in each issue range across a number of policy commitments, perhaps focusing on those which it has identified as important – for example, equal opportunities, housing or social services. Clearly an editor will be unable to include all policy areas in each issue; but if, after a number of issues, housing or social services, for example, has not been featured, the director of that service will undoubtedly contact the editor to point out the 'neglect'. A request from a director to include an item in the newspaper in these circumstances carries a good deal of weight, regardless of the news values of the particular story, since it is endorsed by the editor's need to meet the paper's general objectives of reporting important policy areas.

Finally, members may in some cases veto stories which are highly critical of a policy which is central to the council's overall programme. The exclusion is justified by recourse to the general objectives of the paper, which are to promote council policy. 'If I'm contacted by a Liberal councillor', an editor explained,

> who wants us to carry an article saying how our housing policy on such-and-such an estate has been a complete and unmitigated disaster, I'm not likely to say oh yes, let's go ahead. We're supposed to be promoting the council's policy.

Whether or not exclusion on these grounds is justifiable is a contentious matter and certainly requires acceptance of the prior presumption that the promotion of council policy is legitimate as a comprehensive and overriding objective for a newspaper. The exclusion of certain groups from newspaper coverage, however, is certainly not without precedent. Drawing a comparison with the commercial press, the editor quoted above claimed:

> It's a bit like *The Times* carrying a story about how bad News International is or giving the front page of the *Sun* to the pickets at Wapping to make their case. It's just not going to happen, is it?

In the majority of cases the role of members in editorial matters is not a critical determinant of content. In one local authority, however, members' involvement assumed a more sinister form when the editor was removed for not being sufficiently 'left wing'. Industrial action by some of her colleagues and the support of her NUJ branch proved unable to secure her reinstatement as editor.[16] Clumsy and heavy-handed censorship of this kind deserves to be criticized in the strongest terms, but it is also important to place the incident in perspective as the only occasion, albeit an extreme one, where the involvement of politicians exceeded the largely acceptable role of adviser.

CONCLUSIONS

Three summary conclusions emerge from the preceding discussion.

First, it is unequivocally the case that Labour-controlled local authorities produce more newspapers, more regularly, with more pages, with more lavish and expensive production styles and with higher circulations than their Conservative equivalents. Moreover, Labour newspapers have grown rapidly, with 80 per cent of municipal newspapers established in the last five years being published by Labour authorities.

Second, the contents of Conservative and Labour newspapers are quite different, with Labour emphasizing unemployment and social and welfare issues (policy issues on which the Labour Party nationally is highly critical of central government), which are largely absent from Conservative newspapers. The latter tend to allocate a large part of their editorial space to advertisements and the reporting of leisure activities; the remaining 30 per cent of total space is devoted to much briefer discussion of a narrower range of policy issues than is evident in Labour newspapers.

Third, in the vast majority of cases, overall editorial control rests with officers rather than members. These officers, moreover, are usually public relations specialists who have a professional background in journalism. Members and senior officers may have editorial influence through their ability to initiate stories, but it is limited by competition for scarce space, news values and an editorial commitment to comprehensive coverage of policy areas. On some occasions members may veto content.

Those who allege that local authority newspapers are being used by Labour councils as vehicles for 'propaganda on the rates' may find much evidence in the foregoing to support their case. Most lawyers, however, might argue that whatever evidence exists is at best circumstantial. For their part, local authorities have responded to these charges in one of three ways; the first two involve a denial of the charge, while the third concedes guilt on certain counts but offers mitigating circumstances which warrant dismissal of the case.

First, Labour local authorities can object that Conservative allegations about 'propaganda' are simply so much emotionally charged rhetoric. The purpose of municipal newspapers is to inform the local public about council policy which inevitably reflects the policy preferences of the leading group on council; the latter, because of the democratic electoral mechanism, reflects nothing more objectionable than the electoral preferences of the majority of the voters. On this view municipal newspapers are simply a mechanism through which the public can hold local government accountable by checking its success in implementing voters' policy intentions. Where a preference for Conservative policy predominates among the local electorate and council, the Conservatives enjoy a similar democratic right – some might argue obligation – to inform the public about policy implementation. This is the prize for winning, rather than losing, the democratic game of local politics. It is churlish for the Conservatives, simply because they have lost a succession of local matches, to shout 'foul' and seek to change the rules of the game.

Second, and this elaborates on the first argument, Labour councils have argued that local authorities have not merely an abstract or generalized obligation to inform citizens about policy matters, but a particular brief to offer them information relevant to specific needs. It follows that in areas of bad housing and high unemployment – typically the inner-city areas where Labour authorities predominate – it is appropriate for councils to focus their informational activities on citizens' rights to housing, welfare benefits, social services and so on. As one editor expressed it:

> Unemployment is a recurring theme in our newspaper because it's a recurring theme for 25% of people in the area. We feel we should help them by telling them about the various things that are going on for unemployed people in our area, the various government initiatives about which the council always has a policy, and so therefore it's within our brief to cover it.

This line of reasoning allows Labour authorities to move from the defensive to the offensive by claiming that Conservative councils are neglecting their responsibilities and ignoring legitimate informational needs within their communities. The emphasis on advertising and leisure in Conservative newspapers is of little use to unemployed people with few resources to buy consumer goods or to set aside for entertainment. Municipal newspapers produced by Conservative authorities should, according to this view, begin to emphasize housing, health, unemployment, welfare and social issues and begin to inform local people about their entitlement to benefits and encourage their participation in local affairs.

Finally, Labour local authorities might concede that their municipal newspapers are partial, partisan and focus uncritically on Labour policy, but argue that this is legitimate within the framework of what might be termed a 'liberal' or 'pluralist' theory of the press. The basic assumption of such a theory, albeit crudely stated, is that heterogeneity in the media market is highly desirable. More specifically, it suggests that competition in a free market between the largest possible number of newspapers, promoting the widest possible range of views and opinions and owned by a diverse group of individuals and/or organizations, is the optimum guarantee of a truthful, energetic and efficient press. It is a theory unashamedly based on a simple market model which sees virtue in a plurality of expressed opinions and truth as a consequence of the competition between them. Within the context of this theory a dissenting voice is always welcome, since 'truth', unless constantly challenged by new ideas, can easily regress into orthodoxy. Labour authorities might argue that currently it is orthodoxy which prevails in discussions of local authority affairs. The national press, certainly in its tabloid variant, is conservative by disposition, hostile to local authorities and eager to label, and thereby stigmatize, them as 'the loony left'; the tendency towards monopoly ownership of the national press, moreover, continues apace.

Politically the Conservative Party have held power in central government for more than a decade. During that period they have legally constrained local authority publicity and public relations activities, while employing advertising, marketing and public relations strategies to promote the policies of central government. If, as Conservative politicians suggest, Labour municipal newspapers are partisan, then this is arguably virtue not vice, since such newspapers might serve in some small way to redress the existing imbalance in political discourse and promote that competition of viewpoints which pluralists suggest is necessary to establish 'the truth'.

Chapter 7

Local press reporting of the 1987 general election

The mass media, it seems, can make even the most powerful appear powerless. Even politicians who enjoy a reputation for being 'media performers' profess concerns. 'No Prime Minister', Mrs Thatcher confessed, 'can afford to quarrel with the media, because it is difficult to win.'[1] At a time when elections are judged by politicians and pundits alike to be won or lost on television and in the headlines and editorials of the national popular press, it is perhaps not surprising that many politicians find their relationships with broadcasters and journalists a daunting business.

Some politicians, of course, have more reason than others to express misgivings. The British press is not disinterested in its observations. The 1987 general election was waged by, as well as through, the national press. Speculation in both the tabloid and quality press about the Labour Party's poor electoral prospects and its possible demise subsequent to its electoral defeat was commonplace even before the general election had been called.[2] John Lloyd, writing in the *Financial Times*, felt obliged to deny rumours of an even more significant bereavement – nothing less than the death of socialism itself.[3] Studies of national press coverage of general elections in 1983 and 1987 are diverse in their conclusions, but two consensual points emerge. First, reporting of the general election has typically been accorded a very high news priority in the national press.[4] In the quality newspapers and in some of the tabloids, different aspects of the general election campaign featured as the lead story almost daily during the 3½ weeks of the 1987 campaign period.[5] Indeed, the reporting of the campaign in the national media was so comprehensive that even journalists expressed doubts about 'overkill' in election coverage.[6]

Second, but perhaps more significantly, research confirms the lay observation that national press reporting of general election campaigning has become intensely partisan and in the tabloid press increasingly 'vicious' and 'personalized'.[7] The 1987 general election, at least as it was reported in the national press, has been acclaimed as 'Mrs Thatcher's election', with seven of the eleven national daily papers endorsing her and her party.[8] But even the ostensibly 'non-political' features in tabloids articulate values and sentiments supporting Thatcherism and hostile to the more communitarian mores of socialist ideology.[9]

Yet, if the media can prompt anxieties in the prime ministerial heart, despite such overwhelming endorsement in the national press and the activities of the small army of Conservative Party press officers, hired marketing executives and PR specialists which Margaret Thatacher coordinated, how much more intimidating might media appear to those with less experience of both politics and the media – for example, local politicians trying to communicate with local constituents via local newspapers. In truth, little is known about whether the extent and partisanship of election coverage in the national press are reflected and sustained in local press reporting. Similarly, it is unclear whether local politicians impute to local newspapers and journalists the same ability to influence their political opportunities and outcomes as their national counterparts. Consequently, it is uncertain if, or how, local parties attempt to target newspapers in an effort to exploit them as part of a broader campaigning strategy at the constituency level. Academic studies have neglected the local press, preferring to focus on national newspapers and politicians, and reflecting the widely held view that 'local electioneering has been overtaken by the nationalization of the campaign and the growth of the mass media'.[10]

This chapter addresses some of the questions raised above by reporting the findings of a study of local press coverage of the 1987 general election in ten West Yorkshire constituencies. A particular concern was to explore two aspects of politician/journalist relations in the context of local campaigning in a general election. Expressed broadly, to what extent, and in what way, do local parties try to use local newspapers in constituency campaigning? For their part, how do the local press respond to these party initiatives or, more proactively, initiate coverage of the various candidates and parties in the local constituency contests? These two concerns spawned a number of subsidiary enquiries. Would local newspapers, for example, display the same high levels of interest in the general election as national papers? How might the marginality of a particular contest, or the incumbency status, or the party affiliation of candidates, affect press coverage? Equally, how might parties' previous experience of being reported in the local paper, in and out of election time, or their perceptions of the paper's political commitments, affect their attempts to exploit the local press as part of their overall campaigning strategy?

Three methodological 'tools' were used to generate data for the study. First, extensive semi-structured interviews were conducted with editors and journalists on local newspapers as well as election agents for the three major political groupings (Conservative, Labour, Liberal/SDP Alliance) in the ten West Yorkshire constituencies: Batley and Spen, Bradford North, Bradford South, Colne Valley, Halifax, Leeds East, Leeds North, Leeds West, Pudsey and Wakefield. These ten constituencies were chosen according to four political criteria: the marginality of the particular contest, the incumbency status of candidates, their party affiliation and their seniority within their party and/or their national 'celebrity' status. These were identified as factors which might be influential in attracting media interest in the constituency.

Second, a content analysis was conducted of the weekly paid-for, free and daily newspapers circulating in the selected constituencies for the 3½ weeks of the election campaign. Each of the 1,194 election-related items published (921 articles, 35 editorials and 238 letters) was coded for thirty-eight variables – including partisanship in reporting, status and party affiliation of candidates, subject focus of the item (candidate, national policy or local issues), the type of newspaper (weekly, daily, free), its structure of ownership whether private or chain, the position of the item in the paper, the use of photographs and headlines and the week of the campaign – to assess developments in the quantity and direction of press reporting as the campaign progressed.

Third, election expenses returns were analysed to ascertain proportions of expenditure allocated to different methods of promoting and publicizing the constituency campaign: public meetings, newspaper advertisements, posters, election addresses, leaflets.

LOCAL PARTY CAMPAIGN STRATEGIES AND THE LOCAL PRESS

In the national setting politicians impute great influence to the press to affect electoral fortunes. The Labour Party's decision in 1987 largely to ignore national newspapers and focus on broadcast media was not so much a statement about the presumed inefficacy of the press as a campaigning tool but, on the contrary, an acknowledgement of its influence, which Labour felt had been targeted too frequently against the party.[11] Nationally parties battle against each other to try to influence journalists and thereby to set the electoral agenda.[12] But are politicians as keen to try to influence electoral news agendas at the constituency level? Examination of expenses returns revealed that 'publicity and advertising' were the overwhelming priority for campaign expenditure across all three parties and constituted 70 per cent of Conservative, 80 per cent of Labour and 89.5 per cent of Alliance total expenditure.[13] None of the parties, moreover, devoted more than 3 per cent of expenditure to public meetings, signalling a move away from traditional campaigning methods in the direction of a media-based campaign.[14]

Parties revealed locally a great diversity of attitudes towards the local press and often made quite contrary assessments concerning the potential usefulness of newspapers as an aspect of their constituency campaign strategy. Underlying this diversity, however, four factors seem to structure parties' approaches to the local press. First, the extent to which a newspaper's circulation area 'matched' the relevant parliamentary constituency boundaries was judged to be extremely important. This congruence, or lack of it, in turn had implications for the number and range of papers circulating within a given constituency, the competition between them and parties' possibilities for access to them. A second factor forming parties' attitudes towards the local press was expressed dissatisfaction about their previous treatment by the local newspaper in its reporting of political, especially electoral, affairs. The incumbency or celebrity status of candidates and election agent attitudes towards the local press were the other two factors influential in party attitudes. Each of these will be discussed in turn.

Newspaper circulation areas and constituency boundaries

Parties judged that their potential access to newspapers and therefore the extent to which the local press might form part of their
campaigning strategy were substantially governed by a geopoliti-
cal consideration: namely, the extent to which political and newspaper boundaries or circulation areas overlapped. Four possible
circumstances of newspaper/constituency 'match' were identified.

In constituencies where a newspaper, especially a daily paper,
enjoys a monopoly, high circulation and an extensive local readership – which was the case with the *Halifax Courier* and the
Wakefield Express in Halifax and Wakefield constituencies – access
to that paper becomes a critical issue for the local parties. Strategi-
cally the newspaper is simply too important to ignore. The press
officer for one of the parties contesting the Halifax seat described
the local paper as 'critical' because

> its circulation area coincides almost identically with the con-
> stituency boundary. The *Halifax Courier* goes to virtually every
> house in Halifax and most people read it. So it's the single
> most important media outlet for us and that's the one we
> concentrated on almost exclusively day after day. The *Courier*
> circulates about 40,000 and 25,000 of those will be read in
> Halifax City itself. And 2 to 3 people read each paper, so with
> an electorate of 70–odd thousand that's how important it is.

The *Yorkshire Post* and *Yorkshire Evening Post* illustrate a different, almost entirely reverse circumstance where a single newspaper tries to report the election campaign in a large number of
constituencies (more than seventy) throughout the entire Yorkshire region. Even though the *Yorkshire Post*'s reporting is focused
on Leeds, most election agents even in Leeds considered that the
prospects of 'catching the editor's eye' and securing coverage in
the paper was slim. The Conservative agent for a Leeds constituency expressed with characteristic Yorkshire bluntness her scepticism about the possibility of securing both coverage for her candidate in the *Yorkshire Post* and the interest of the paper's readership
in matters political:

> The *Yorkshire Post* covers a hell of an area and they simply
> don't have the space. If they started putting a report in on the
> 3 or 4 PPCs in every constituency the paper would be full of

nothing but electoral news and then of course nobody would buy the damned thing.

A number of election agents had anticipated that, because the *Yorkshire Post* was a regional paper with a substantial and widespread circulation, it would play what they described as 'the regional newspaper game', tending to focus its reporting on national events and showing interest only in the most senior figures on the local political scene. If their guess was right, this would reduce further any possibilities of access to the paper for campaigning purposes.

In some constituencies there was no local daily newspaper for parties to target. In Batley and Spen, for example, only two weekly papers, the *Batley News* and the *Spenborough Guardian*, circulate within the constituency boundaries, which set severe limits on the scope for local parties' press campaigns. An election agent claimed that the party 'identified the two weekly papers as the major outlets for us. . . . There was going to be one major story a week that we would need to manufacture and place in each of the papers.' Given these circumstances of newspaper/constituency fit, a party's most ambitious projection for its press strategy was to generate six favourable stories in the local press by using six press releases across the entire three weeks of the campaign period.

Finally, a local paper which reports more than one constituency may try to achieve balanced coverage of the parties across a number of constituencies. This can create considerable difficulties for parties trying to target newspapers. A Conservative agent explained the problems eruditely:

> The *Wharfe Valley Times* spreads itself over a number of constituencies. . . . So we've got to watch that a Conservative in another constituency isn't being used to balance up say a Liberal or a Labour here so that we don't get good coverage. . . . In advance of the election we realised that to get good coverage we would have to fight not only the opposition for space . . . but our own Conservative candidates in other constituencies. We would have to produce qualitatively better material if we were going to win space.

In summary, the lack of 'match' between media and political boundaries and the number of newspapers circulating within or across a particular constituency had significant implications for parties' press strategies. In some constituencies the possibilities for access to newspapers were so slight that they became irrelevant in campaigning terms, while in others the existence of a local paper distributed to the home of virtually every voter meant that a media strategy geared to gaining access to that paper was considered to be critical by local parties.

Party dissatisfaction with press electoral reporting

Parties expressed a near-unanimous dissatisfaction with local press reporting of their party and candidate during the campaign; only one of the thirty agents interviewed did not offer a long list of grievances when questioned. For their part, journalists and editors professed an unequivocal commitment to at least a procedural equality of coverage for each party. The *Halifax Courier* designated a journalist to analyse the paper's daily output of election news by measuring text in column inches and counting the number of letters in favour or against particular parties, to check for any imbalances in political reporting. Another editor expressed a commitment to similar routines to guarantee equity across the parties:

> We have very strict rules about the coverage of general and local elections. We are in touch with the political agents before the start of the actual campaign and we outline to them what we propose to do by way of coverage. The three major parties will get the same coverage, and that means the same number of photographs of the same size, the same number of meeting reports, and exactly the same amount of press coverage, and we go to the point of measuring it literally in column inches.

Despite these procedures, parties routinely registered very similar complaints about press reporting. Because the grievances against the press were so widely held, they cannot easily be attributed simply to sour grapes and seem to question Goldenberg and Traugott's observation that 'winners' attributed success to good candidates, while 'losers' attributed their failure to media bias.[15] In many parties, anticipation of poor coverage, based on their previous experiences with local press, did much to curtail their enthusiasms for developing a press media campaign strategy. Parties routinely voiced six complaints against local newspapers.

First, dissatisfaction was prompted by omission in the reporting of candidates. An agent complained that she had issued weekly press releases over the three-year period since her candidate's selection, but not a single one had been published. She had discussed the matter with the editor, who had been helpful in explaining how to compose an eye-catching press release. But following this pedagogic procedure nothing was published. Agents suggested, however, that press reporting in the year prior to the election was crucial to establish the candidate's identity in the constituency. Consequently, failure to report candidates during this period was considered cause for complaint even if coverage during the three weeks of the campaign had been meticulously fair. 'We got some semblance of fair coverage in the end,' a Labour agent complained, 'but only because we were vigilant. . . . But the damage had been done in the 18 months beforehand and in the May elections prior to the General Election. The paper had done their damnedest and succeeded.'

Second, agents complained about newspapers' use of layout and editing techniques, objecting that reports of their candidates were always 'tucked away at the back'; others objected to misrepresentative headlines and the alleged manipulation of the letters page to partisan advantage.

Third, some agents were concerned by inaccuracies in the reporting of candidates, with the wrong name, party or constituency being on occasion attributed to candidates. An SDP agent complained: 'My candidate had been missed off the list of speakers at a public meeting, had been wrongly described as a Conservative candidate and had been wrongly attributed to the Bradford North constituency.' There was a commonly expressed suspicion that such mistakes were too frequent to be mere 'errors'.

Fourth, it was alleged that the press reported some candidates in a highly unfavourable way. In a Bradford constituency the Labour Party agent complained that his candidate had been persistently described as a member of the 'hard' or 'loony' left and that such references were electorally disadvantageous. The Bradford *Telegraph and Argus*, for example, published a quite extraordinary article in the week following the election. The article carried a photograph of the three newly elected Bradford MPs, Pat Wall (who has subsequently died), Max Madden and Bob Cryer, under the headline 'Whatever next! Eating babies?' The text began by claiming: 'Last Thursday night Bradford joined Brent, Lambeth,

Haringey and Greater Manchester as one of those places dominated by the loony left.' The article continued by asking: 'What are our credentials for membership of this elite group of loonies? Well, we've got a Labour council for one thing and our sex equality officers and our gypsy policy together would be enough to qualify Bradford.'[16] It is unclear whether this particular article was intended as a serious piece of journalism or was written with tongue planted firmly in cheek; the latter seems more likely, but a number of points must be made. If it is 'tongue-in-cheek journalism', it does none the less target three Labour MPs, each of whom is politically on the left of the Labour Party. Throughout the election campaign the newspaper referred to two of the candidates as being 'hard' left. Pat Wall received particular admonition as the '54-year-old star villain of Conservative election broadcasts. . . . It is true that he was a founder member of Militant.' The article, moreover, alleged a number of potentially damaging political associations for the Labour MPs concerned – allegations about their anti-democratic intentions and their supposed support for unpopular political parties like Sinn Fein. The Labour agent for one of the new MPs complained to the *Telegraph and Argus*; and it might be presumed that, since he judged the article to be serious journalism, many readers may have done likewise, and that consequently the article could have damaged the reputations of the MPs concerned.

Fifth, party dissatisfaction was evident when agents considered that a local newspaper was giving excessive and/or more favourable coverage to opposition candidates. Invariably most agents felt that the opposition was receiving superior coverage. A Leeds Conservative agent claimed: 'The *Yorkshire Post* was hopeless. . . . We couldn't get anything in but every day there was something about Meadowcroft [the Liberal Alliance candidate];' while an SDP agent in Bradford alleged: 'Coverage of the Conservative Party was fantastic, two or three pages at a time.' The Labour agent compalined that 'On election day itself when the *Batley News* came out I don't think they had a picture of our candidate in . . . whereas the Conservative candidate had three or four photos . . . including one on the front page.'

Finally, agents occasionally denounced local papers for their outright partisanship. Certain newspapers expressed their political preferences unequivocally. The *Heckmondwike Herald*, for example, in its issue of the Friday before the election took the unprecedented step of publishing an editorial in the lead story position on the front page. The editorial, headlined inappropriately in red letters, announced: 'Great Britain, by the Editor'. The text opened:

> Local electors are confronted with a choice between a Socialist or a Conservative vote. The SDP/Alliance, as far as this constituency is concerned, can be written off. . . . No one wants to be taxed higher and for some of that money to be spent on loony left profligacy. . . . Free enterprise with the Conservatives leads to more competition, more jobs, and increased choice and reasonably priced products for the public to buy. . . . Labour policies lead to stagnation, strife, debt and inflation. We unreservedly and strongly urge all our readers to vote for the positive next move forward with Elizabeth Peacock and the Conservative Party. This country and all its people can be made great again.[17]

Editorials are, of course, intended to be opinionated rather than 'balanced', but there were no editorials supporting Labour published in any newspapers.

These six reported aspects of press coverage – omission, manipulation of editorial layout, inaccurate reporting, negative coverage of parties/candidates, excessive and favourable coverage of the opposition parties/candidates and straightforward partisanship – were mentioned singly or in combination by almost every agent. This represents a substantial party dissatisfaction with local press reporting of the campaign. Some candidates offered structural explanations for the differential treatment of candidates similar to those outlined above which focused upon limited opportunities for access; there were simply too many candidates for everyone to get good coverage. Others offered surprisingly pragmatic explanations and conceded that perhaps their candidate lacked the charisma and glamour of others. The overwhelming majority of agents, however, stated that the paper quite simply had partisan attachments which militated against impartial coverage. The allegation seemed self-evident. A Labour agent claimed: 'It's obvious to everyone how biased local papers are. The *Huddersfield Examiner* is a Liberal paper. . . . Coverage has been absolutely diabolical against the Labour Party.' The Conservative agent for the same constituency confirmed that the '*Examiner* is patently

Liberal in its editorial', but added: 'Quite a few of its journalists are Socialists.'

Two important points should be noted about these various allegations concerning press coverage. First, expressed dissatisfaction with press reporting was not confined to a particular party. In one Leeds constituency all agents expressed suspicion of partisan reporting by the *Yorkshire Evening Post*; each agent, however, held a different view about the direction of that partisanship. Second, parties responded to these difficulties in quite contrary ways. Some parties simply gave up on the enterprise, while others persisted and stepped up their efforts since they had no other positive press strategy. Few complained to editors, believing it could make matters worse. 'How can I put it?' an agent speculated. 'You are trying to limit damage. You know what to expect from the paper and you don't want to make it worse. In the end our paper gave us as bad as we'd expected.' Five agents reported complaining to editors with little or no effect. The Conservative Party, following the failure of the Conservative incumbent to secure re-election, complained about two articles on the poll tax published in the *Halifax Courier*. The paper took the complaint extremely seriously and instigated an investigation chaired by an ex-editor of the *Birmingham Post*. But whatever the outcome of any such investigation it is clearly too late to undo any harmful effects of the original reporting.

Local newspapers and local candidates

All parties believed that incumbents or candidates who enjoyed a national reputation were advantaged in gaining access to the local media. A Liberal agent claimed that 'The press will undoubtedly take more notice of you if you can stick the magic letters MP after someone's name.' Agents in all three parties also reported that it was relatively easy to get coverage in both local and national media with a national celebrity. Denis Healey's agent confessed: 'I've had too simple a task. He's so well known. There's this great thing about him, his eyebrows. If anyone just drew two eyebrows on a piece of white paper and asked anyone who it was they could tell you.' In Leeds East, Healey's constituency, none of the parties contesting the seat spent more than a small percentage of their allowed legal maximum. It seems all three major parties considered the outcome a foregone conclusion and were unprepared to 'waste' money.[18] This phenomenon was unique to Healey's constituency, although a number of other seats in the research sample were considered 'safe'.

Agents claimed, however, that generally the press's preference for certain types of story was more important than the merits of particular candidates in securing coverage. Serious or sustained discussions of policy matters, for example, typically came a poor second to more whimsical 'quirky' stories. Consequently, a Liberal agent capitalized on the discovery of someone called Michael Meadowcroft who was invited to meet Michael Meadowcroft MP for a press 'photo opportunity'. One of the more prominent press photographs of Bob Cryer featured him in the driving seat of his vintage car, which he used in the campaign. This press emphasis on the 'quirky' rather than more substantive stories suggests that the amount of coverage candidates receive may be influenced as much by their willingness to comply with the demands of local newspapers for a certain sort of story as by their standing as a celebrity or incumbent.

Election agent attitudes to the local press

The factors outlined above establish the context within which local parties' press strategies are formulated but they detail only the necessary but not sufficient conditions for an effective campaign. Agents' attitudes towards local newspapers proved important in structuring both the extent and duration of the constituency campaign. Two antithetical appraisals of the significance of local newspapers emerged, which, for the sake of convenience, may be termed 'traditionalist' and 'modernist'.[19]

Traditionalists considered the local press unimportant to the outcome of the campaign and knew little about the structure and organization of local newspapers, media audiences or the impact of press reporting on that audience. They judged local newspapers to be largely beyond their control and preferred direct communication strategies such as leafleting and canvassing. Traditionalists were not confined to any particular party or associated with any particular type of candidate, although they seemed to predominate among agents who were older, both chronologically and professionally.

Modernists made a quite contrary assessment of local newspapers. They considered them extremely important to the outcome of the campaign, were usually very knowledgeable about local newspapers and often professed experience of working as a journalist or in public relations. They believed that press content could be influenced by the local party and tended to see newspaper reporting of politics as a consequence of negotiation between political and journalistic personnel. Not surprisingly, it was commonplace in campaigns where modernist attitudes prevailed for the campaign team to include an experienced press officer.

In summary, local parties' assessments of the potential effectiveness of the local press in a constituency campaign seemed to depend upon a range of factors including the status of their candidate, their appraisals of the impartiality of the local press and their judgements concerning the opportunities to gain access to local newspapers. Party agents of a traditionalist disposition, however, on occasion simply judged that the game was not worth the candle and ignored the local press without regard to the possibilities or constraints inherent in their party's media environment.

LOCAL PRESS REPORTING OF THE 1987 GENERAL ELECTION

National press reporting of general elections is characterized by the near-'saturation' coverage which the topic enjoys and a growing partisanship favouring the Conservative Party. The observation of Sidney Jacobson, former editor of the defunct *Daily Herald*, that relations between the government and the press were bad and getting worse, and should under no circumstances be allowed to improve, is sadly nothing more than an anachronism. But how did the local press report the election and how extensive was local coverage of the election? Were the many forms of dissatisfaction expressed by parties about press coverage – concerning alleged partisanship, an emphasis on candidates rather than political issues and a national rather than a local focus to reporting – justified when newspaper content was examined?

The general election was accorded a highly variable news priority across the different types of local newspaper. The regional morning paper, the evening paper, the weekly paid-for papers and the free weekly papers in our survey formed a gently descending hierarchy of interest in election concerns – see Table 7.1.

Table 7.1 Number of items of election coverage

Paper title	Paper type	Circu- lation	Article	Editorial	Letter	Row total
Batley News	Weekly	12,843	29	2	16	47 (3.9%)
Colne Valley Chronicle	Weekly	3,100	23	–	1	24 (2.0%)
Hebden Bridge Times	Weekly	4,000	15	–	8	23 (1.9%)
Heckmondwike Herald	Weekly	12,230	45	4	22	71 (5.9%)
Holme Valley Express	Weekly	5,500	20	–	3	23 (1.9%)
Spenborough Guardian	Weekly	12,230	45	4	22	71 (5.9%)
Todmorden News	Weekly	5,156	21	1	12	34 (2.8%)
Wakefield Express	Weekly	29,380	38	–	2	40 (3.4%)
Wharfedale and Airedale Observer	Weekly	6,000	15	–	–	15 (1.3%)
Bradford Star	Free	109,655	7	–	7	14 (1.2%)
Brighouse, Spen. and Mirfield Advertiser	Free	49,301	–	–	–	–
Colne Valley News	Free	10,200	–	–	–	–
Halifax Shopper	Free	45,000	–	–	–	–
Holme Valley News	Free	10,108	–	–	–	–
Leeds Skyrack	Free	54,134	4	–	1	5 (0.4%)
Leeds Weekly News	Free	216,000	5	–	9	14 (1.2%)
Midweek Extra (Wakefield)	Free	68,300	1	–	–	1 (0.1%)
Spenborough and Calder Weekly News	Free	60,000	1	–	–	1 (0.1%)
Wharfe Valley Times	Free	46,530	32	–	1	33 (2.8%)
Halifax Evening Courier	Evening	36,595	231	4	78	313 (26.2%)
Yorkshire Post	Morning	87,000	389	20	56	465 (38.9%)
Column total			921 (77.1%)	35 (2.9%)	238 (19.9%)	1,194 (100.0%)

At the bottom of that hierarchy were the free newspapers, which seemed largely to ignore the election. Across the 3½ weeks of the campaign the ten free newspapers analysed published only 68 election-related items (50 articles and 18 letters), compared to 348 items in the 9 weekly papers and 778 items in the 2 daily/evening papers. If the *Wharfe Valley Times*, which showed considerable interest in the general election and published 32 articles, was removed from the sample, then the free press would have published only 18 articles across 9 titles throughout the entire campaign. Four free newspapers – the *Colne Valley News*, the *Holme Valley News*, the *Halifax Shopper* and the *Brighouse, Spenborough and Mirfield Advertiser* – carried no election coverage throughout the whole campaign period. Two other free papers, the *Midweek Extra* and the *Spenborough and Calder Weekly News*, which both enjoyed distributions in excess of 60,000, carried only a single item of election coverage. Even the larger free newspapers, the *Bradford Star* (109,655) and the *Leeds Weekly News* (216,000), each reported only a minimal 14 election items, of which 7 and 9 respectively were letters. No editorials discussing the election were published in any free newspapers, and only two items of election coverage appeared on free newspaper front pages. Free newspaper indifference to the election developed apace as the campaign progressed, with the number of items published plummeting from 32 in the second week to a mere 14 in the final week of the campaign.

Free newspapers' lack of interest in the general election seems to support the criticisms often voiced by journalists and editors working in the traditional paid-for sectors of the local press, that 'freebies' are 'thin' on editorial and hard news. One editor, with a discernible lack of measure, described their content as 'rubbish' and argued: 'They only want editorial to fill the gaps round the adverts.' Perhaps more interestingly, if paradoxically, the free press's manifest indifference to the election stands in stark contrast to the image of free newspapers that we presented in Chapter 4 as 'news hungry' and willing, because of their lack of editorial and financial resources, to publish 'information subsidies' in the form of press releases issued by local authority public relations departments or other sources.[20] During the election, however, when political parties both locally and regionally were issuing large numbers of press releases relating to what was the top story of the day in national news agendas, the free press paid the election only scant attention.

The morning daily, the *Yorkshire Post*, displayed by far the most enthusiasm for the election and published extensive coverage of the various constituency campaigns within its circulation area, which encompasses the entire Yorkshire region. The 25 issues of the newspaper analysed contain 465 election-related items, 20 editorials focused on the election and 22 lead stories on the front page featuring some aspect of election news. The general election was the paper's overwhelming news priority for the duration of the campaign.

The evening paper, the *Halifax Courier*, similarly considered the election to be extremely newsworthy. The paper carried 313 election items during the campaign. While an election story formed the headline lead item in only 2 of the 21 papers sampled, a further 11 issues carried a front-page election section, bordered with a thin black line, sporting a specially designed logo and occupying between an eighth- to a half-page. The *Halifax Courier*, unlike the *Yorkshire Post*, published less election items during the final week of the campaign (103 items compared to 131 in week two), when it might have been anticipated that coverage would climax towards election day. This retreat from election stories coincides with, and perhaps reflects, the impact of a strong complaint from the local Conservative Party concerning alleged partisanship in reporting.

The paid-for weekly newspapers, as a distinct category within the local press, published substantially more election material than their free weekly counterparts but less than the two daily papers. The weeklies were, however, extremely variable in the attention they paid to electoral concerns. The *Heckmondwike Herald* and its sister paper the *Spenborough Guardian* both published 71 election items during the campaign and featured the election as the front-page lead in four of the five issues of each paper analysed. The *Batley News* (47 items) and the *Wakefield Express* (40 items) also devoted considerable space to the reporting of the campaign. The *Wharfedale and Airedale Observer* (15 items) and the *Holme Valley Express* (23 items), however, were less enthusiastic about election concerns; but, since these figures represent only four issues of these papers, election news was none the less a relatively high priority even in these latter papers.

A number of other indicators suggest that the local press, with the exception of free newspapers, considered the election campaign deserving of coverage.

First, when election news was reported, it was given a prominent position within the paper. Front-page placings were achieved by 22 per cent of articles in the daily press, 18 per cent in the paid-for weeklies and 4 per cent in the free newspapers. An average 20 per cent of articles were ranked sufficiently newsworthy to be placed on the front page, with a further 63 per cent of items placed between the front and centre pages. Second, a high proportion (29 per cent) of election articles were accompanied by photographs, and 71 per cent of these were placed in the top half of the page. Third, nearly all the newspapers analysed, with the exception of *Midweek Extra*, the *Spen and Calder Valley News* and the four other papers not reporting any election news, designated a particular page or part of a page for election reports. An average of 57 per cent of items were published on these special election pages, but some newspapers made a particular feature of election news; the *Yorkshire Post*, for example, published 70 per cent of its election items on its featured election page.

Finally, local newspaper interest in the election increased as the campaign progressed. The reductions in reporting by free newspapers and the *Halifax Courier* during the final week of the campaign, which were noted above, are hidden by the general increase in reporting by the great majority of newspapers – see Table 7.2.

Table 7.2 Number of items of election coverage in local newspapers across the campaign period

Newspaper type	Week of the campaign			Row total
	First	*Second*	*Third*	
Free	22	32	14	68 (5.7%)
Weekly paid-for	96	106	146	348 (29.1%)
Daily	219	274	285	778 (65.2%)
Column total	337 (28.2%)	412 (34.5%)	445 (37.3%)	1,194 (100.0%)

Another feature of local press coverage over the campaign period is worth noting. The various items of election coverage (editorials, articles and letters) each increased across the 3½ weeks of the campaign, but because they increased differentially, they constituted a shifting proportion of the total number of election items – see Table 7.3. Readers' letters, for example, represented 11.9 per cent of election items in week one, 21.6 per cent in week two, but 24.5 per cent by week three. These data reveal a rapid growth in readers' interest in the election, possibly prompted by the newspapers' earlier reporting.

Table 7.3 Different types of local newspaper election coverage across the campaign period

Item type	Week of the campaign			Row total
	First	Second	Third	
Article	288	311	322	921 (77.1%)
Editorial	9	12	14	35 (2.9%)
Readers' letters	40	89	109	238 (19.9%)
Column total	337 (28.2%)	412 (34.5%)	445 (37.3%)	1,194 (100.0%)

In summary, local newspapers accorded the general election a relatively high priority in their news agendas, and their coverage increased as the campaign progressed. Different types of newspaper displayed quite substantial variations in their coverage of the election, with the daily morning papers showing the greatest commitment to reporting the story, followed by the daily evening paper and finally the weekly paid-for press. For their part, local free newspapers proved an exception to this general treatment of election matters and seemed largely to ignore the campaign and its concerns.

A major concern expressed by parties about press reporting focused not so much on the quantity of published material but on its quality, which was usually measured by the varying degrees of alleged partisanship evident in its content. Measurement and analysis of partisanship in press reporting are a highly complex matter. A number of indicators were used to make an assessment. Each item of election coverage was measured to assess which party formed the predominant focus of the report. Additionally, the number of quotations of spokespersons by the different parties, the number of pictures featuring members of the various political parties and the number of negative and positive appraisals concerning the different parties were counted for each item of election coverage.

The evidence concerning partisanship in press reporting seems rather confusing at first sight, but a number of points are unequivocal.

The Conservative Party enjoyed the lion's share of press reporting of the local election – see Table 7.4. The Conservative Party was the predominant focus of 422 (35 per cent) election items compared to 294 (25 per cent) Labour and 193 (16 per cent) Alliance. The local press emphasis on the Conservative Party cannot, moreover, be explained simply by assuming an abundance of pro-Conservative editorials, reflecting the widely held view – albeit unsupported to date by evidence – that editors in the local press are inherently conservative, at least with a small 'c' – see Table 7.5.

Table 7.4 The predominant party focus of published election items

	Frequency	Percentage
Conservative	422	35.3
Labour	294	24.6
Liberal/SDP	193	16.2
No one	285	23.9
Total	1,194	100.0

Table 7.5 Newspaper focus on political parties by item type

Item type	Conservative	Labour	Liberal/SDP	No one	Row total
Article	317	224	170	210	921 (77.1%)
Editorial	7	15	3	10	35 (2.9%)
Letter	98	55	20	65	238 (19.9%)
Column total	422 (35.3%)	294 (24.6%)	193 (16.2%)	285 (23.9%)	1,194 (100.0%)

When articles reporting election coverage are analysed, to the exclusion of editorials and letters, the same tendency to feature the Conservative Party above its competitors, obtains. Three hundred and seventeen (34 per cent) articles focused predominantly on the Conservative Party, with 224 (24 per cent) and 170 (18 per cent) featuring the Labour Party and the Alliance respectively. Table 7.5 reveals two other points of great interest; the first relates to editorials.

Editorials are surprising mostly by their absence. For only 35 to be published in 10 weekly free, 9 weekly paid-for and 2 daily papers, across the 3½ weeks of the campaign period, is not the level of editorial activity that might have been anticipated given the popularity of the election in national news agendas. The general prevalence of editorializing is actually much lower than even these figures suggest when it is acknowledged that 20 editorials were published by a single newspaper, the *Yorkshire Post*, 4 were published by the *Halifax Courier* and the remaining 11 by the weekly paid-for papers. Equally surprising, because of the imbalance, is the political emphasis of editorials, with 15 focusing on the Labour Party, 7 on the Conservatives and only 3 on the Alliance.

The second point of interest emerging from Table 7.5 is the large number of published letters (98 or 41 per cent of the total) focusing on the Conservative Party. Parties in interview commonly alleged manipulation of the letters page to party advantage, and consequently this finding might reflect partisan letter selection. It may also, of course, reflect a superior Conservative Party organization in providing the local press with a greater number of well-written letters on topics of reader interest. Equally, it may simply reflect a different emphasis in parties' press campaigns to target the letters page.

The Conservative Party's high profile is sustained across all types of newspaper – see Table 7.6. Free, weekly paid-for and daily papers each featured the Conservative Party most prominently in their electoral coverage, this emphasis being most notable in the two daily papers.

Three other indicators help to assess alleged press partisanship. First, the number of quotations by spokespersons of the different parties and referenced in press reporting were counted. Again the Conservative Party seems to have benefited disproportionately from press attention. The local press published 546 quotations by

Conservative politicians in 172 items of election coverage, whereas the Labour Party enjoyed only 413 quotations published in 146 items. The Alliance lagged substantially behind, with 332 quotations in 114 items.

Table 7.6 Focus on political parties by newspaper type

Paper type	Conservative	Labour	Alliance	No one	Row total
Free	22	17	13	16	68 (5.7%)
Weekly paid-for	117	82	53	96	348 (29.1%)
Daily	283	195	127	173	778 (65.2%)
Column total	422 (35.3%)	294 (24.6%)	193 (16.2%)	285 (23.9%)	1,194 (100.0%)

Second, the number of pictures featuring members of political parties, accompanying the different items, was measured. The Conservative Party again opened a considerable lead on its opponents. The local press published 141 pictures of Conservative candidates accompanying 135 items of electoral coverage, compared to equivalent figures of 98 pictures and 92 items for the Labour Party and 89 pictures and 82 items for the Alliance.

To suggest that the Conservative Party has been the major beneficiary of press coverage however, leaves aside any judgement about the political direction of that coverage. The Conservative Party may feature in more articles than the Labour Party simply because local newspapers are either more eager to criticize the party or, conversely, more enthusiastic and positive towards the party. The nature as well as the quantity of reporting is important. None the less the prominence with which parties are featured in, or excluded from, election reporting does have implications for balance and partisanship. The local press's consistent neglect of the Alliance in election reporting, its failure to quote the party's spokespersons with the same frequency as those of the other main parties and the absence of supporting photographic material featuring Alliance members combined to create a substantial imbalance against the Liberal/SDP Alliance in press reporting. There is perhaps some truth after all in the adage that there is no such thing as bad publicity, whereas being consigned to the margins of press coverage may have quite damaging electoral consequences. The routine exclusion of the Alliance, in tandem with the press's tendency to focus reporting on one of the other two parties, helped sustain the impression of a two-party contest in which third parties are patronized as 'trying hard' but with little hope of success. It also confounds, quite unequivocally, editors' protestations of at least a quantitative equality of treatment across the parties.

Table 7.7 Positive appraisals of political parties in local newspaper election coverage

Newspaper	Conservative		Labour		Alliance	
	No. of items	Total comments	No. of items	Total comments	No. of items	Total comments
Batley News	8	12	10	18	3	8
Colne Valley Chronicle	6	27	5	26	5	28
Hebden Bridge Times	4	15	5	16	6	11
Heckmondwike Herald	22	66	15	29	4	7
Holme Valley Express	5	16	5	26	4	27
Spenborough Guardian	22	66	15	35	4	7
Todmorden News	5	17	7	21	8	20
Wakefield Express	11	23	12	28	7	19
Wharfedale and Airedale Obs.	2	4	1	2	2	2
Bradford Star	1	2	2	4	1	1
Leeds Skyrack	0	0	0	0	1	2
Leeds Weekly News	5	11	1	2	0	0
Midweek Extra	0	0	0	0	0	0
Spen. and Calder Weekly News	0	0	0	0	0	0
Wharfe Valley Times	6	16	3	14	3	14
Halifax Courier	49	93	54	109	33	72
Yorkshire Post	89	145	53	90	26	58
Totals	235	513	188	420	107	276

The third indicator of partisanship is therefore critical: the number of positive and negative appraisals of the major political groupings contained in local press coverage.

Significantly, the Conservative Party received 513 positive references in press reporting, compared to 420 for the Labour Party and a mere 276 for the Alliance – see Table 7.7.

Conservatives, however, were also the recipients of more frequent press admonitions; and when negative comments towards each of the parties are analysed, assessments of partisanship become more equivocal – see Table 7.8.

Table 7.8 Negative appraisals of political parties in local newspaper election coverage

Newspaper	Conservative		Labour		Alliance	
	No. of items	Total comments	No. of items	Total comments	No. of items	Total comments
Batley News	13	23	16	38	5	5
Colne Valley Chronicle	7	24	4	6	5	15
Hebden Bridge Times	8	34	6	12	5	7
Heckmondwike Herald	30	75	23	52	9	13
Holme Valley Express	7	24	4	6	5	15
Spenborough Guardian	30	75	23	52	9	15
Todmorden News	13	44	7	14	6	8
Wakefield Express	11	38	9	20	6	10
Wharfedale and Airedale Obs.	2	4	2	4	1	1
Bradford Star	3	4	3	5	3	3
Leeds Skyrack	2	5	0	0	0	0
Leeds Weekly News	0	0	1	2	1	2
Midweek Extra	0	0	0	0	0	0
Spen. and Calder Weekly News	0	0	0	0	0	0
Wharfe Valley Times	8	20	7	12	3	5
Halifax Courier	99	237	65	119	23	36
Yorkshire Post	126	232	171	379	48	70
Totals	359	839	341	721	129	205

There were 839 negative comments directed to the Conservative Party, 721 to Labour and 205 towards the Alliance. The low figure for the Alliance seems to reflect nothing more positive than the relative neglect which the two parties seem to have suffered from the local press throughout the campaign period. It is worth noting, however, that the Alliance is the only political grouping to have received more positive (276) than negative (205) appraisals. The higher Conservative negative appraisal seems at first glance paradoxical. The party generally enjoyed greater press exposure than its competitors and more positive commentary in the press, but suffered a correspondingly high negative appraisal. Perhaps such negative commentary is an inevitable burden for the party in government; the opposition strategy seeks to undermine the credibility of the government's record. Alternatively, it may reflect what Blumler has called 'the modern publicity process', which has, as one of its central features, a tendency for parties to advance their campaign by denigrating the opposition rather than by promoting their own policies.[21] An editorial in the *Halifax Courier* offered a similar analysis, claiming: 'This has been a campaign of negatives. Of character assassination. Of knocking policies rather than promoting one's own.'[22]

The question of the extent of press partisanship becomes a little clearer, however, if the performance of individual papers is examined; aggregate figures for all newspapers sampled tend to hide the nature of particular newspaper reporting.

The *Halifax Courier*, for example, carried only 93 positive appraisals of the Conservative Party, which were more than counterbalanced by 237 negative appraisals. The Labour Party, however, enjoyed 109 positive appraisals by the *Courier* set against only 119 negative appraisals. On this reckoning, the *Halifax Courier* may be judged pro-Labour in its reporting. The *Yorkshire Post* illustrates the reverse case. The Conservative Party scores 145 positive comments and 232 negative comments, while Labour's meagre 90 positive appraisals are offset by a massive 375 negative comments. The *Yorkshire Post* appears to have spoken strongly against the Labour Party in its reporting. If this calculus is repeated for each of the papers listed in Tables 7.7 and 7.8, it becomes clear that local newspapers across West Yorkshire reflected a plurality of partisan commitments in their reporting of the general election. Some papers endorsed the Labour Party in their reporting, others the Conservatives, creating a rough or proximate even-handedness on the part of the local press across the two parties. But while political balance may prevail across a range of newspapers circulating in a number of West Yorkshire constituencies, local parties in particular constituencies must deal with a specific newspaper which may well be partisan in its political coverage.

Moreover, not all items of election coverage reveal equivalent degrees of partisanship – see Table 7.9.

Table 7.9 Number of negative and positive appraisals of parties according to item type

	Conservative Party		Labour Party		Alliance	
	Positive	Negative	Positive	Negative	Positive	Negative
Article	177	251	150	230	94	81
Editorial	9	6	0	27	0	6
Letter	49	102	38	84	13	42

Table 7.9 reveals a proximate parity of local press treatment of the Conservative and Labour parties in election coverage contained in articles, but substantial partisanship in editorializing. The Conservative Party, across the 21 newspapers in the sample, enjoyed 9 editorials in its favour, with only 6 offering criticism. The Labour Party and the Alliance, however, had no editorials in their favour but 27 and 6 respectively against them. Editorials are, of course, extremely important. They embody the newspaper's authentic and essential voice, and accordingly the partisanship reflected in editorials must be judged especially significant.

Local press partisanship in the reporting of the general election was consequently infinitely more complex than parties had imagined, varying across constituencies, newspapers and the type of item reported. Partisanship was also infinitely more ripe than aggregate figures suggest, with newspapers' pro-Labour and pro-Conservative postures cancelling each other out and suggesting a numerical parity of treatment.

The *Yorkshire Post* was undoubtedly the most overtly partisan of any of the newspapers in the sample. Its espousal of the Conservative cause is worthy of closer examination.

The *Yorkshire Post*'s partisanship, as noted above, is evident from the very high number of negative appraisals of the Labour Party published in the routine election coverage. The headlines, carrying the lead stories of the day, however, betray even more clearly the paper's sentiments. Twenty-two of the 25 issues analysed featured election news as the lead story; all 22 supported the Conservative Party – see Table 7.10.

Table 7.10 Headlines in the *Yorkshire Post*, 15 May 1987 to 12 June 1987

Date	Headline
15 May 1987	Mrs Thatcher's battle cry: fight every hour
16 May 1987	Only one choice says Premier: nightmare warning to Britain
18 May 1987	Nine die in mid-air collision
19 May 1987	Big brother computer at city council
20 May 1987	Main parties swing into action: Tory pledge 'power to the people'
21 May 1987	Parties go to war over patriotism: Union Flag 'belongs to the Tories'
22 May 1987	Mrs Thatcher savages opposition parties' defence policies: Britain 'safe only in Tory hands'
23 May 1987	Grammar schools set for return: Labour denounces 11-plus shake-up
25 May 1987	Tories will 'walk it' claims Tebbit: main parties squeeze out Alliance
26 May 1987	'Prison policies laughable' says minister: Hurd pounces on Alliance police split
27 May 1987	Premier says Labour will put Britain in union chains: 'threat of the left'
28 May 1987	'Grevious errors' outburst at defence policy: President's Kinnock bombshell
29 May 1987	'White flag policies' condemned
30 May 1987	Council puts skids under £17 million pound centre
1 June 1987	Parties launch personal attack: Thatcher rides out Labour's offensive
2 June 1987	'Uncaring' Mrs Thatcher fights back: we have the guts – Premier
3 June 1987	For bulldog read the bully boys
4 June 1987	'Hung Parliament on the cards after all': opinion poll jolts Tories
5 June 1987	Yorkshire woman tests Kinnock on unions: Labour gain but Tories stay safe
6 June 1987	Premier's bubbling Britain
8 June 1987	Labour close gap in key marginals
9 June 1987	Reagan in plea over Gulf war
10 June 1987	Thatcher plea to Labour supporters: put country before party urges Premier
11 June 1987	Polls agree on Tory win
12 June 1987	Mrs Thatcher back in Number 10

The *Yorkshire Post*'s support for Conservatism, like the party's own campaign propaganda, was presidential in style and centred very closely around the personality and qualities of Mrs Thatcher. In the headlines cited in the table, where a Conservative politician is mentioned, on only two occasions (Hurd and Tebbit) is it not 'Mrs Thatcher' or 'the Premier'. Similarly, the 25 issues of the paper analysed published 2 photographs of Alliance politicians on the front page, 3 of Labour politicians (including 1 of Kinnock), but 12 of Conservative politicians, 9 of which featured Mrs Thatcher.

The text of the articles beneath the headlines invariably set Mrs Thatcher as the subject of the piece and typically began with 'Mrs Thatcher' or, bestowing on her the authority deriving from her office, 'The Prime Minister'. The language of the reporting was often highly charged, bellicose, uncompromising and adversarial. Military metaphors were deployed with regularity, and consequently politicians were described as 'going to war' and 'attacking' other politicians who, in turn, were 'thrown on the defensive'. The lead article in the *Yorkshire Post* on 16 May 1987 was typical. 'Mrs. Thatcher stormed into the election campaign last night', it announced, 'with ferocious attacks on what she called the "nightmare" of a Socialist government and the dangers of voting for the Alliance.'

The image of Mrs Thatcher in these reports captures neatly the tensions within the authoritarian populism of the new Conservatism and her own leadership style. She is presented as a caring politician – her only fault, if fault it is, being her over-protectiveness towards others and her concern to alert them to the dangers of 'socialism' which may not be readily apparent to them. Yet on 20 May 1987 the *Yorkshire Post* announced her intention to dismantle the state, 'change the face of British politics' and devolve 'power to the people'. Some things in British politics, however, never change, and Mrs Thatcher and Conservatism were identified squarely in reports with the national interest; indeed, they were presented as synonymous. The *Yorkshire Post* lead on 27 May was fairly representative and embraced much of the imagery of the party leader detailed above: 'Mrs. Thatcher launched a sweeping attack on the "socialist" Labour Party last night by saying that Britain could not afford to risk a Labour government or return to union chains.' Two days later a similar lead story combined the caring, protective aspect of Mrs Thatcher's public image with the strong, responsible, militaristic elements in her press persona. Under the headline 'White flag policies condemned', the text claimed that 'Britain's 55,000 front-line troops in Germany would suffer the brunt of a nuclear attack under a "ban the bomb" government, Mrs Thatcher said last night.' The *Yorkshire Post*'s uncritical celebration of Mrs Thatcher's leadership style and Conservative Party policy is also evident in the paper's editorials. On 13 June 1987 an editorial headed 'A great triumph' declared: 'Margaret Thatcher has thoroughly deserved her sweeping victory and an historic third term. . . . It is our opinion that she is in fact as widely admired and respected here at home as she is abroad.' Such unashamed congratulations for Conservatism have no counterpart for the Labour Party (the 'Labour–Marxist coalition party' as the *Yorkshire Post* prefers to call it), with its 'television commercials designed to bamboozle the people' and 'to preach the politics of hate'. Attacks on the Labour Party in *Yorkshire Post* editorials were, like reporting of the Conservative Party, typically presidential in style, focusing on Neil Kinnock and stressing his alleged weaknesses. Mrs Thatcher's strong leadership of the Conservative Party was contrasted starkly in the *Yorkshire Post* with the 'weak' leadership of the Labour Party. Kinnock was 'too lightweight and unclever for the Marxists', who now 'litter the opposition benches of the new Parliament'; and if he 'does not toe the extremist line . . . he will be out on his neck'.[23] His deputy and Shadow Chancellor, Roy Hattersley, was little better. He 'appears to have only the most faltering grasp of economics', but was none the less 'a relatively benign and harmless figure'.[24]

The *Yorkshire Post* alleged, however, that the party was led by a coalition of its 'Marxist wing' and 'powerful left-wing leaders' in the 'trade union movement' who steer it from the back and would compromise Kinnock's ability to implement policies hostile to their interests. Consequently, 'how would the Kinnock government be allowed to control mass secondary picketing and violence at private work places, not least in areas such as Brent?'[25] The 'true face of the new Labour Party' is in reality 'the snarling militancy revealed at recent Labour Party conferences and in many constituencies and town halls'.[26] It constituted nothing less than a terrible conspiracy against the electorate. This quiet, sinister and powerful 'Marxist' leadership was responsible for most that was bad about the Labour Party. It was this group which during the coal dispute tried 'to justify the picket line and pit village violence and seemed to long for a Scargill victory'.[27] They subscribed to defence policies which 'would throw the Western Alliance into confusion and the Red Army marchers into paroxysms of mirth',[28] and an industrial relations policy which sought 'to take away the power that the Tories have given to the workers and hand it back to the trade union barons and their satraps'.[29] Fortunately, the Conservative Party won the election in 1987, and

> Britain has been saved from a disaster course. NATO has been saved from dangerous confusion. The economy has been saved from the ravages of Socialist ideology. The near victory against inflation will not be reversed. The Labour–Marxist coalition party will have to send Mr. Healey off to Moscow to apologise to the Russians for failing to answer their prayers.[30]

These editorial remarks must be judged, at the risk of committing understatement, as far from disinterested in their observations. Party claims of partisanship in reporting are clearly confirmed in some instances. As noted above, the political commitments of local newspapers were not identical, and the overall sample of West Yorkshire papers revealed a very rough balance between the press coverage of the two major parties. In any given constituency, however, the local party may well have been reported by a local paper unsympathetic to its political objectives. Throughout the West Yorkshire region, the Alliance was largely neglected by the local press in its election coverage.

Parties expressed three other concerns about press coverage which can be assessed by the data from content analysis. First, election agents suggested that newspapers might play the 'regional newspaper game' and focus on 'national' to the neglect of 'local' political issues and consequently restrict access opportunities to the newspaper. Second, agents claimed that the focus of election reporting might be on 'gimmicky' or 'quirky' stories about candidates rather than systematic discussion of policy issues. Finally, it was alleged that incumbent candidates and those enjoying a celebrity status locally or nationally might receive disproportionate press attention compared to ordinary prospective parliamentary candidates (PPCs).

Parties' claims that local papers might be swamped by the news agendas of the national papers, and fail to offer their readers a distinctive local agenda, seem initially to be confirmed by the data – see Table 7.11.

Table 7.11 National or local focus of election items

	Frequency	Percentage	Cum. percentage
Local	378	31.7	31.7
National	504	42.2	73.9
Predominantly local	155	13.0	86.9
Predominantly national	157	13.1	100.0

Table 7.11 signals that 55.3 per cent of published election items in the local press were 'national' or 'predominantly national' in focus; but different local papers reveal quite distinctive emphases in their balance between local and national news – see Table 7.12.

Table 7.12 National and local emphases in general election reporting by newspaper

	Local	National	Predom. local	Predom. national	Row total
Batley News	23	10	1	13	47
Colne Valley Chronicle	11	7	5	1	24
Hebden Bridge Times	7	4	7	5	23
Heckmondwike Herald	22	14	19	16	71
Holme Valley Express	10	7	5	1	23
Spenborough Guardian	22	14	19	16	71
Todmorden News	13	6	5	10	34
Wakefield Express	16	6	6	12	40
Wharfedale and Airedale Obs.	13	—	1	1	15
Bradford Star	2	5	3	4	14
Leeds Skyrack	2	1	1	1	5
Leeds Weekly News	—	11	3	—	14
Midweek Extra	1	—	—	—	1
Spen. and Calder Weekly News	1	—	—	—	1
Wharfe Valley Times	9	6	9	9	33
Halifax Courier	136	86	46	45	313
Yorkshire Post	90	327	25	23	465
Column total	378	504	155	157	1,194

The morning daily paper, the *Yorkshire Post*, is overwhelmingly national in orientation to news and confirms agents' speculations that it might play the regional newspaper game. Seventy per cent of published items were national in emphasis, with a further 5 per cent of election news being 'predominantly national'; only 25 per cent of items are classified local or predominantly local. By contrast, the other daily, the evening paper, the *Halifax Courier*, displays a preference for a local emphasis in election reporting. Forty-three per cent of stories are local, with a further 15 per cent predominantly local, whereas only 27 per cent and 14 per cent of items were judged national or predominantly national respectively. The local emphasis of the *Courier* is confirmed by its headlines and lead stories during the campaign. Eighteen of the 21 papers sampled featured lead stories which were local in emphasis; only 2 featured election stories.

The paid-for weekly press revealed an even greater preference for local news, with the *Wharfedale and Airedale Observer* featuring 86 per cent local stories, a further 7 per cent predominantly local and no stories with a wholly national focus. Even the *Heckmondwike Herald* and the *Spenborough Guardian*, with a lower-than-average emphasis on purely local news, published a majority of stories with a local flavour when the 'predominantly local' items were included.

The balance between national and local news in the free press is hard to assess because of the paucity of published election materials. *Leeds Weekly News*, however, published 78 per cent national stories, and the *Bradford Star* 63 per cent national or predominantly national stories, but these figures – untypical for the free press – probably reflect little more than the extent to which these free papers are composed by 'lifting' items from their sister daily papers in the same chains – the *Yorkshire Post* and the *Telegraph and Argus*.

In summary, local newspapers tend to reveal varying preferences for national news. The morning regional *Yorkshire Post* is by far the most national in its orientation to news, followed by the daily evening paper and finally the paid-for weeklies. The majority of free newspapers in the sample emphasized local aspects of the election where they reported it, but the editorial influence of chain membership was clear in some instances.

These newspaper preferences for local or national foci in news reporting are complicated, however, when, across all types of newspaper, different item types (editorials, letters, articles) reveal statistical correlations with distinct national or local emphases – see Table 7.13.

Table 7.13 National and local emphases in general election reporting by item type

	Local	National	Predom. local	Predom. national	Row total
Article	332	338	122	129	921 (77.1%)
Editorial	4	27	2	2	35 (2.9%)
Letter	42	139	31	26	238 (19.9%)
Column total	378 (31.7%)	504 (42.4%)	155 (13.0%)	157 (13.1%)	1,194 (100.0%)

Editorials are overwhelmingly national in orientation. In large part, this reflects the twenty editorials in the *Yorkshire Post*, with its substantial national focus. None the less 82 per cent of editorials are national or predominantly national in focus, compared with equivalent figures of 69 per cent and 50 per cent for readers' letters and journalists' articles respectively. These data suggest a disjuncture between readers' and journalists' interests. Readers (judged and identified by their letters) seem relatively more interested in national than local matters, while journalists (judged by the news values and content of their articles) seem to prefer a more local focus to election news. For their part, editors appear to be more in touch with their readers' concerns than their colleague journalists'.

A second concern expressed by parties suggested that the press might focus on candidates rather than political issues and might prefer 'gimmicky' stories rather than considered discussions of policy matters. On both accounts the data offer some, but limited, support for party claims. Sixty-seven per cent of published items, for example, focused predominantly on political issues rather than candidates. However, reporting was less issue-oriented than appeared at first when the foci of different types of reporting were analysed – see Table 7.14.

Table 7.14 reveals that, while the majority focus of newspaper articles remained political issues, 354 or 39 per cent of articles were none the less candidate-based. It is editorials (32 or 91 per cent) and readers' letters (201 or 88 per cent) which are overwhelmingly concerned with political issues, again indicating the possibility of differences between journalists' and readers' interest in candidates and political issues.

Table 7.14 Focus on candidates or politics in election reporting by item type

	Candidate	Politics	Neither	Row total
Article	354	565	2	921 (77.1%)
Editorial	3	32	—	35 (2.9%)
Letter	37	201	—	238 (19.9%)
Column total	394 (33.0%)	798 (66.8%)	2 (0.2%)	1,194 (100.0%)

Party concerns that the press might focus on the more trivial or gimmicky aspects of candidates issues, rather than offering serious discussion of the campaign, similarly receive only qualified support from the data, with only 230 (19.3 per cent) of items classified as gimmicky. When the type of item (article, letter, editorial) is analysed, however, the picture is slightly modified. While the majority of articles (699 or 75 per cent) emphasized serious discussion of campaign issues, a substantially larger proportion of editorials (34 or 97 per cent) and letters (231 or 97 per cent) were focused upon various issue aspects of the campaign, suggesting a more 'serious' reader engagement with electoral matters.

Finally, parties expressed the belief that the local press might focus disproportionately on incumbent candidates and those who enjoy a certain celebrity status in the locality or, less commonly, nationally, at the expense of ordinary prospective parliamentary candidates (PPCs).

Papers did reveal some preference for incumbent candidates. Excluding minority candidates, there were 30 main candidates in the ten constituencies, of whom 6 were incumbents: 4 Conservatives, 1 Alliance and 1 Labour. Consequently, excluding other considerations, it might be expected that 20 per cent of items would focus on incumbents. Incumbents, however, were featured in 319 (26.7 per cent) of items. Incumbents feature more frequently and disproportionately in articles, when the different items of election coverage are analysed, with 277 (30.1 per cent) of 921 articles focusing on incumbents – 50 per cent higher than the figure which might have been anticipated. This may simply reflect other inequities in reporting. Four incumbents were Conservative, and, given the press prominence accorded to the party noted above, it may be that the preference shown to incumbents simply reflects Conservative Party predominance in press reporting.

What is striking is the relative neglect of PPCs in the press reporting. Twenty-five candidates (80 per cent) were PPCs but they featured in only 474 election items (39.7 per cent). Again, PPCs were more likely to appear in articles (429 or 46.6 per cent) rather than editorials (1 or 2.85 per cent) and letters (44 or 18.5 per cent); but none the less the figure of 47 per cent is well below the 80 per cent of all candidates in the field which they represent. The local press seems to have judged PPCs to be only marginally newsworthy.

Party expectations that the local media might focus on political 'celebrities' was, interestingly, both confounded and confirmed. Local candidates who enjoyed a national reputation made only scant appearances in the local press – see Table 7.15. Another analysis found, however, that national political celebrities brought in to bolster the campaign of local candidates featured in 48 per cent of all items.

Table 7.15 Local/national parliamentary celebrity featured within the item

	Frequency	Percentage	Cum. percentage
Healey	33	2.8	2.8
Shaw	9	0.8	3.6
Meadowcroft	7	0.6	4.2
Cryer	19	1.6	5.8
Healey/Shaw/Meadowcroft	1	0.1	5.9
None	1,124	94.1	99.9
Meadowcroft/Cryer	1	0.1	100.0
	1,194		

CONCLUSIONS AND SUMMARY

In 1987 local parties approached the local press with justifiable trepidation. They consider local newspapers often unsympathetic, if not hostile, to their political objectives and consequently perceive them as partisan in their coverage of electoral matters. Some local parties also reveal great sophistication in their understanding of the way the structure of the media and political organizations can militate against their possibilities for gaining access to the local press as a vehicle for their campaign propaganda. In brief, they regard local political communications as an uphill task; opportunities are few, and the local press may be partisan. The task, however, can be marginally ameliorated if the party selects a candidate who displays certain characteristics such as incumbency or celebrity status within the constituency.

The content analysis of press coverage confirmed some party suspicions – for example, concerning partisanship – although it also revealed that the allegations of partisanship are not as readily or simply proved and are infinitely more complex than parties imagined. Varying degrees and directions of partisanship (measured in part by the balance between negative and positive appraisals of parties in press reporting) were discernible in different newspapers and types of election coverage – that is, articles, letters and editorials. Across the entire sample of newspapers, a degree of political balance prevailed, but it seems clear that in particular constituencies local parties faced politically hostile newspapers. Editorials generally were stridently partisan, and yet on other matters – their emphasis on political issues rather than candidates, their preference for serious engagement with issues rather than quirky stories and their orientation towards national aspects of the campaign – they achieved a greater proximity to readers' interest and concerns in election matters than their journalistic colleagues managed. To some extent, journalists seemed keen to present their readers with a diet of local news, while the latter's news agendas seemed more structured by national concerns. Again the relationships are highly complex, with different newspapers expressing varying attitudes to each of these matters.

What is unequivocal is the overall high news priority given to the election issue. The daily morning paper devoted most coverage to election matters, followed by the evening paper and finally the weekly paid-for press. The local free press largely ignored the election. Interestingly, the same rank ordering of newspapers which characterized the extent of election coverage was also evident in newspapers' national orientation towards news and the degree of partisanship evident in reporting. Papers publishing the most prolific election coverage were also the most partisan and national in orientation towards election news.

Similarities between local and national press reporting of the general election are therefore quite clear and reflected both in the high profile accorded to election news and in the partisanship with which it was reported. There are, however, enormous differences in the way the story was treated in local and national news agendas. The local press obviously reported the campaign in local constituencies in much greater detail than the national press and, despite its commitments, displayed a much greater ideological pluralism than was evident in the national press. Few local politicians, compared to their national counterparts, felt that their success or failure in the election rested in any great part on the content of local newspaper headlines. Local parties are, however, becoming increasingly aware of the campaign potential of the local media, and many parties targeted local newspapers as part of their overall campaigning strategy. Local party campaigning via local newspapers seems bound to proliferate.

The local press: what future?

Writers who have studied the local or community press have tended to focus on its localism to provide a special framework for understanding its essential nature. Explanations of the local press and what it does are typically given in terms of the way relationships between local politics and business interact with the producers of the local paper, which results in a special type of journalistic output – the local newspaper. Macroscopic issues such as ownership of the media, technological change and ideological hegemony, which are the routine concerns of analysis of the mass media, are ignored.

Our examination of the British local press indicates that no explanation of its nature can be successfully formulated in terms of purely local factors. Such a formulation may have seemed to be adequate three decades ago, when the traditional local and evening paid-for newspaper was the only form of the local press. This had been in existence for more than a century, generally in the same form, even though papers may have been subsumed into regional or even national chains. The mahogany-panelled offices, the massive rattling presses and the Linotype machines, with their hanging pots of molten lead and pressed-brass manufacturers' name-plates on them, were a solid physical metaphor for the continuity and stability of the local press.

The content of such papers, heavily reliant on the local government structure which then encapsulated the police, the fire brigade, the ambulance service and the medical officer of health, provided a construct of a local community as a neatly defined polity coterminous with the circulation area of the local newspaper. This local government structure was a source of organized events in terms of council meetings and elections which provided a regular supply of narrative accounts of the democratic process. It provided ritual events associated with the mayor, the mayoress's charity and the bench of aldermen which constructed the idea of a community as the basis for the polity; and through its minutes, its reports and the activities of its public relations departments it provided an account of itself which the press could then process into news. The local press and local government were thus both engaged in the production of the idea of a community for the differing but coincidental contingent interests of the personnel of each.

There was a large overlap of worthies between this local government structure and the local parts of the legal system and central government structures. Magistrates were based on small localities and were often councillors and aldermen. Many of the individuals on hospital management boards were the same as those on the council and on the bench of magistrates. The routine activities of these agencies and the special rituals they organized were all part of the depiction of the local community which the press routinely constructed.

In the same way, churches, schools, allotments and garden societies, amateur dramatics groups, CND branches, covens of naturists, rings of Rotarians, fraternities of farmers, players of football, cricket, lacrosse, bowls, darts and baseball, and teams of harriers looked to the local newspaper to provide them with publicity, while the paper looked to them for readers. The names of such voluntary organizations would typically be derived from the place-names of their areas of membership, and these would be derived from the local government structure, in terms of the name of either a town or a ward.

Local newspapers defined their markets in readers in terms of such local polities: the *Congleton Chronicle*, the *Swinton Journal*, the *Coventry Standard* or the *Huddersfield Examiner*. The newspaper gave advertisers access to these readers. The main source of income for the local press was and is advertising fees. The limit on journalistic activity was that it had to be undertaken at a minimum cost, which would be less than the income from cover sales and advertising, but that it would be sufficiently well done to maximize readership, and therefore both cover sales and advertising revenue. The outcome of this situation was one in which the coverage of local life was the outcome of interaction between the press and a limited number of local 'spokespeople'. This produced a version of the life of the locality which enhanced the status quo. It reproduced in the form of neatly packaged narratives the versions of events promulgated by these spokespeople. It constructed their rituals as the rituals of 'the community', and reinforced the significance of the boundaries of local government units with the notion that they defined an area with a strongly defined and particular character and special local interests.

It was possible to see this depiction of the local press purely in terms of local forces and a local market, and as part of a stable set of relationships which could adequately be understood in terms of these factors. Our account of the local press in Thatcherite and post-Thatcherite Britain shows that this is not so, however, and the reasons for this can be adduced under three headings: changes in the nature of the politics and structure of local government; the effects of new technology; and the operation of the market. We will examine these factors in order.

POLITICAL CHANGE

In the early 1970s the Heath government changed the structure of local government in Britain by eliminating many of the smaller local authorities, which were subsumed into a system which left the county councils intact but introduced large metropolitan counties for the major conurbations. The pattern was similar to that established by the Macmillan government ten years earlier in forming the Greater London Council. Both of these reforms were supported by Margaret Thatcher but opposed by the Labour Party.

By the 1980s, however, the gradual movement of the wealthier sections of the population to the countryside meant that Labour began to gain control of these larger metropolitan counties, and Mrs Thatcher developed an enthusiastic loathing for what she had so recently helped to bring into existence. Labour in the meantime had learned to love what it had previously wanted to smother at birth. The Thatcher government promptly set about the elimination of the metropolitan counties.

The net effect of the Local Government Act (LGA) 1986 and the subsequent Local Government Finance and Housing Acts has been to hijack many of local government's key functions to an increasingly centralist state located in Whitehall and Westminster.

Consequently, the neat definitional equation of local government boundaries with the circulation areas of local newspapers has been eroded. A major consequence of this development is that local newspapers have been deprived of their bread-and-butter news sources. We can identify cases where the elimination of local authorities has been followed fairly rapidly by the closure of local weekly newspapers.

One of the responses to this process of downgrading local government has been the attempt, especially by Labour authorities, to mount a propaganda counter-offensive by developing public relations departments and producing their own magazines and civic newspapers. These publications constitute one of the alternatives to the traditional commercial local press. Since 1988, however, the municipal press has been subject to considerable pressures, reflecting the financial squeezing of local authorities and the impact of controls imposed by central government against the so-called 'propaganda on the rates' – a principle which does not seem to extend to 'advertising on the taxes' so widely practised by central government.

We are arguing that the secular process of political centralization over the past two decades – undertaken by the Conservatives in government, opposed by Labour in opposition but left unaltered by them when in government – has removed one of the elements in the apparently stable structure of the traditional local press. In particular, the traditional local weekly press was especially dependent on the borough, urban district and rural district councils: precisely those authorities which have been removed.

NEW TECHNOLOGY

New technology had two clear and visible consequences from the early 1970s. It seemed to promise a greater variety in the nature of the local press, because the end of hot-metal typesetting and printing reduced the set-up and running costs involved in newspaper and magazine production. There was a gradual growth of commercial free newspapers and of an alternative radical press. As we have shown, the free newspaper expansion came primarily from the activities of business people with little or no background in newspaper production. They were motivated primarily by the profits available from advertising. Such publications often had their origins in property guides financed by estate agencies. Even where newspapers were clearly the prime concern, as in the case of Eddie Shah's free newspapers, the Messenger Group, and *Today*, the enterprise was driven by concern for production innovation rather than for the content of the papers. This may explain its failure.

The alternative press, as we have shown, expanded as a cooperatively owned and radically inclined local press which produced forms of writing, an articulation of concerns and a method of reporting based on investigation and campaigning which had not previously been a characteristic of any section of the provincial newspaper industry. But although much energy was injected into this sort of activity, the alternative press has remained marginal and has generally lost its radical character. One of the reasons for this is the decline in the activities of local authorities and the squeeze on their expenditure. Such magazines often received grants from local Labour councils and were often dependent on advertising revenue from the same source. Bereft of most of this support, most alternative magazines have now had to seek the income elsewhere.

THE MARKET

To understand what has happened to the free press, the alternative press and the traditional local newspaper we need to look at the way the market affects newspaper production, distribution and ownership. The only way that newspapers increase their income is by selling more copies and by increasing the amount of advertising space they sell. Income from sales accounts for only 13 per cent of total revenue; it is therefore clear that any major increase in income must come from increased advertising. The key to this is to increase the number of readers for whom the paper gives access to advertisers. Three strategies have been used by the owners of newspapers to succeed in this endeavour: a move to free newspapers; the expansion of the circulation area of newspapers; and buying up competing newspapers and newspaper chains, especially in adjacent areas. Large traditional newspaper firms have bought up competing free newspapers or have started their own to beat off the competition.

But newspaper publishers do not simply wish to increase their income; their prime concern is profit and market control. Profit is increased by reducing costs, and reductions in labour costs have been achieved by rationalization of groups of small newspapers into single entities, sometimes with district news sections. This reduces wage and distribution costs, fits in with the centralizing tendencies in politics and, by establishing monopoly over larger districts, provides the firm with market control and stability. At the same time, the power of the trades unions has been weakened so that reductions in personnel, new technology agreements and resistance to wage increases have been made easier and have given the owners and managers control over the labour market.

Members of the alternative press have had to seek their survival through increased advertising and have either gone under or moved into areas of journalism primarily concerned with entertainment, consumerism and style. Meanwhile, the pull of labour-market forces on journalists and graphic designers working in this field has always drawn them towards national magazines and to the broadcast media.

The consequence has been that, while the traditional local press has declined, the variety which promised to engulf it has proved illusory. A new sort of commercial local press has developed: owned by conglomerates, driven by the need for advertising, employing fewer journalists who are low-paid and producing news which is geared to low-cost production in the interests of sustaining more advertising.

The localism of the local press is increasingly illusory; the market, ownership, the political system and cultural influences such as notions of style are increasingly homogenized and centralized. There is in prospect no visible countervailing tendency which would suggest a reinvigoration of the local press as a means of scrutinizing or informing a system of local politics which has been stifled and undermined.

All of these developments are to be regretted, since vibrant and autonomous local government in tandem with an independent and well-resourced local press are important ingredients of a democratic polity. What is interesting to note is how little comment these developments have occasioned from academic scholars interested in media studies or from politicians who have recently shown increasing interest in press standards and quality. At the national level there has been a lively debate about the extent to which competition and market forces should be left unfettered by statutory intervention at a time when standards of journalism, not to mention of common decency, are said to be falling rapidly. Recent Labour Party conferences have supported motions advocating limited ownership of the national press and the establishment of funds to support newspapers offering an alternative moral and ideological diet to the right-wing racist pornography pervasive in the national tabloids. Private members' bills seeking a right of reply and to protect citizen privacy prompted government promises of an enquiry and the Calcutt proposals for a statutory press council with powers to guarantee such matters. It is perhaps testament to the extent to which most academic observers and politicians regard the local press as insignificant that they have not considered extending such proposals into local media arenas. We would argue that an ailing, but not terminally ill, local press would be revitalized by a fund established to support local newspapers offering an alternative to the existing bill of fare; by restrictions on monopoly ownership of the local press; by guaranteed working conditions and rights for journalists (not least to belong to a trade union); and by the establishment of a critical watchdog press council, funded from sources other than the Newspaper Society, with a specific brief to monitor the quality and journalistic integrity of the local press. The executive body of the Press Complaints Committee established in January 1991 contains only a single editor from the regional press. We suggest that these measures would help improve journalistic standards of the local press, the quality of local democracy and, because Britain is ultimately a unitary state, the nature of democracy within the polity as a whole. These are ambitious aspirations, but what we are proposing is the first dose of medicine long overdue but necessary to get the patient back on its feet.

We gratefully acknowledge the valuable assistance of Sandra McTaggart who conducted the content analysis of newspapers on which some of the discussion in this chapter is based.

Municipal free newspapers in England, Scotland and Wales for general distribution

Authority	Type of authority	Political control	Paper's name	No. of years published	Frequency
Aberdeen	District	Labour	Bon Accord	4	Quarterly
Avon	County	Labour	Avon Report	13	Monthly
Barnet	London borough	Cons.	Barnet Borough News	7	Monthly
Basildon	District	Cons.	Link	20	Monthly
Blackburn	District	Labour	Shuttle	4	Monthly
Boston	District	Cons.	Boston Gazette	1	Monthly
Buckinghamshire	County	Cons.	Swan	10	3 issues per annum
Calderdale	M. district	Labour	Annual Report	5	Annual
Cambridge	District	Labour	City Herald	2	Quarterly
Camden	London borough	Labour	Camden Magazine	4	Monthly
Carlisle	District	Labour	Council News	5	Annual
Chester	District	Cons.	Morning News	5	Quarterly
Chesterfield	District	Labour	Our Town	1	Bi-monthly
Chester-le-Street	District	Labour	District News	12	Annual
Coventry	M. district	Labour	Coventry Contact	3	Quarterly
Cumbernauld and Kilsyth	District	Labour	District News	19	Annual
Cumnock and Doon Valley	District	Labour	District Reporter	3	Biannual
Derbyshire	County	Labour	Insight	4	Quarterly
Derbyshire, North East	District	Labour	NED News	5	Bi-monthly
Dundee	District	Labour	Update	2	Biannual
Durham	County	Labour	Durham County Reporter	10	Biannual
Dyfed	County	Labour	Annual Report	4	Annual
East Hampshire	District	Cons.	Envoy	3	3 issues per annum
East Kilbride	District	Labour	Newsletter	8	Annual
East Lothian	District	Labour	Focus on East Lothian	4	Quarterly

Authority	Type of authority	Political control	Paper's name	No. of years published	Frequency
East Yorkshire	District	Cons.	Newsletter	13	Quarterly
Eastleigh	District	Cons.	Progress	12	Annual
Edinburgh	District	Labour	District News	1	10 times per annum
Fareham	District	Cons.	Fareham Today	3	Biannual
Gosport	District	Cons.	Gosport Coastline	17	Biannual
Guildford	District	Cons.	Annual Review	10	Annual
Hackney	London borough	Labour	Hackney Herald	7	Bi-monthly
Harlow	District	Labour	Harlow News	20	Monthly
Hertsmere	District	Cons.	Hertsmere Connection	13	Biannual
Horsham	District	Cons.	Horsham District News	2	Annual
Hounslow	London borough	Labour	Your Hounslow	12	Quarterly
Hull	District	Labour	Civic News	2	Bi-monthly
Ipswich	District	Labour	Angle	2	Monthly
Islington	London borough	Labour	Islington People	1	Monthly
Knowsley	M. district	Labour	Knowsley News	13	Quarterly
Leicester	District	Labour	Leicester Link	2	Monthly
Lewisham	London borough	Labour	Outlook	14	Monthly
Longborough	District	Labour	Longborough News	13	3 times per annum
Maidstone	District	Cons.	Maidstone Borough News	8	Weekly
Manchester	M. district	Labour	Manchester Magazine	24	Monthly
Middlesbrough	District	Labour	Middlesbrough News	11	Quarterly
Newcastle	M. district	Labour	City News	6	Quarterly
Norwich	District	Labour	Norwich Citizen	1	Quarterly
Nottingham	District	Labour	Nottingham Arrow	8	Monthly
Nuneaton and Bedworth	District	Labour	N&B Civic News	12	Annual

Authority	Type of authority	Political control	Paper's name	No. of years published	Frequency
Reading	District	Cons.	Reading Revue	2	Monthly
Redbridge	London borough	Cons.	Redbridge Newsletter	3	Biannual
Redditch	District	Labour	First issue? Sept. 1986		Quarterly
Rochford	District	Cons.	Rochford News	7	Quarterly
Scunthorpe	District	Labour	Scunthorpe Scene	4	Biannual
Sefton	M. district	Cons.	Sefton Citizen	1	Annual
Sheffield	M. district	Labour	Sheffield News	7	Monthly
Slough	District	Labour	Slough Citizen	3	Biannual
Southend on Sea	District	Cons.	Civic News	3	Quarterly
Southwark	London borough	Labour	Southwork Sparrow	6	Monthly
Stafford	District	Cons.	Civic News	4	Biannual
Stirling	District	Labour	Stirling Tribune	7	Quarterly
Stockton	District	Labour	Stockton News	5	3 times per annum
Strathclyde	Regional council	Labour	Strathclyde Reporter	12	Bi-monthly
Sunderland	M. district	Labour	In Touch	15	Monthly
Thamesdown	District	Labour	Thamesdown News	13	Monthly
Thurrock	District	Labour	Thurrock Talk	1	9 times per annum
Tonbridge and Malling	District	Cons.	Here and Now	13	Quarterly
Warrington	District	Labour	Warrington News	6	Quarterly
Watford	District	Labour	Watford Our Town	17	Bi-monthly
Waverley	District	Cons.	Waverley News	6	Biannual
Welwyn	District	Labour	District News	13	Bi-monthly
Wigan	M. district	Labour	Wigan Metro News	13	Biannual
Wrekin	District	Labour	Wrekin Report	6	Bi-monthly

West Yorkshire newspapers monitored for study of local press coverage of 1987 general election

Paper title	Proprietor	Status	Paper type	Circulation/ distribution	Constituencies covered
Batley News	United Newspapers Plc	Chain	Weekly	12,843	Batley and Spenborough
Colne Valley Chronicle	Huddersfield District Newspapers	Independent	Weekly	3,100	Colne Valley
Hebden Bridge Times	Halifax Courier Ltd	Independent	Weekly	4,000	Halifax; Calder Valley
Heckmondwike Herald	John H. Hirst & Co. Ltd	Independent	Weekly	12,230	Batley and Spenborough
Holme Valley Express	Huddersfield District Newspapers	Independent	Weekly	5,500	Colne Valley
Spenborough Guardian	John H. Hirst & Co. Ltd	Independent	Weekly	12,230	Batley and Spenborough
Todmorden News	Halifax Courier Ltd	Independent	Weekly	5,156	Halifax
Wakefield Express	Yorkshire Weekly Newspaper Group	Chain	Weekly	29,380	Wakefield
Wharfedale and Airedale Observer	William Walker & Sons, Otley, Ltd	Independent	Weekly	6,000	Leeds West; Leeds East; Leeds North-East
Bradford Star	Westminster Press Group	Chain	Free	109,655	Bradford North; Bradford South
*Brighouse, Spenborough and Mirfield Advertiser	John H. Hirst & Co. Ltd	Independent	Free	49,301	Batley and Spenborough
*Colne Valley News	Huddersfield Examiner Ltd	Independent	Free	10,200	Colne Valley
*Halifax Shopper	Halifax Courier Ltd	Independent	Free	45,000	Halifax
*Holme Valley News	Huddersfield Examiner Ltd	Independent	Free	10,018	Colne Valley
Leeds Skyrack	Yorkshire Weekly Newspaper Group	Chain	Free	54,134	Leeds West; Leeds East; Leeds North-East
Leeds Weekly News	United Newspapers Plc	Chain	Free	216,000	Leeds West; Leeds East; Leeds North-East

Paper title	Proprietor	Status	Paper type	Circulation/ distribution	Constituencies covered
Midweek Extra (Wakefield)	Yorkshire Weekly Newspaper Group	Chain	Free	68,300	Wakefield
Spenborough & Calder Weekly News	United Newspapers Plc	Chain	Free	60,000	Batley and Spenborough
Wharfe Valley Times	Ackrill Newspaper Group	Independent	Free	46,530	Leeds West; Leeds East; Leeds North-East
Halifax Courier	Halifax Courier Ltd	Independent	Evening	36,595	Halifax; Calder Valley
Yorkshire Post	United Newspapers Plc	Chain	Morning	87,000	All Yorkshire constituencies

*Newspapers which contained no articles concerning the 1987 general election.

Notes

1 THE LOCAL PRESS: DEFINING THE NEW BOUNDARIES

1 See e.g. D. Murphy, *The Silent Watchdog: The Press in Local Politics*, London, Constable, 1976; R. Burke, *The Murky Cloak: Local Authority Press Relations*, Croydon, Charles Knight, 1970; H. Cox and D. Morgan, *City Politics and the Press*, Cambridge, Cambridge University Press, 1974; I. Jackson, *The Provincial Press and the Community*, Manchester, Manchester University Press, 1971; A. Beith, 'The press and English local authorities', B.Litt. thesis, Nuffield College, Oxford, 1968; D. Hill, 'Democracy and participation in local government', Ph.D. thesis, Leeds University, 1966. There are more recent studies by D. Simpson, *The Commercialization of the Regional Press*, Aldershot, Gower, 1981; A. Hetherington, *News in the Regions*, Basingstoke, Macmillan, 1989. The latter deals with local radio and regional television as well as the local press. Other recent studies have rarely extended beyond book chapters or articles. See e.g. D. Murphy, 'The local press', in B. Pimlott and J. Seaton (eds), *The Media in British Politics*, Aldershot, Gower, 1987, pp. 90–110; and B. Franklin, 'Press reporting of the West Yorkshire Metropolitan County Council', *Local Government Studies*, May/June 1991, pp. 20–41. For a study of the local press in Israel see D. Caspi, *Media Decentralization: The Case of Israel's Local Newspapers*, New Brunswick, Transaction Books, 1986.

2 *Benn's Directory*, Tonbridge, Benn's Business Information Services, 1988.

3 Recent ABC figures published in *UK Press Gazette*, 15 May 1989.

4 M. Ward, '*Daily News*: up and running well', *UK Press Gazette*, 5 October 1987.

5 A. Bairner, 'Local newspapers and international news: the press in Northern Ireland', paper presented to the annual conference of the Political Studies Association, University of Warwick, April 1989, p. 5.

6 See e.g. *The Local Government Elector*, the Maud Report on the

management of local government, vol. 3, London, HMSO, 1987, p. 28.

7 MORI, 'Residents' attitudes to rates and services', research report for London Borough of Richmond-upon-Thames, November 1984, p. 12.

8 The Press Council, *The Press and the People*, 34th annual report, London, 1987, p. 288.

9 Recent ABC figures published in *UK Press Gazette*, op. cit.

10 N. Hartley, P. Gudgeon and R. Crofts, 'Concentration of ownership in the provincial press', research paper for the Royal Commission on the Press, Chair Professor O. R. McGregor, Cmnd 6810–5, London, HMSO, 1977, pp. 32, 33, 35. See also D. Simpson, 'How control has shifted on regional newspapers', *Journalism Studies Review*, July 1980, p. 16.

11 P. Golding, 'Limits to Leviathan: the local press and the poll tax', paper presented to the annual conference of the Political Studies Association, University of Warwick, April 1989. See the result of similar research conducted in Birmingham and reported in *AFN News*, September/October 1987, p. 6.

12 *Harlow News*, March 1986.

13 Advertising Association, *Advertising Statistics Yearbook*, London, 1988, p. 42. Also *AFN News*, August/September 1988, p. 16.

14 ibid., p. 16.

15 *AFN News*, April/May 1988, p. 11.

16 A. Hetherington, 'News in the regions', paper presented to the annual conference of the Political Studies Association, University of Warwick, April 1989, p. 7. See also Hetherington, *News in the Regions*, p. 125.

17 S. Hall, *The Voluntary Sector under Attack*, London, Islington Voluntary Action Council Publications, 1989, p. 7.

18 Goldsmiths' College Media Research Group, *Media Coverage of London Councils: Interim Report*, London, 1987, p. 1; Association of London Authorities, *It's the Way They Tell 'Em: Distortion, Disinformation and Downright Lies*, London, April 1987; and R. Todd, 'The media and the people', Henry Hetherington Lecture, London School of Economics, June 1987.

19 M. Brynin, 'The young homeless: Pressure groups, politics and the press', *Youth and Policy*, May 1987, pp. 24–34.

20 The Press Council, *The Press and the People*, p. 328.

21 J. Porter, 'Distribution of frees in Europe', *AFN News*, June/July 1986, p. 7.

22 The Press Council, *The Press and the People*, pp. 334–5.

23 M. Ward, 'The *Daily News*: up and running well', *AFN News*, September/October 1987, pp. 4–6.

24 The Press Council, *The Press and the People*, p. 275.

25 Simpson, *The Commercialization of the Regional Press*, op. cit.

26 M. Hollingsworth, *The Press and Political Dissent: A Question of Censorship*, London, Pluto Press, 1986, appendix 1, pp. 301–25.

27 The Press Council, *The Press and the People*, p. 271.

28 J. Morgan, 'Frees millionaire sells remainder of empire', *UK Press Gazette*, 18 February 1988.
29 J. Morgan and M. Broughan, 'Heady days for Thomson', *UK Press Gazette*, 9 May 1988.
30 A. Garth, 'The free concept which paid off', *UK Press Gazette*, 15 August 1988.
31 The Press Council, *The Press and the People*, pp. 314–326.
32 T. Kelly, 'Red Rose free aims for 300,000 print run', *UK Press Gazette*, 8 June 1988.
33 E. Holden, 'The politics of new technology in the provincial press', paper presented to the annual conference of the Political Studies Association, Plymouth Polytechnic, April 1988, pp. 10–12.
34 The Press Council, *The Press and the People*, p. 273. For the Press Council's report on new technology see *The Press and the People*, 33rd annual report, London, 1986.
35 D. Goodhart and C. Wintour, *Eddie Shah and the Newspaper Revolution*, London, Coronet, 1986, chapter 1.
36 R. Nicholson, 'We must not waste valuable opportunity', *UK Press Gazette*, 4 April 1988.
37 T. Loynes, 'The year of decision', *UK Press Gazette*, 22 December 1986.
38 J. Morgan, 'Survey shows DI deals range from nil to £40', *UK Press Gazette*, 7 September 1987.
39 D. Swingewood, 'Sheffield chiefs reject talks in new tech row', *UK Press Gazette*, 23 February 1987.
40 Loynes, 'The year of decision', p. 15. See also Goodhart and Wintour, *Eddie Shah and the Newspaper Revolution*, pp. xi–xii.
41 Local Radio Workshop. *Nothing Local about It: London's Local Radio*, London, Comedia, 1982, p. 10.
42 Hetherington, 'News in the regions', p. 2.
43 T. Kelly, 'Six BBC stations to axe 28 jobs in North', *UK Press Gazette*, 6 June 1988.
44 C. Mowbray, 'The station now departing . . .', *Guardian*, 28 July 1986.
45 T. Kelly and D. Pike, 'IR mergers seen as the new way forward', *UK Press Gazette*, 13 October 1986.
46 *Broadcasting in the 1990s: Competition, Choice, Quality*, London, HMSO, 1988.
47 Douglas Hurd, 'A boring mishmash? That's not my plan', *Guardian*, 1 February 1988.
48 T. Kelly, 'Community stations boost news', *UK Press Gazette*, 1 May 1989.
49 Hetherington, 'News in the regions', op. cit., p. 3. See also T. O'Malley, *Switching Channels*, London, Campaign for Press and Broadcasting Freedom, 1988, pp. 18–21.
50 *Broadcasting in the 1990s*, para. 6.17.
51 ibid., para. 6.11.
52 See e.g. N. Ryan, 'Quality is the casualty', *UK Press Gazette*, 21

November 1988; S. Prebble, 'White lies', *Listener*, 17 November 1988, pp. 4–6.

53 B. Franklin, *Public Relations Activities in Local Government*, Croydon, Charles Knight, 1988, especially chapters 1 and 3.

54 ibid., pp. 59–60.

55 ibid., p. 80.

56 T. Baistow, *Fourth Rate Estate: An Anatomy of Fleet Street*, London, Comedia, 1985, p. 67.

57 Franklin, *Public Relations Activities in Local Government*, p. 87.

58 Murphy, *The Silent Watchdog*, chapters 1 and 2.

59 M. Cockerell, P. Hennessy and D. Walker, *Sources Close to the Prime Minister*, London, Macmillan, 1984, pp. 57–8. See also M. Cockerell, 'The sincerity machine', *PR Week*, 17–23 November 1988, pp. 13–15; and R. Cobb, 'Behind Big Brother', *PR Week*, 13 February 1989, pp. 14–15.

60 T. O'Sullivan, 'Ingham refuses to back ethics code', *PR Week*, 27 April 1989, p. 5.

61 B. Franklin, 'Central government information vs local government propaganda', *Local Government Chronicle*, 26 August 1988.

62 Golding, 'Limits to Leviathan', p. 9.

63 ibid., p. 11.

64 B. Franklin, 'Public relations, the local press and the coverage of local government', *Local Government Studies*, July/August 1986, p. 31.

65 C. Gardner, 'How they buy the bulletins', *Guardian*, 17 September 1986. See also R. Cobb, 'PR has radio taped', *PR Week*, 21 April 1989, pp. 12–14.

66 'Free to launch without staff journalist', *UK Press Gazette*, 1 September 1986.

67 C. Heathcote, 'The disappearing council reporter', *Newstime*, September 1986, p. 9.

68 J. Slattery, 'Keep out!', *UK Press Gazette*, 13 May 1987; and C. Benfield, '*MEN* set to plug daily gap if rival enters fray', *UK Press Gazette*, 6 October 1986.

69 N. Fountain, *Underground: The London Alternative Press 1966–1974*, London, Comedia, 1988.

70 K. Myers, *Understains: The Sense and Seduction of Advertising*, London, Comedia, 1986, p. 125.

71 C. Landry, D. Morley, R. Southwood and P. Wright, *What a Way to Run a Railroad: An Analysis of Radical Failure*, London, Comedia, 1985, especially chapters 3 and 4; C. Aubrey, 'Beyond the free press: recent developments in the radical press', in B. Whitaker (ed.), *News Limited: Why You Can't Read All about It*, London, Minority Press Group/Comedia, 1984, pp. 167–76; and C. Aubrey et al., *Here Is the Other News: Challenges to the Local Commercial Press*, London, Minority Press Group, 1980.

2 THE CORPORATION AND THE PARISH PUMP

1 I. Jackson, *The Provincial Press and the Community*, Manchester, Manchester University Press, 1971.
2 D. Murphy, *The Silent Watchdog: The Press in Local Politics*, London, Constable, 1976; D. Murphy, 'Control without censorship', in *The British Press: A Manifesto*, London, Macmillan, 1978, pp. 171–92; D. Murphy, 'The local press', in B. Pimlott and J. Seaton (eds), *The Media in British Politics*, Aldershot, Gower, 1987, pp. 90–110; B. Whitaker, *News Limited: Why You Can't Read All about It*, London, Minority Press Group/Comedia, 1984.
3 Murphy, *The Silent Watchdog*, 'Control without censorship' and 'The local press', all op. cit.
4 Whitaker, *News Limited*, op. cit.
5 R. E. Park, *The Immigrant Press and its Control*, New York, Harper, 1929; L. Wirth, *The Ghetto*, Chicago, University of Chicago Press, 1928; Janowitz, *The Community Press in an Urban Setting*, Chicago, University of Chicago Press, 1967.
6 D. L. Paletz, P. Reichert and B. MacIntyre, 'How the media support local government authority', *Public Opinion Quarterly*, XXXV, 1, spring 1971, pp. 80–94; W. Breed, 'Social control in the newsroom', *Social Forces*, 33, 1955, pp. 326–35; H. Molotch and M. Lester, 'News as purposive behavior', *American Sociological Review*, 39, 1, 1974, pp. 101–12; G. Tuckman, 'Making news by doing work: routinizing the unexpected', *American Journal of Sociology*, 79, 1, 1973, pp. 110–31.
7 J. Curran and J. Seaton, *Power without Responsibility*, London, Routledge, 1988, pp. 250–3.
8 ibid., p. 250.
9 Royal Commission on the Press 1974–7, Chair Professor O. R. McGregor, *Final Report*, Cmnd 6810, London, HMSO, July 1977.
10 ibid., p. 250.
11 ibid., p. 250.
12 ibid., pp. 251–2.
13 'Paper suspends publication', K. Collins, 'Another free for the Midlands', and 'NEP relaunches its new-look Focus', *Journalist's Week*, 11, 23 March 1990, pp. 3, 7.
14 EMAP, annual report, 1989, p. 3.
15 ibid., p. 3.
16 ibid., p. 3.
17 ibid., p. 8.
18 Reed International, annual report, chief executive's review of operations, 1989.
19 International Thomson, annual report to shareholders, 1988, p. 5.
20 *Financial Times*, 29 September 1989.
21 ibid.; *Investors Chronicle*, 6 October 1989; *Daily Telegraph*, 13 October 1989.

3 THE TRADITIONAL LOCAL PRESS

1 See J. Curran and J. Seaton, *Power without Responsibility*, London, Routledge, 1988, pp. 7–30.
2 P. Hollis, *The Pauper Press*, London, Oxford University Press, 1970.
3 ibid., pp. 23–44.
4 H. Christian, 'Journalists' occupational ideologies and press commercialization', in H. Christian (ed.), *Sociological Review Monograph 29: Sociology of Journalism and the Press*, University of Keele, 1980, pp. 259–306.
5 J. Aitchison, *Writing for the Press*, London, Hutchinson, 1988.
6 ibid., p. 1.
7 ibid., p. 1.
8 ibid., p. 1.
9 ibid., p. 3.
10 ibid., p. 3.
11 ibid., p. 10.
12 ibid., p. 10.
13 ibid., p. 13.
14 P. Schlesinger, *Putting 'Reality' Together*, London, Constable, 1978.
15 'John jets in from desert ordeal', *Manchester Evening News*, 15 August 1990, p. 1.
16 'Skier killed in avalanche: trip ends in tragedy after Paul switches his holidays', *Stockport Express Advertiser*, 11 February 1988.
17 'Tenerife brawler jailed', *Stockport Express Advertiser*, 11 February 1988.
18 'Cuts may hit elderly', *Stockport Express Advertiser*, 11 February 1988.
19 'Flasher sought by police', *North Wales Weekly News*, 16 August 1990.
20 'Mum fears the worst in bin mystery', *North Wales Weekly News*, 16 August 1990.
21 'Anxious wait for Gulf families', *North Wales Weekly News*, 16 August 1990.
22 'Desert escape drama: ex-Bury man tells of Kuwait freedom dash', 'Couple hear from son in Baghdad', 'Early flight home for holiday student', *Bury Times*, 17 August 1990.
23 'We won't quit Saudi war zone', *Rossendale Free Press*, 18 August 1990.
24 'Shoe jobs toe-hold: managers set up rescue package for crash company', *Rossendale Free Press*, 18 August 1990.
25 'Big stores shut-down', *North Wales Weekly News*, 16 August 1990.
26 'Metals firm to close', *Glossop Chronicle*, 16 August 1990.
27 Curran and Seaton, *Power without Responsibility*, op. cit., pp. 47–54.
28 'Protests flare in Romania', 'Rebel's return', ' "Closed Shop" Labour Row', *Evening Mail*, 18 December 1989.
29 P. Marston, 'Five make a return crossing', *Evening Mail*, 18 December 1989.
30 C. Johnston, 'We're set for war says Tornado Ted: warning of fighting by the weekend', *Manchester Evening News*, 21 August 1990.

31 L. Bullas, 'Golfers can stymie water company's business park', *Manchester Evening News*, 21 August 1990.
32 R. Fitzwalter, 'The master builder', *Bradford Telegraph and Argus*, 4 April 1970. See R. Fitzwalter and D. Taylor, *Web of Corruption*, London, Granada, 1981.
33 For an account of the press coverage of the Stalker affair see D. Murphy, *The Stalker Affair and the Press*, London, Unwin Hyman, 1990.
34 'Two-shots claim in McRae death riddle', *Press and Journal*, 31 March 1990.
35 ibid.
36 See all editions of *Manchester Evening News* for 2 April 1990.
37 'The road to ruin', *Yorkshire Evening Post*, 3 March 1989.
38 ' "Arogant media" ', *Manchester Evening News*, 9 October 1987.

4 FREE NEWSPAPERS: SOME OF THE NEWS THAT'S FIT TO PRINT - AND MUCH THAT ISN'T

1 J. Cunningham, 'Frees are jolly good business', *Guardian*, 1 August 1988.
2 Quoted in N. Hartley, P. Gudgeon and R. Crofts, 'Concentration of ownership in the provincial press', research paper for the Royal Commission on the Press, Chair Professor O. R. McGregor, Cmnd 6810–5, London, HMSO, 1977, p. 92.
3 S. Barnes, 'Why do people on a diet read more free papers?', *AFN News*, October/November 1986, p. 8.
4 See e.g. J. Slattery, 'Frees must invest in editorial', *UK Press Gazette*, 27 February 1989.
5 M. Costello, 'From free sheets to papers of real value', *AFN News*, February 1990, p. 12.
6 'Free to launch without staff journalists', *UK Press Gazette*, 1 September 1986.
7 J. Slattery, 'Community press: how to spread the buzz word', *UK Press Gazette*, 26 October 1987.
8 'Frees' respectability does not come cheaply', *UK Press Gazette*, 26 October 1986.
9 I. Fletcher, 'The future is free', *AFN News*, April/May 1988, p. 10.
10 Hartley et al., 'Concentration of ownership in the provincial press', op. cit., p. 32.
11 ibid., p. 33.
12 ibid., p. 35.
13 M. Brynin, 'The unchanging British press', *Media Information Australia*, 47, February 1988, pp. 23–37.
14 Lionel Pickering speaking on BBC Radio 4 programme *The Free Press*, broadcast 15 July 1986, produced by John Abberley, BBC Radio Stoke, presented by Larry Harris.
15 Eddie Shah, ibid.

16 C. Lawrance, 'A decade of success', *UK Press Gazette*, 12 February 1990.
17 J. Porter, 'Distribution of frees in Europe nears 200 millions', *AFN News*, June/July 1986, p. 7.
18 Fletcher, 'The future is free', op. cit., p. 11.
19 S. Barnes, 'Advertising: frees lead on', *AFN News*, June/July 1987, p. 6.
20 Lawrance, 'A decade of success', op. cit.
21 J. Morgan, 'Frees millionaire sells remainder of empire', *UK Press Gazette*, 18 February 1988.
22 J. Morgan and M. Boughan, 'Heady days for Thomson', *UK Press Gazette*, 9 May 1988.
23 A. Garth, 'The free concept which paid off', *UK Press Gazette*, 15 August 1988.
24 J. Slattery, 'TRN pays £25m for Trader group', *UK Press Gazette*, 19 June 1989.
25 *A–Z of Britain's Free Newspapers and Magazines*, Gloucester, Association of Free Newspapers, 1990, pp. 3–5.
26 Lawrance, 'A decade of success', op. cit.
27 ibid.
28 ibid.
29 ibid.
30 *Targeting for Profit*, Gloucester, Association of Free Newspapers, 1986, p. 1.
31 *A–Z of Britain's Free Newspapers and Magazines*, op. cit., p. 7.
32 ibid., p. 8.
33 Slattery, 'Community press: how to spread the buzz word', op. cit., p. 14.
34 M. Ward, '*Daily News*: up and running well', *UK Press Gazette*, 5 October 1987.
35 'Maxwell to study new free London dummies', *UK Press Gazette*, 9 November 1987.
36 J. Slattery, 'Keep out!', *UK Press Gazette*, 13 May 1987.
37 'The rise of the city free', *AFN News*, June 1990, p. 14.
38 '*Daily News* entering new phase', *AFN News*, February 1989.
39 'Birmingham battleground', *UK Press Gazette*, 9 October 1989.
40 Ward, '*Daily News*: up and running well', op. cit.
41 ibid.
42 'Birmingham battleground', op. cit.
43 '*Daily News* claims it's number one', *AFN News*, May 1990, p. 16.
44 Ward, '*Daily News*: up and running well', op. cit.
45 D. Swingewood, '*Brum Post* was keen to sell to free', *UK Press Gazette*, 12 September 1988.
46 J. Slattery, 'Ingersoll shows hand with 39 new papers', *UK Press Gazette*, 21 August 1989.
47 'Jobs shake-up as Focus falters', *UK Press Gazette*, 12 February 1990.
48 H. Conroy speaking on BBC Radio 4's *The Free Press*, op. cit.
49 Slattery, 'Community press: how to spread the buzz word', op. cit.

50 C. Heathcote, 'The disappearing council reporter', *Newstime*, September 1986, p. 9.
51 B. Franklin, 'Public relations, the local press and the coverage of local government', *Local Government Studies*, July/August 1986, p. 26.
52 Unpublished report by the Society of County and Regional Public Relations Officers, September 1985.
53 Society of County and Regional Public Relations Officers, op. cit., p. 4. See also A. Godfrey, 'Press reporting by remote control', *Local Government Review*, 28 April 1984, p. 328.
54 B. Franklin, *Public Relations Activities in Local Government*, Croydon, Charles Knight, 1988, p. 69.
55 B. Franklin, 'Watchdog or lapdog? Local press reporting of the West Yorkshire Metropolitan County Council', *Local Government Studies*, January/February 1991.
56 B. Franklin and J. V. S. Turk, 'Information subsidies: agenda-setting traditions', *Public Relations Review*, spring 1988, pp. 29–41.
57 Franklin, *Public Relations Activities in Local Government*, op. cit., p. 81.
58 ibid., p. 82.
59 'Post GLC: the big PR gap', *UK Press Gazette*, 31 March 1986.
60 'Free newspapers should ban PR campaign', *AFN News*, April/May 1986, p. 7.

5 THE ALTERNATIVE LOCAL PRESS

1 J. Curran and J. Seaton, *Power without Responsibility*, London, Routledge, 1988.
2 D. Murphy, *The Silent Watchdog: The Press in Local Politics*, London, Constable, 1976; D. Murphy, 'The local press', in B. Pimlott and J. Seaton (eds), *The Media in British Politics*, Aldershot, Gower, 1987, pp. 90–110.
3 *Manchester Free Press*, 21, p. 1.
4 *Manchester Free Press*, 19, p. 1.
5 *Leeds and Bradford Other Paper*, 620, 16 February 1990.
6 *Manchester Free Press*, 43, p. 10.
7 *New Manchester Review*, 58, 2–15 June 1978, pp. 4–5.
8 ibid.
9 ibid.
10 ibid.
11 ibid.
12 'Mystery over Fieldhouse probe', *New Manchester Review*, 66, 6–19 October 1978, p. 4.
13 'Costly tune from boys in blue', *New Manchester Review*, 66, 6–19 October 1978, p. 4.
14 'Jim Anderton, the secret Tory', *New Manchester Review*, 71, 15 December–11 January 1979, p. 5.
15 'Police probe case for prosecution', *New Manchester Review*, 73, 26 January–8 February 1979, p. 4.

16 ibid.
17 ibid.
18 ibid.
19 B. Whitaker, *News Limited: Why You Can't Read All about It*, London, Minority Press Group/Comedia, 1984.
20 ibid., pp. 139–66.
21 'Call for action on missing money', *Venue*, 145, 20 November–3 December 1987, p. 11.
22 'More questions than answers', *Venue*, 149, 22 January–4 February 1988, p. 10.
23 S. Khanum, 'Rape in marriage law must be seen to work for women', 'Women step up security measures' and 'Black man awarded £6,000 damages for police assault', and Q. Bradley, 'Emergency workers' control', all from *Leeds Other Paper*, 620, 16 February 1990, pp. 4, 2, 6, 7 respectively.
24 A. Spinoza, 'Laughing gear', *City Life*, 90, 20 November–4 December 1987, pp. 10–11; D. Higgitt, 'Big Ben', *Venue*, 145, 20 November–3 December 1987, pp. 12–13.

6   THE MUNICIPAL FREE PRESS

1 House of Commons Debates, 25 March 1986, cols 883–4.
2 Cited in A. Chaudhuri, 'Government gets tough on council political publicity', *PR Week*, 27 November 1986.
3 See also B. Adams, 'The council newspaper: a public interest', *Municipal Review*, 45, 539, November 1974, p. 252.
4 Simon Hughes, House of Commons Debates, 25 March 1986, col. 890; see also Alan Beith's remarks, col. 896.
5 Tony Banks, House of Commons Debates, 22 January 1986, cols 337–8.
6 Royal Commission on the Press 1974–7, Chair Professor O. R. McGregor, *Final Report*, Cmnd 6810, London, HMSO, July 1977, p. 15.
7 The questionnaire was initially circulated by the local government group of the Institute of Public Relations (IPR) between May and the end of June 1986. We would like to acknowledge our gratitude to the local government group of the IPR for their assistance and co-operation with our research on the local press.
8 Central Policy Unit, *Sheffield News* survey, unpublished report, May 1988. See also the report of a similar survey of 870 households conducted by J. McClounan for Strathclyde Regional Council, February 1987.
9 C. Heathcote, 'The disappearing council reporter', *Newstime*, September 1986, pp. 9–10.
10 Adams, 'The council newspaper: a public interest', p. 252.
11 Goldsmiths' College Media Research Group, *Media Coverage of London Councils: Interim Report*, London, 1987.

12 Editorial, *Manchester Magazine*, May 1987, p. 3. See also P. Hetherington in the *Guardian*, 28 April 1987, p. 3.

13 Adams, 'The council newspaper: a public interest', p. 252; and '*Islington People*: breaking the silence at County Hall', *PR Week*, 13–19 November 1986, p. 10.

14 B. Franklin, *Public Relations Activities in Local Government*, Croydon, Charles Knight, 1988, chapters 1 and 4.

15 H. Dutch, *Annual Report of the Public Relations Department*, Strathclyde Regional Council, 1986.

16 'Council mag blacking ends', *UK Press Gazette*, 18 May 1987.

7 LOCAL PRESS REPORTING OF THE 1987 GENERAL ELECTION

1 *Daily Telegraph*, 30 July 1986.

2 See e.g. *Financial Times*, 23 March 1987.

3 ibid.

4 M. Harrop, 'The press and postwar elections', in I. Crewe and M. Harrop (eds), *Political Communication: The General Election Campaign of 1983*, Cambridge, Cambridge University Press, 1986, p. 141.

5 M. Harrop, 'The press', in D. Butler and D. Kavanagh (eds), *The British General Election of 1987*, Basingstoke, Macmillan, 1988, pp. 184–5.

6 C. Dunkley, 'Why broadcasters go in for election overkill', *Financial Times*, 17 June 1987.

7 Harrop, 'The press and postwar elections', p. 141.

8 Harrop, 'The press', p. 163.

9 J. Seabrook 'What the papers show', *New Society*, 5 June 1987, pp. 16–18.

10 D. Butler and D. Kavanagh, *The British General Election of 1979*, Basingstoke, Macmillan, 1980, p. 292.

11 D. Swingewood, 'Kinnock is geared to TV not newspapers', *UK Press Gazette*, 1 June 1987.

12 J. G. Blumler, M. Gurevitch and T. J. Nossiter, 'Setting the television news agenda: campaign observation at the BBC', in Crewe and Harrop, *Political Communication*, pp. 104–25.

13 S. McTaggart, 'Local parties and campaign expenditure in ten West Yorkshire constituencies in the 1987 general election', unpublished paper, Centre for Television Research, 1989.

14 ibid. See also M. Atkinson, 'The 1983 election and the demise of live oratory', in Crewe and Harrop, *Political Communication*, op. cit., p. 38.

15 E. Goldenberg and M. Traugott, *Campaigning for Congress*, Congress Quarterly Press, Washington, 1984.

16 *Telegraph and Argus*, 16 June 1987.

17 *Heckmondwike Herald*, 5 June 1987, front page. The same editorial appeared in the sister paper, the *Spenborough Guardian*.

18 McTaggart, 'Local parties and campaign expenditure', op. cit.

19 For a fuller discussion of these two orientations to the local media see B. Franklin, 'Local parties, local media and the constituency campaign', in I. Crewe and M. Harrop (eds), *Political Communications: The General Election Campaign of 1987*, Cambridge, Cambridge University Press, 1989.

20 B. Franklin, 'Public relations, the local press and the coverage of local government', *Local Government Studies*, July/August 1986, pp. 25–34.

21 J. G. Blumler, 'Elections, the media and the modern publicity process', in M. Ferguson (eds), *Public Communication: The New Imperatives*, London, Sage, 1989, pp. 102–13.

22 Editorial, *Halifax Courier*, 10 June 1987.

23 Editorial, *Yorkshire Post*, 13 June 1987.

24 Editorial, *Yorkshire Post*, 5 June 1987.

25 Editorial, *Yorkshire Post*, 4 June 1987.

26 *Yorkshire Post*, 13 June 1987.

27 *Yorkshire Post*, 10 June 1987.

28 Editorial, *Yorkshire Post*, 27 May 1987.

29 Editorial, *Yorkshire Post*, 4 June 1987.

30 *Yorkshire Post*, 4 June 1987.

Select bibliography

A–Z of Britain's Free Newspapers and Magazines, Gloucester, Association of Free Newspapers, 1990.

Adams, B., 'The council newspaper: a public interest', *Municipal Review*, 45, 539, November 1974, p. 252.

Advertising Association, *Advertising Statistics Yearbook*, London, 1988.

Association of London Authorities, *It's the Way They Tell 'Em: Distortion, Disinformation and Downright Lies*, London, April 1987.

Aubrey, C., 'Beyond the free press: recent developments in the radical press', in B. Whitaker (ed.), *News Limited: Why You Can't Read All about It*, London, Minority Press Group/Comedia, 1984, pp. 167–76.

Aubrey, C., *et al.*, *Here Is the Other News: Challenges to the Local Commercial Press*, London, Minority Press Group, 1980.

Bairner, A., 'Local newspapers and international news: the press in Northern Ireland', paper presented to the annual conference of the Political Studies Association, University of Warwick, April 1989.

Baistow, T., *Fourth Rate Estate: An Anatomy of Fleet Street*, London, Comedia, 1985.

Barnes, S., 'Why do people on a diet read more free papers?', *AFN News*, October/November 1986, p. 8.

—, 'Advertising: frees lead on', *AFN News*, June/July 1987, p. 6.

Beith, A., 'The press and English local authorities', B.Litt. thesis, Nuffield College, Oxford, 1968.

Benfield, C., '*MEN* set to plug daily gap if rival enters fray', *UK Press Gazette*, 6 October 1986.

Blumler, J. G., 'Elections, the media and the modern publicity process', in M. Ferguson (ed.), *Public Communication: The New Imperatives*, London, Sage, 1989, pp. 102–13.

Blumler, J. G., Gurevitch, M. and Nossiter, T. J., 'Setting the television news agenda: campaign observation at the BBC', in I. Crewe and M. Harrop (eds), *Political Communication: The General Election Campaign of 1983*, Cambridge, Cambridge University Press, 1986, pp. 104–25.

Broadcasting in the 1990s: Competition, Choice, Quality, London, HMSO, 1988.

Brynin, M., 'The young homeless: pressure groups, politics and the press', *Youth and Policy*, May 1987, pp. 24–34.

—, 'The unchanging British press', *Media Information Australia*, 47, February 1988, pp. 23–37.

Burke, R., *The Murky Cloak: Local Authority Press Relations*, Croydon, Charles Knight, 1970.

Caspi, D., *Media Decentralization: The Case of Israel's Local Newspapers*, New Brunswick, Transaction Books, 1986.

Chaudhuri, A., 'Government gets tough on council political publicity', *PR Week*, 27 November 1986.

Cobb, R., 'Behind Big Brother', *PR Week*, 13 February 1989, pp. 14–15.

—, 'PR has radio taped', *PR Week*, 21 April 1989, pp. 12–14.

Cockerell, M., 'The sincerity machine', *PR Week*, 17–23 November 1988, pp. 13–15.

Cockerell, M., Hennessy, T. and Walker, D., *Sources Close to the Prime Minister*, Basingstoke, Macmillan, 1984.

Costello, M., 'From free sheets to papers of real value', *AFN News*, February 1990, p. 12.

Cox, H. and Morgan, D., *City Politics and the Press*, Cambridge, Cambridge University Press, 1974.

Cunningham, J., 'Frees are jolly good business', *Guardian*, 1 August 1988.

Curran, J. and Seaton, J., *Power without Responsibility*, London, Routledge, 1988.

Dunkley, C., 'Why broadcasters go in for election overkill', *Financial Times*, 17 June 1987.

Dutch, H., *Annual Report of the Public Relations Department*, Strathclyde Regional Council, 1986.

Fletcher, I., 'The future is free', *AFN News*, April/May 1988, p. 10.

Fountain, N., *Underground: The London Alternative Press 1966–1974*, London, Comedia, 1988.

Franklin, B., 'Public relations, the local press and the coverage of local government', *Local Government Studies*, July/August 1986, pp. 25–34.

—, *Public Relations Activities in Local Government*, Croydon, Charles Knight, 1988.

—, 'Central government information vs local government propaganda', *Local Government Chronicle*, 26 August 1988, pp. 10–14.

—, 'Local parties, local media and the constituency campaign', in I. Crewe and M. Harrop (eds), *Political Communication: The General Election Campaign of 1987*, Cambridge, Cambridge University Press, 1989, pp. 110–24.

—, 'Watchdog or lapdog? Local press reporting of the West Yorkshire Metropolitan County Council', *Local Government Studies*, January/February 1991, pp. 20–44.

Franklin, B. and Turk, J. V. S., 'Information subsidies: agenda-setting traditions', *Public Relations Review*, spring 1988, pp. 29–41.

'Free to launch without staff journalist', *UK Press Gazette*, 1 September 1986.

Gardener, C., 'How they buy the bulletins', *Guardian*, 17 September 1986.

Garth, A., 'The free concept which paid off', *UK Press Gazette*, 15 August 1988.

Goldenberg, E. and Traugott, M., *Campaigning for Congress*, Washington, Congress Quarterly Press, 1984.

Golding, P., 'Limits to Leviathan: the local Press and the poll tax', paper presented to the annual conference of the Political Studies Association, University of Warwick, April 1989.

Goldsmiths' College Media Research Group, *Media Coverage of London Councils: Interim Report*, London, 1987.

Goodhart, D. and Wintour, C., *Eddy Shah and the Newspaper Revolution*, London, Coronet, 1986.

Hall, S., *The Voluntary Sector under Attack*, London, Islington Voluntary Action Council Publications, 1989.

Harrop, M., 'The press and postwar elections', in I. Crewe and M. Harrop (eds), *Political Communication: The General Election Campaign of 1983*, Cambridge, Cambridge University Press, 1986.

—, 'The press', in D. Butler and D. Kavanagh (eds), *The British General Election of 1987*, London, Macmillan, 1988.

Hartley, N., Gudgeon, P. and Crofts, R., 'Concentration of ownership in the provincial press', research paper for the Royal Commission on the Press, Chair Professor O. R. McGregor, Cmnd 6810–5, London, HMSO, 1977.

Heathcote, C., 'The disappearing council reporter', *Newstime*, September 1986, pp. 9–10.

Hetherington, A., *News in the Regions*, London, Macmillan, 1989.

—, 'News in the regions', paper presented to the annual conference of the Political Studies Association, University of Warwick, April 1989.

Hill, D., 'Democracy and participation in local government', unpublished Ph.D. thesis, Leeds University, 1966.

Holden, E., 'The politics of new technology in the provincial press', paper presented to the annual conference of the Political Studies Association, Plymouth Polytechnic, April 1988.

Hollingsworth, M., *The Press and Political Dissent: A Question of Censorship*, London, Pluto Press, 1986.

Hurd, D., 'A boring mishmash? That's not my plan', *Guardian*, 1 February 1988.

Jackson, I., *The Provincial Press and the Community*, Manchester, Manchester University Press, 1971.

Kelly, T., 'Six BBC stations to axe 28 jobs in North', *UK Press Gazette*, 6 June 1988.

—, 'Community stations boost news', *UK Press Gazette*, 1 May 1989.

Kelly, T. and Pike, D., 'IR mergers seen as the new way forward', *UK Press Gazette*, 13 October 1986.

Landry, C., Morley, D., Southwood, R. and Wright, P., *What a Way to Run a Railroad: An Analysis of Radical Failure*, London, Comedia, 1985.

Lawrance, C., 'A decade of success', *UK Press Gazette*, 12 February 1990.

The Local Government Elector, the Maud Report on the management of local government, vol. 3, London, HMSO, 1987.

Local Radio Workshop, *Nothing Local about It: London's Local Radio*, London, Comedia, 1982.

Loynes, T., 'The year of decision', *UK Press Gazette*, 22 December 1986.

McTaggart, S., 'Local parties and campaign expenditure in ten West Yorkshire constituencies in the 1987 general election', unpublished paper, Centre for Television Research, 1989.

Morgan, J., 'Survey shows DI deals range from nil to £40', *UK Press Gazette*, 7 September 1987.

—, 'Frees millionaire sells remainder of empire', *UK Press Gazette*, 18 February 1988.

Morgan, J. and Broughan, M., 'Heady days for Thomson', *UK Press Gazette*, 9 May 1988.

MORI, 'Residents' attitudes to rates and service', research report for London Borough of Richmond-upon-Thames, November 1984.

Mowbray, C., 'The station now departing . . .', *Guardian*, 28 July 1986.

Murphy, D., *The Silent Watchdog: The Press in Local Politics*, London, Constable, 1976.

—, 'The local press', in B. Pimlott and J. Seaton (eds), *The Media in British Politics*, Aldershot, Gower, 1987, pp. 90–110.

Myers, K., *Understains: The Sense and Seduction of Advertising*, London, Comedia, 1986.

Nicholson, R., 'We must not waste valuable opportunity', *UK Press Gazette*, 4 April 1988.

O'Malley, T., *Switching Channels*, London, Campaign for Press and Broadcasting Freedom, 1988.

O'Sullivan, T., 'Ingham refuses to back ethics code', *PR Week*, 27 April 1989, p. 5.

Pelly, T., 'Red Rose free aims for 300,000 print run', *UK Press Gazette*, 8 June 1988.

Porter, H., *Lies, Damn Lies and Some Exclusives*, London, Coronet, 1984.

Porter, J., 'Distribution of frees in Europe nears 200 millions', *AFN News*, June/July 1986, p. 7.

Prebble, S., 'White lies', *Listener*, 17 November 1988, pp. 4–6.

The Press Council, *The Press and the People*, 34th annual report, London, 1987.

Royal Commission on the Press 1974–7, Chair Professor O. R. McGregor, *Final Report*, Cmnd 6810, London, HMSO, July 1977.

Ryan, N., 'Quality is the casualty', *UK Press Gazette*, 21 November 1988.

Schlesinger, P., *Putting 'Reality' Together*, London, Constable, 1978.

Seabrook, J., 'What the papers show', *New Society*, 5 June 1987, pp. 16–18.

Simpson, D., 'How control has shifted on regional newspapers', *Journalism Studies Review*, July 1980, pp. 10–23.

—, *The Commercialization of the Regional Press*, Aldershot, Gower, 1981.

Slattery, J., 'Keep out!', *UK Press Gazette*, 13 May 1987.
—, 'Community press: how to spread the buzz word', *UK Press Gazette*, 26 October 1987.
—, 'Frees must invest in editorial', *UK Press Gazette*, 27 February 1989.
Swingewood, D., 'Sheffield chiefs reject talks in new tech row', *UK Press Gazette*, 23 February 1987.
—, 'Kinnock is geared to TV not newspapers', *UK Press Gazette*, 1 June 1987.
Tiffen, R., *News and Power*, Sydney, Allen & Unwin, 1989.
Todd, R., 'The media and the people', Henry Hetherington Lecture, London School of Economics, June 1987.
Ward, M., '*Daily News*: up and running well', *UK Press Gazette*, 5 October 1987.
Whitaker, B., *News Limited: Why You Can't Read All about It*, London, Minority Press Group/Comedia, 1984.
Wintour, C., *The Rise and Fall of Fleet Street*, London, Hutchinson, 1989.

Index

CPSIA information can be obtained at www.ICGtesting.com
Printed in the USA
LVOW11*2110130416

483500LV00006B/17/P